A Transforming Vision

A Transforming Vision

Knowing and Loving the Triune God

Edited by
GEORGE WESTHAVER

scm press

Published in 2018 by SCM Press
Editorial office
3rd Floor, Invicta House,
108–114 Golden Lane,
London EC1Y 0TG, UK
www.scmpress.co.uk

SCM Press is an imprint of Hymns Ancient & Modern Ltd
(a registered charity)

Hymns Ancient & Modern® is a registered trademark of
Hymns Ancient & Modern Ltd
13A Hellesdon Park Road, Norwich,
Norfolk NR6 5DR, UK

The author and publisher acknowledge with thanks permission to
reproduce:
The Ghent Altarpiece by Hubert and Jan van Eyck, 1432, St Bavo's
Cathedral, Ghent.
The Chapel rood in Pusey House by Temple Moore, 1914, Oxford.
'The Return of the Dove to the Ark' by Sir John Everett Millais,
1851, Ashmolean Museum, Oxford. Image © Ashmolean
Museum, University of Oxford.
'Convent Thoughts' by Charles Allston Collins, 1851, Ashmolean
Museum, Oxford. Image © Ashmolean Museum, University
of Oxford.
Pentecost Cope Hood by Ninian Comper and the Society of the Sisters
of Bethany, c.1900, Victoria and Albert Museum, London.
Image © Victoria and Albert Museum.

British Library Cataloguing in Publication data

A catalogue record for this book is available
from the British Library

978 0 334 05568 6

Typeset by Manila Typesetting Company
Printed and bound by
CPI Group (UK) Ltd

Contents

Preface

GEORGE WESTHAVER

Blessed and Glorious Trinity, Father, Son and Holy Spirit, Thee, Holy and Undivided, do we confess and praise with heart and mouth; to Thee be glory for ever, Alleluia.

The Transforming Vision conference and the papers collected in this volume grew out of an aspiration to promote theological study according to the originating principles of Pusey House, Oxford, and the ideals of the Oxford Movement. Pusey House was founded in 1884 to be a centre of theological study, worship and pastoral care, and as a fitting memorial to Dr E. B. Pusey, Regius Professor of Hebrew and Canon of Christ Church from 1828 to his death in 1882. Alongside John Keble and John Henry Newman, Pusey emerged in the 1830s as one of the leaders of the Oxford Movement and their efforts, theological, ecclesiastical and social, to renew the life of Church of England. After Newman became a Roman Catholic and Keble returned to parish life to live out a Tractarian ideal as a scholar priest, the mantle of leadership fell more and more to Pusey, who remained in Oxford at Christ Church. Canon H. P. Liddon, Pusey's biographer and one of the founders of Pusey House, hoped that the institution bearing Dr Pusey's name would be both 'a home of sacred learning and a rallying point of the Christian faith'. For Pusey, the special character of sacred learning means appreciating that 'knowledge of God and of His ways' is both 'our highest knowledge' and at the same time our 'indistinctest' or most elusive form of knowing: 'for that which is most elevated must most surpass our comprehension; it belongs to another sphere, and just touches, as it were, upon that wherein we dwell; its centre is not in this world, and so we cannot surely it encompass'.[1] Grappling with the same paradox, Newman described religious doctrine as having an 'illuminated' and an 'unilluminated' side: 'Religious Truth is neither light nor darkness, but both together.'[2] For Newman, Pusey and their colleague John Keble, religious knowledge has the character of a mystery or a sacrament; this knowledge is not a collection of facts or concepts but a dynamic encounter with the living God in whom truth and life are one. The outward form of theological knowledge, the human words or symbols by which this truth is expressed, reveal and point to a reality which is both the light that makes any thinking about God possible or fruitful, and a truth that grasps us before we can grasp it.

This sacramental approach to religious knowledge has two direct consequences, both of which shaped the conference at Pusey House in the summer of 2016. First, religious knowledge is necessarily closely allied with an attitude of awe and wonder, with a sensibility shaped by worship and prayer. For the leaders of the Oxford Movement, worship was not simply an act of piety but the way by which all the aspects of the human character, including our powers of reason and under-standing, are brought into relation with God. For the Tractarians, the movement of the heart towards God and the knowledge of God were fundamentally connected.[3] Second, a sacramental understanding of how God is both known and loved sharpens our awareness not only of the insufficiency of all human knowing and loving but also of the all-sufficiency and superabundance of grace in the sacramental life of the Church. Summarizing the work of Bishop Joseph Butler, largely forgotten now but a key inspiration for the Oxford Fathers, Newman commented that every part of the Christian Dispensation 'runs up into mystery'.[4] This was not a statement of despair or an excuse for slop-piness but an encouragement to an appropriate and illuminating rev-erence and care when contemplating either the gift of Revelation in Scripture (the Book of God's words) and in the created order (the Book of God's works), or in the sacraments, which they understood to be the chief means by which the life of Christ is communicated by the Holy Spirit to the members of his body.

This brief reflection on the theology of the Oxford Movement explains something of what led to the choice of both the subject and the form of the conference held at Pusey House between 29 June and 1 July 2016: 'A Transforming Vision: Knowing and Loving the Triune God'. First, the way that the doctrine of the Trinity takes us to the heart of Christian theology, worship and life suggested that this subject would be a good choice for the first of what we plan to be a series of confer-ences. Second, the study of Christian theology in the last half-century has seen a major renaissance in Trinitarian thought, which has been expressed in attempts to connect Trinitarian theology to all aspects of Christian faith and practice. The way in which contemplating the doc-trine of the Trinity leads to a consideration of how the study of theol-ogy is also an invitation to share and grow in the life that is both the goal and the principle of that study, fits with the Oxford Movement's emphasis on the intrinsic connection between theology, worship and sanctification. For Pusey, Keble, Newman and their colleagues, movement towards God comes with transformation, with being born of God and becoming progressively more like God.

While not all the speakers at the conference would either endorse or share all of the principles or emphases of the Oxford Movement, the themes and ideas described above animate and guide the reflections on Trinitarian thought and life that appear in this volume. All the authors acknowledge and grapple in different ways with the tension between what we can know about God the Holy Trinity and how an overconfidence in the powers of human apprehension can distort or conceal the truth and the life we seek. An awareness of this challenge and of the corporate character of all our knowing led us to invite speakers from different traditions in the hope that we might approach something more of a catholic fulness in our response to the revelation and dynamic reality of the Divine Love. The speakers at the conference also consider in different ways how reflection about what it means to know and to love God raises the question of participation in the life of the Holy Trinity. While the theme of participation is one of the unifying themes of the conference, one also finds caution about making simplistic connections between whatever we understand about the triune life of God and discerning the image of the Trinity in either the human person or in the life of the Church. We find a similar caution about making simplistic connections in discussions about social Trinitarianism. On the one hand, there is a shared understanding that it makes sense to consider how the Bible, philosophical reflection and the created order suggest that human flourishing is ordered according to some resemblance with the fountain of all life. On the other hand, there is a caution about making God simply a bigger or more perfect instance of our social aspirations, or about collapsing the distinction between the Creator and the creature in a way that leads to some form of implicit pantheism.

The emphasis of the Oxford Movement on the way worship and prayer are intrinsic to the task and goal of theology led to our decision to have the conference unfold within the normal pattern of daily worship that orders our life at Pusey House. The conference began with a Solemn Eucharist for the Feast of St Peter and St Paul and with a sermon that reminded us that 'this is where for the Church our doctrine of God *begins* – in the apostles' experience and testimony to God's act and initiative.' The way the conference was framed by the daily Mass and daily offices, with Orthodox Vespers one evening, is reflected in this volume by the interspersing of the sermons offered by the conference preacher, the Bishop of Ebbsfleet, the Rt Revd Jonathan Goodall. We also see in many of the papers this volume brings together a natural movement from reflection on the doctrine of the Trinity to a consideration of how the life of the Church is ordered and sustained by the gift of the sacraments and the life of prayer. The authors of the chapters that follow describe also the connection between what we know about God and how we live and make moral decisions, and how we both apprehend the revelation of God as the Holy Trinity and respond to that revelation in works of music and art as well as in dogmatic theology.

For those who are willing to live out one of the recurring themes of T. S. Eliot's *Four Quartets*, that 'In my end is my beginning', the best introduction to this volume is the concluding chapter by Rowan Williams. There he reflects on the themes of the conference, three days of both speaking about God the Holy Trinity and considering 'the territory we inhabit', with the help of three questions: 'Where do we look?'; 'Where do we stand?'; 'How are we united with God?' In what is probably a perfect expression of the kind of oversimplification the authors encourage us to avoid, the chapters in this volume are organized according to a Trinitarian shape, with three main parts between an introductory part and Rowan Williams' concluding reflections. The preliminary material also includes a tribute to John Webster, sometime Professor of Divinity at the University of St Andrews, Lady Margaret Professor of Divinity in Oxford and Professor of Systematic Theology at Wycliffe College, University of Toronto. John had an important role in encouraging the organization of the conference and had already produced the abstract of the paper he planned to deliver before he died suddenly in the weeks leading up to the conference. We were particularly grateful to Oliver O'Donovan for stepping in at the last minute and offering a fine paper in memory of his long-time colleague and friend. The tribute included here by Andrew Moore, another friend of John, preceded in the conference his introduction to Oliver O'Donovan's paper.

The introductory part of this volume, 'Surveying the Mystery', begins as the conference did, with a reflection on God the Holy Trinity in the context of worship and with the celebration of the sacrament of Holy Communion, and ordered by the apostolic witness of Sts Peter and Paul. The other two introductory chapters offer in different ways a helpful overview of some of the key themes of the conference as described above. Jarred Mercer's investigation of Hilary of Poitiers' Trinitarian theology leads him to reflect on the question of participation through the lens of Hilary's ideas about the mutual indwelling of Christ and the Church, in the Incarnation and in the Eucharist. He considers also the dangers of projection when attempting to speak about God and suggests how classic sources and concepts can guide our approach to social Trinitarianism. Jeremy Begbie's investigation of how an appreciation of music can shape our understanding of 'Trinitarian space' helps to bring to light the change of perspective that a fruitful consideration of Trinitarian theology requires. His analysis reveals both the way any knowledge of the Trinity must be both high and elusive, and also how disciplined and careful thought can help us to see more clearly and live more faithfully.

Following on from the introductory chapters in Part 1, Part 2 of the book, 'Foundations', brings together four chapters reflecting on the foundational sources of Trinitarian theology – the Bible and the witness of the Fathers of the Church. In the first chapter of this part, Hans Boersma takes us to the christological centre of Trinitarian theology, reflecting on Origen's and Chrysostom's complementary but distinct approaches to the divine hospitality manifest in the encounter between Abraham and the three divine visitors in Genesis 18 and 19. Boersma invites the reader not just to reflect on the divine hospitality but to participate in it: 'Let us give attention to make our acts such . . . that we, known by the Trinity, might also deserve to know the mystery of the Trinity' (Origen). In their 'relational and reciprocal' complementarity, the two New Testament chapters in this part reflect on and model related emphases of Trinitarian theology. Markus Bockmuehl considers the theme of knowing and loving in the Gospels, arguing that 'knowledge of God saves above all where it denotes God's knowledge, the unknowing human knower being divinely known by the Father through the Son in the Spirit'. Jenn Strawbridge amplifies this theme, suggesting that 'love in its fullest sense expands to subsume true knowledge', that in St Paul's writings an awareness of the imperfection of human knowing produces not despair but hope, leading through longing and sighing 'to the knowledge that only the Spirit and only Christ can fully know and intercede for us with God'. In his masterly chapter, Kallistos Ware emphasizes the centrality of Trinitarian reflection in the theology of the East – 'Between the Trinity and hell, there lies no other choice' (Florensky). In particular, he argues that the Cappadocians avoid both tritheism and modalism to emphasize theologically and pastorally 'the *koinonia* of the three who are joined in mutual love'. In the final chapter of this part, Paige Hochschild focuses on the theology of Augustine of Hippo and his 'logic of Trinitarian renewal'. There she considers how the idea of worship mediates between the wisdom that is summed up in the person of Christ, 'in whom are hidden all the treasures of wisdom and knowledge', and true human wisdom, which is a kind of 'participation in this wisdom, to which we cling by the Holy Spirit, who is charity spread abroad in our hearts'.

The middle part of the volume, 'Explorations', offers a series of historical and theological explorations of Trinitarian thought, considering also the importance of artistic and liturgical expressions. Against the backdrop of misunderstandings of Thomas Aquinas' Trinitarian theology, Richard Conrad examines the *Summa Theologiae* to argue that for Thomas, the reason why the triune God 'goes out' in the acts of creation and salvation is a 'journey home' that is the perfection of the image of God in the human being – a participation in the Divine Love, a conformity to the Divine Wisdom, and eternal friendship with God.[5] In his chapter on the English divine Richard Hooker and the sources of his theology in the pre-scholastic Greek patristic tradition, Gary Thorne offers another perspective on participation. He argues that Hooker's Trinitarian and Incarnational doctrine of the sacraments and of creation offers 'a way of seeing and interpreting the whole of experience as theophany and sacrament, making us partakers of the divine within the created order and leading us to know our happiness by living the life of God the Holy Trinity'. Gavin Dunbar also reflects on the liturgical tradition of the English Church and the Book of Common Prayer. He argues that Thomas Cranmer crafted a verbal image of the Trinitarian 'Throne of Mercy', which replaced the visual images that disappeared from English altars and churches in the iconoclasm following the Reformation. He examines the dynamic of continuity and change in Cranmer's liturgical reforms, arguing that it 'provides a frame within which the Church's own mission of witness and service in the world may be better understood within a Trinitarian context'. In the final chapter in this part, Ayla Lepine takes the reader on a tour of Oxford, inviting us to look with her at a number of Victorian and early twentieth-century British works that 'represent something bespoke and personal as a response to the ultimate, changeless, perfect vitality of God' and offer a purgative and reshaping 'horizon of engagement with Trinitarian theology'. The importance of this work of purgation is a recurring theme in this volume.

The final part of the book, 'The Trinity in Prayer, in Life and in the Church', brings together chapters that emphasize how Trinitarian thought is both shaped by and leads to prayer and contemplation, action and ethical reflection. It opens and closes with sermons by the conference preacher, the Bishop of Ebbsfleet, in which he invites the reader to share in the first disciples' transforming encounter with Christ and to live in the Church as a foretaste of a new creation, shaped by a threefold movement of love 'which the Father originates, the Son undertakes, and the Holy Spirit enables'. In another chapter that anchors theological reflection in the life of the Church, Andrew Louth argues that it is essential to understand Sergii Bulgakov's theology and his 'conception of the self-revelation of the Godhead in the double figure of Wisdom-Glory' not primarily as a theological expression of nineteenth-century idealism but as the prayer of a priest, 'reflecting on and interpreting what he is doing when he is standing before the altar, celebrating the Divine Liturgy'. Continuing in this vein of considering how Trinitarian doctrine emerges with prayer, Lucy Gardner argues that for Hans Urs von Balthasar, 'Christian prayer, the Church's Spirit-empowered participation in Christ's prayer to the Father, and contemplation in particular, appears to provide not only a resource for Christian theological reflection, but in a sense also both its horizon and its content.' Two of Gardner's conclusions, that 'Theology cannot merely describe the process of our transformation, it must contribute to it', and that 'there is ultimately no division between contemplation and action', serve as a helpful bridge to the contributions by Lydia Schumacher and Oliver O'Donovan. In her chapter, Schumacher leads us back to Aquinas, offering a 'constructive account' of how his doctrine of the Trinity 'may serve as a model for human participation in the life of the triune God', and seeking to establish 'the Christian doctrine of the Trinity as the ultimate foundation for enabling us to live the human lives – and be the human beings – we were designed by God to be'. In the final chapter of this part, Oliver O'Donovan examines the role of ethics in 'discourse about the Trinity', arguing that 'it takes a Trinitarian God to elicit purposeful human action' and inviting us to 'live out the conformity between God's gracious act and our responsive action'. The book concludes as the conference did, with Rowan Williams' overview and reflections on three days of thinking, talking and praying together.

In some ways the division of the chapters into the parts described here is an arbitrary one, as they all reflect in different ways on biblical or patristic sources, all include elements of historical theology, and all raise questions about moral action, prayer and the life of faith. Nonetheless, this division of the chapters can help us to see how they serve to interpret one another or how the different authors approach similar questions from different perspectives or offer different emphases.

It is our hope that this collection from the Transforming Vision conference, as well as others like it in the future, will contribute in a small way to that serious, disciplined and patient recovery of the Church's memory that shapes and encourages a renewed and renewing encounter with the risen and ascended Christ, present in the Church and the world by the Holy Spirit.

Notes

1   E. B. Pusey, 'Lectures on Types and Prophecies of the Old Testament: written mainly in July–August, 1836', unpublished manuscript, Pusey House, Oxford, LBV-151, p. 2.

2   John Henry Newman, 'On the Introduction of Rationalistic Principles into Religion', No. 73, *Tracts for the Times*, iii (London: J. G. & F. Rivington, 1839), p. 9.

3   Andrew Louth discusses the importance of this unity at length in *Discerning the Mystery* (Oxford: Clarendon Press, 1989), pp. 2ff.

4   Newman, *op. cit.*, p. 18.

5   This sentence is a paraphrase of the author's Abstract for the chapter.

Acknowledgements

This collection offers the harvest of many hands and many hours of labour. Behind the book lies the Transforming Vision conference held at Pusey House between 29 June and 1 July 2016, and the work and support that made the conference possible. We are especially grateful to the speakers and those who have contributed to this book, and who also contributed to the social life of the conference. Simon Jones put us in contact with Christine Smith, and David Shervington at SCM Press has worked generously and patiently with us to bring the project to fruition. Paul Oliver and Daniel Matore gave long hours to proofread and to assist with the editing and formatting of the papers.

In addition to those whose papers are collected here, we would like to thank Douglas Hedley, Alister McGrath and Robin Ward, for both presenting papers at the conference and for offering generous assistance and encouragement. David Harris had a crucial role in inspiring, shaping and helping to organize the conference, and then tirelessly produced numerous versions of all the publicity material and web pages. Andrew Pinsent offered essential advice and guidance gleaned from his years of running successful conferences, which saved us many headaches and helped things run more smoothly. Sarah Clarkson oversaw and helped to coordinate and organize myriad practical tasks and details with good humour and great competence. Karen Westhaver helped to make sure that our creditors were paid. Maks Adach organized and directed the musical contributions to the daily services and prepared the service booklets. Our sacristan, Sam Aldred, saw that the services were conducted in good order and with reverence. The librarian of Pusey House, Anna James, both assisted with the preparations for, and the day-to-day life of, the conference (including the provision of very welcome *pains au chocolat* at the breakfasts). Finally, all the conference participants, by their presence, questions and conversation helped to inspire and shape this book.

The conference would not have been possible without the partnership of St Cross College. St Cross provided the catering and made available the common room and hall each day. We are especially grateful to Mark Jones, Suzy Hodge, Flori Olteanu, Lara Summerhill, Paul Wicking and all who worked with them. We are also grateful to Johannes Zachhuber and to the Faculty of Theology and Religion and the University of Oxford for their support.

Louis Harris printed and helped to prepare a small mountain of paper, and Michael Lessman produced a fine conference booklet. We are also grateful for the team of stewards who greeted participants, answered questions and performed a great variety of necessary work, and to Sam Maginnis, who helped to coordinate their efforts. In addition to those mentioned above, this team included: Fr Sam Cross, Thomas Fink-Jensen, James Roberts, Fergus Butler-Gallie, Sophy Tuck, Jenny Lander, Jon Askonas, Jozef Kosc, Isaac Frisby, John Ritzema, John Smallman, Kvetoslav Krejci and Matthew Cashmore.

The conference was made possible with the help of generous grants from the Anglican Foundation, the Fellowship of St Alban and St Sergius, the St Theosevia Centre for Christian Spirituality, the Anglican and Eastern Churches Association, the John Bishop Charitable Trust and the Prayer Book Society. Throughout the project, the members of the governing body of Pusey House were consistent in their enthusiasm and encouragement.

George Westhaver, Principal
Mark Stafford, Chaplain
Pusey House, Oxford

John Webster – A Tribute

ANDREW MOORE

Many of us here, when we first heard about this conference and saw its list of speakers, would have been particularly attracted by the opportunity to hear Professor John Webster. Sadly, as everyone will know, John died, suddenly and unexpectedly, a few short weeks before the conference began. Many of us knew him – in person or through his writings – and grieve for him, so it seems right that we spend a few moments recollecting John and his contributions to the Church before I introduce Professor O' Donovan's paper.

In an interview published in the American journal *The Christian Century* in 2008, John was asked how he would account for the renewed interest in systematic theology over the last decade or two. He replied:

> The renewed confidence that constructive theology is possible and worthwhile is probably the biggest change in theological culture since I was a graduate student in the late 1970s. The confidence has many roots: the steady decline of models of theology in which 'critical appraisal' is the dominant task; receptiveness toward and fresh engagement with classical thinkers, patristic, medieval and Reformation; a sense that the Enlightenment is only one episode in the history of one (Western) culture and not a turning point in the history of humankind; the work of a number of gifted and independent-minded theologians now at the height of their powers who have shown the potency of constructive doctrinal work.[1]

Typically, Webster doesn't say who he has in mind under those descriptions, though some educated guesses might be made. For example, the 'gifted and independent-minded theologians . . . now at the height of their powers' who helped renew confidence in constructive theology would undoubtedly have included Oliver O'Donovan. But John certainly would not have allowed the thought to enter his head that, getting on for ten years after that interview, he himself would be among the ranks of those constructive theologians, themselves at the height of their powers, who would be inspiring and training a new, younger generation, to continue and to develop the work that had begun in the 1980s.

Raised in Yorkshire, John was a fine example of that county's people – modest, to the point, and not naturally tolerant of snobbishness or hierarchy. So when his interviewer asks, 'Why should ordinary Christians care about such seemingly recondite matters as how to articulate the immanent being of the Trinity?', John's answer is that of a sanctified Yorkshireman: 'There aren't any "ordinary" Christians; there are saints, a few of whom are appointed to the task of thinking hard about and trying to articulate the common faith of the church.' Since the question and the answer relate directly to the theme of this conference, allow me to quote his response in full.

> We don't usually need to use formal theological language and concepts in the everyday life of the church in prayer, preaching and service. But like any other important human activity, faith has to achieve a measure of conceptual clarity if it is to understand and express itself, and part of that process is the development of abstract concepts like Trinity, Incarnation and substance. What's important is that we don't treat such concepts as if they were improvements on the ordinary ways in which the saints express the faith; they are simply shorthand terms, a tool kit which helps us keep certain crucial aspects of the gospel alive in the mind and worship of the church. Theology and theological abstractions matter because the gospel matters, because the gospel concerns truth, and because living in and from the truth involves the discipleship of reason.

John was personally very encouraging to Fr George Westhaver when he took up his post as Principal here at Pusey House (they had become friends when they were both in Toronto). He wanted to see Pusey House flourish as a centre of catholic learning and teaching in the traditions of the Church of England. Shortly after John had moved to St Andrews to take up the Chair of Divinity, a graduate student commented to me that John seemed to have become 'more catholic'. This took me somewhat by surprise, more for my interlocutor's rather narrow sense of what catholic Christianity could be than for what the comment said about John. For later in the interview from which I have been quoting, in response to the question, 'If you were just starting out in theology today, what topics and issues would you want to tackle?', John replied, 'What I didn't get round to doing when I set out: lots of exegesis, lots of historical theology, mastering the big texts of the traditions of the church.' Isn't that an answer with which Dr Pusey would have been in wholehearted agreement? 'Lots of exegesis, lots of historical theology, mastering the big texts of the traditions of the church.' Wasn't it precisely that to which Dr Pusey sought to recall the Church of England?

When I last saw John – a month before his death – he spoke in much the same terms of his scholarly priorities; life was too short for secondary literature (not that he didn't read it). John was and remained an Anglican theologian in the Reformed tradition, and like John Owen (the four-hundredth anniversary of whose birth is celebrated this year), whose work was a major recent focus of John's own, he was as likely to quote favourably from Thomas Aquinas as from John Calvin. Give or take a capital 'C' – a difference inexpressible in spoken English – John would have joined earnestly with the words of the Collect for Pusey House: 'Grant that this House . . . may ever serve to thy glory, by the maintenance of the Catholic Faith, and by the preaching of thy Holy Gospel, through the same thy Son, Jesus Christ our Lord.'

In human terms, that John has been taken from us seems a great loss to the Church; but we submit ourselves to God, and give thanks for his life. Let us therefore spend a few moments in prayer.

Heavenly Father, we give heartfelt thanks for the life and ministry of your servant, John Bainbridge Webster, and we praise you for all the ways that you have blessed us and your whole Church through his life and learning. Give to us, we pray, the same patience and docility in wrestling with your truth, the same courage in proclaiming the gospel, and the same wisdom and generosity in meeting our neighbour, through Jesus Christ, our Lord and Saviour.

May he rest in peace
and rise in glory.

Note

1   *The Christian Century*, 3 June 2008, pp. 32–4.

PART ONE

Surveying the Mystery

Sermon

Trinitarian Communion

JONATHAN GOODALL

Solemn Eucharist for St Peter and St Paul, Wednesday 29 June
Lectionary: Zechariah 4.1–6a, 10b–14; Acts 12.1–1; Matthew 16.13–19

Surely it can be no accident that this conference is beginning with a celebration of the apostles Peter and Paul: Peter the first disciple called by Jesus in the narratives of the synoptic Gospels, the rock of the Church; and Paul, the 'last of all', as he calls himself (1 Cor. 15.8), neither a disciple nor one of the Twelve but nonetheless 'the Apostle', the missionary par excellence.

The New Testament tells us about their callings and labours, and gives us their teachings, but it does not tell us about their ends. Ancient tradition tells us they were both martyrs, victims of the savage persecution against Christians in Rome, and thus founders of the Church in the imperial city, and for this reason it became the Church that presides in love and is rich in mission. Moved by an inner strength, by an *apokálypsis* (a revelation) that could only come from God, whether at Caesarea Philippi or Damascus, they had believed that Jesus was the Messiah, the Son of God. The first- and last-called, two lives offered for the cause of Jesus and the Gospel; so different in personality and earthly witness but so united by the manner of their deaths that their traditional image – a tight embrace, face to face and seen in half-profile – must have been well known before the famous fourth-century marble found at Aquileia was carved. 'Whether it was I or the other apostles,' says St Paul, 'God's grace was the way we proclaimed Christ raised from the dead, and God's grace was the way you have come to believe' (1 Cor. 15.10–12).

And this is where, for the Church, our doctrine of God *begins*: in the apostles' experience and testimony to God's act and initiative. They are the eyewitnesses of God's self-revelation and self-proclamation in the person of Jesus Christ. When God the eternal Son came in human form, he gathered people to himself, he called them close, to teach them, to challenge them to repent, to help them to see and believe. He invited them to stand in *his* shoes, to see the world, human sin and human need, God himself, and his mercy, through *his* eyes. He drew them into a quality of relationship where following means carrying his cross, sharing his suffering, being baptized with his baptism, dying to self and living to God. The apostles found themselves immersed in a frightening and exhilarating mystery, something they could barely comprehend, much less control. They were being caught up into the movement of the Son's love, in the Spirit, for the Father – the 'movement of his own self-offering' as ARCIC put it – and into all that that transforming vision would mean and promise and cost.

It was discipleship that involved repeat learning: being called, standing alongside Christ, misunderstanding, falling and failing, being forgiven and recalled; until, on the far side of the most devastating failure, they find themselves alongside the risen Christ who now tells them that, filled with his Spirit, they are to go, to baptize others in the name of the 'threefold love' and to teach others to grow in holiness. They are to go and invite others to join them standing in Christ's place, praying Christ's prayer, breathing Christ's Spirit.

And it is out of that experience – fellowship, mission and above all baptism and the Eucharist – that doctrine about the Christian God, the Christlike God, arises. Learning repeatedly to identify with Christ and his sacrifice, using his words in order to return love to the same Father, seeking the anointing and energy of his Spirit, the Church of God came to understand that it lives in and from the Holy Trinity. It is a living presence so deep and real that the early Christians could easily grasp that – to use the title of the Anglican-Orthodox Commission's 2006 report – the Church is the 'church of the triune God', totally shaped and marked and filled with the Trinity. 'The Church', says Origen, 'is *full* of the Trinity', and moreover, 'he who is in the church inhabits the universe' (*Selecta in Psalmos* 23.1, PG 12:1265B).

What is revealed – and learnt – through the mystery of Christ's Incarnation is precisely that Christ is not a single individual but a divine person and as such is the fullest possible relation to the Father and the Holy Spirit. Likewise, the Father and the Holy Spirit do not simply verify the identity of Jesus Christ as the only-begotten Son of the Father, on whom the Holy Spirit rests (Matt. 3.16–17 and par.; John 1.29–34); they are also united with the incarnate Son in the fullest possible relation, present in him from his conception and into the new creation. The life he reveals, the life that is revealed through him, the life that is given in him, is a participation in an eternal and perfect communion of irreducibly distinct persons in love, a permanent freedom of mutual self-offering of each, and of all of them to the world (John 10.17–18; 17.4; Phil. 2.6–11; Heb. 9.14).

So while we shall hear in the coming days a great deal to help us to think through and explore this overwhelming mystery, we need at all times to recall that the place of the Holy Trinity's fullness in the world, and the place where the gathering together of creation begins, is in the Church, which De Lubac calls the 'mysterious extension of the Trinity in time' (*Ecclesia Mater*, 237), among the adopted sons and daughters of the Father, a people united by the unity of the Trinity (St Cyprian, *De orat. Dom.*, 23).

And of course it is here, in the celebration of the Holy Eucharist, that our life in the Holy Trinity comes most energetically and joyfully to life. Here we take on ourselves Christ's Spirit, we speak with his words and ask his Father that the life that is in his Son will also come alive in us. And it is also from here, from this living fullness of eucharistic experience, that the work of ministry and mission flows most transformingly for the salvation and healing of the world.

So today we are giving thanks for the revelation of God as Holy Trinity in the experience and in the teaching of the apostles, especially in Peter and Paul, the twin pillars of the Church. And we are giving thanks that that life has not come to us in words alone but through the eucharistic identity of Christian communities throughout history. In societies painfully racked between globalization and individualism, the Church must offer this witness of communion in every aspect of its mission. It is a reality that comes from nowhere in this world but is a mystery rooted in the presence of the triune God himself. The spiritual and theological deepening of the doctrine of the Trinity by contemporary theology will help lay a new foundation for a rediscovery of the mystery of the triune God as the source, the model and the ultimate goal of both the human and the non-human world.

Eucharistic Priority in Trinitarian Theology: Retrieving a Patristic Idea

JARRED MERCER

Introduction

'Who would the Saviour *have to be* . . . to rescue human beings?', reads the description on the back of a very influential and important book on Christology. This statement in many ways encapsulates what I think is an epidemic in contemporary theology: God in God's self, *Theos*, is no longer a suitable object of *theo*logical enquiry. Theology has in too many ways become another consumer service for our own perceived needs or agendas: we are no longer understood in relation to God but God in relation to us – God is who we *need* God to be. This is particularly evident in the way Trinitarian theology has become an essential ecclesiological and anthropological prolegomenon. Human communion, it is assumed, must *reflect* the triune communion. So Miroslav Volf contends: 'Today, the idea that the church as a community should take its shape from the communion within the Holy Trinity enjoys the status of an almost self-evident presupposition.'[1]

Contemporary discussions typically assume that this seemingly self-evident link inherently necessitates that triune relations exist as a 'model' for human ones. The Trinity must be *relevant* in some way; it must 'say' something to the human condition and to the interrelations of human beings in society.[2]

The need felt by many theologians to restore the doctrine of the Trinity to 'relevance' has led to, I believe, not only problematic solutions but a misdiagnosis of the problem itself, principally by assuming that the purpose of Trinitarian theology is to be relevant to human relations at all, and further by replacing a foundation of classic Trinitarianism, Creator–creature *distinction*, with an epistemological *gap* between the human and divine, something that is to be bridged through human conceptualization projected on to God. This projection creates a vision of the Trinity that is necessarily anthropocentric, and makes bold presumptions regarding the ability of the human mind to access the divine. Through these processes, divine and human relations have become *comparable* things and, I will argue, Trinitarian doctrine is led into the very irrelevance it has sought to avoid.

This chapter seeks to contribute to contemporary discussions through exploring how the Eucharist is for Hilary of Poitiers a fundamental point of access to knowing the triune God. Hilary gives a *eucharistic priority* to Trinitarian theology; that is to say, there is a *primacy* for the grammar of God as triune given to the Eucharist.[3] His journey of thinking towards God takes eucharistic shape. Hilary is a choice source for constructing Trinitarian theology in this way, as his perspective is quite unique among theologians of his time.[4]

Hilary's offering of the Eucharist as a point of access into Trinitarian theology levels both strong critique against and constructive insight into our current situation, as it confronts the *way* contemporary theologians conceive of the Trinity functioning as precursor to anthropology – in other words, how *divine* relations and *human* relations are related to each other.

The Current Conversation: Socialization and the Need for 'Relevance'

The most prominent Trinitarian model contemporary theologians use to answer this question, and the one that shows the most utility for Trinitarian 'relevance', is most certainly 'social Trinitarianism'. This view holds that the Trinity is a tightly interwoven community of distinct persons on a very close analogy to that of human persons, allowing Trinitarian 'society' to serve as a model for human society.

In considering the Trinitarian impetus for human relations, social Trinitarianism has become the 'typical pattern of Trinitarian reflection';[5] indeed, Kilby notes, 'it has become the new orthodoxy'.[6] The basic assumption in social Trinitarianism is that the classical understanding of God as one substance and three persons is irrelevant, and in most cases, deeply problematic, for political, social and ecclesial life. Kilby traces a pattern of 'abstraction followed by application' throughout the various social theories: at some point the discussion moves away from the biblical narratives (Creation, Incarnation, Cross, Resurrection etc.) towards abstract concepts of persons, relations and *perichoresis* (a word now used to explain the mutual indwelling of the Father, Son and Spirit as an 'interpenetration' of three persons in one another).

These abstractions are then taken as the heart of Trinitarian doctrine, and an attempt follows to give these abstractions relevance to human life.[7] Here from the outset a major difficulty must be noted: this method is every bit as abstractive as those it critiques as being irrelevant through abstraction.

Reconceiving the Problem: Relevance and Idolatry of the Self

One key way this is true is how certain language, for example that of person, is used univocally of God and humanity,[8] particularly since this was precisely what the Cappadocians – who many of these theologians credit with their view of personhood[9] – were writing against in Eunomius![10] In the modern appropriation of this view, God is seen to relate to us, is seen as 'relevant' to us, because he is actually in a sense very much like us.[11] This type of univocality results in a human projection on God that might indeed see the true 'defeat' of Trinitarian theology.[12]

The idea of *perichoresis*, as appropriated in social Trinitarianism, logically necessitates the same sort of conclusion, particularly as expressed in theologians such as Moltmann[13] and LaCugna.[14] This sort of theological argument also makes a move beyond traditional understandings of the Creator–creature relationship, so that the life of God simply becomes the life of the world.[15] *Perichoresis*, connected with the overarching need in modern theology to relate the Trinitarian life to human community, yields to a breakdown in Creator–creature distinction that is at the very foundation of classical Trinitarian theology (the freedom in which social Trinitarianism can refer to the inner life of God indicates this). This insider information about the divine life is then referred back to the human condition, so that God's inner life is seen to have direct implications for what is not God.[16]

Jean-Luc Marion vividly elucidates something at the core of the problem described here in contemporary Trinitarianism, and indeed, of any conceptualization of the divine *tout court*:

> If my eventual concepts designating God say nothing about God, they say something about *me* insofar as I am confronted by the incomprehensible: they say what it is that I am able to consider, at least at a given moment, as an acceptable representation of God; they articulate, therefore, the conception that I make for myself of the divine – a conception that imposes itself on me as the best since it

defines precisely what is maximal or optimal for me. In short, the concepts that I assign to God, like so many invisible mirrors, send me back to the image that I make up for myself of divine perfection, which are thus images of myself. My concepts of God turn out in the end to be idols – idols of myself.[17]

Human finitude places restrictions on how the infinite God can be known, and no matter how tightly one presses an analogy between the inner life of God and human society, the relations of Trinitarian persons cannot be fully expressed in human community (this Volf readily admits).[18] Even given the demand for the Trinitarian life to 'say something' to human relations, the distinction between the divine and human does not allow whatever the life of the Trinity is 'saying' to be heard. The inability of humanity to discern the inner life of the divine, coupled with a general refusal to admit this inability, inevitably results in the projection of human understanding on to God.[19] Without this anthropomorphizing projection, 'models' of communion based on the Trinitarian life simply cannot communicate to human life.

This is why these Trinitarian theologies, though their goal is to be utterly practical, always remain inevitably abstract and conceptual. So Kilby observes:

> It is . . . the abstraction, the conceptual formula, the three-in-oneness, that many theologians want to revivify, and if one is going to make an abstraction, a conceptual formula, relevant, vibrant, exciting, it is natural that one is going to have to project on to it, to fill it out again so that it becomes something the imagination can latch on to.[20]

Rather than achieving a presentation of the divinizing of humanity, or participation in the divine life, these theologies risk the inverse of *humanizing* the Trinity in a desperate attempt to claim 'relevance' of Trinitarian constructs for human ways of being.

Hilary's eucharistic Trinitarianism rejects this sort of abstraction and anthropocentrism. A close reading of his argument will provide the groundwork for retrieving eucharistic priority in Trinitarian theology today.

Hilary's Polemical Setting: The 'Example of Unity'

Hilary's polemical opponents were 'Homoians', from the Greek *homo-ios* (like), because they forbade any use of *ousia* (essence) language, and said Scripture only taught that the Son is 'like' the Father, without any further supplementation. They therefore argued that the Father and the Son are one in agreement of will only, and not in nature. They used the connection made by Christ in John 17.21 between human and divine union in their favour (Jesus' prayer that the Church 'may be one, even as you, Father, are in me and I in you'). The Homoian chain of logic was to project human relations on to God, like much of contemporary argumentation.[21] They referenced Acts 4.32, which says the multitude of believers were one in heart, and 1 Corinthians 3.8, in which the one that plants and the one that waters are united through their common working for salvation, and argued these are unities of will, not nature.[22] They then concluded that this must be true of the divine life as well.

Hilary suggests that the structure of Christ's prayer provides for a more faithful reading of the passage. The prayer is that 'they may be one' but this is ordered by an 'example of unity' (*exemplo unitatis*), so that 'as the Father is in the Son and the Son in the Father, so through the pattern of this unity all might be one in the Father and the Son.'[23] The logical movement of Christ's prayer is divine to human. This, however, creates serious obstacles. Humans do not have direct access to the divine – there is an infinite ontological distinction between Creator and creature for Hilary. God is incomprehensible, and though he is known in revelation, this knowledge is qualified as condescended to human ways of knowing: God is known in a *humane* way.[24] The key then to the relation of divine and human communion is answering how these infinitely distinct realities can interrelate – how they can *know* one another. Hilary finds the Homoian answer of human projection on to God radically insufficient. For Hilary, there must be a properly *theological* answer, in the strict sense of the word, for interpreting Jesus' words in John 17.

The 'Nature' of Unity

Hilary's argument begins by saying that the unity of the Church directly correlates to that of the Father and the Son because both unions are *natural*. Nature derives from birth for Hilary. The Son is of one nature with the Father because he is begotten of the Father and a father cannot generate a son of a different nature from his own.[25] In generation, he gives all that he is to his son so that they are equal and of the same nature.[26] Though Christians are united in faith, as in Acts 4.32, this is nevertheless a *natural* unity, as 'all were born again to innocence, immortality, knowledge of God, and the faith of hope.'[27] As there is a 'birth' into one faith, there is natural union, as nature corresponds to birth. The baptized 'have been regenerated *to a nature* of one life and eternity' and 'are one by regeneration in an identical nature'.[28] For Hilary, the unity of the Father and Son is the 'example' for Christians then, not because the triune unity sets a model to follow after, or patterns a way of being for humanity but because both human unity and divine unity are *natural*.

Hilary continues in *Trin*. 8.8 stating that this unity comes 'from the nature of the mysteries' (*ex natura sacramentorum*) in all those who 'have put on Christ' in one baptism:[29] the 'nature' of the sacraments is the source of this unity, and Christ himself its habitation. Humans are naturally united *sacramentally* but this sacramental nature has its source in Christ, and so we begin to move towards a proper theological, or theocentric, key to understand divine–human relations, as opposed to the Homoian anthropocentric practice of projection.

The Incarnation as Gift of the Trinity

Natural union through 'birth' into one nature is a birth *into Christ* for Hilary. In its most basic appropriation this refers to Christ's Incarnation. In assuming human nature to himself Christ has united humanity to the divine. Because of Christ's words ('I in them and you in me'), which qualify the natural union of humanity ('that they may be one'), Hilary contends that if his opponents do not believe that the Father and the Son are united by nature, they must also deny natural union between Christ and humanity, in other words, promote a docetic Christology and, in effect, deny human salvation, as salvation depends on the uniting of real, actual human life to God in Christ.[30] He also enforces the inverse of this argument. According to the Homoians' own logic of human projection on the divine, this natural union of Christ with humanity necessitates natural union in the Father and the Son, on the authority of their own favoured prooftext of John 17.21.

Human union with God and with one another rests for Hilary on the Incarnation. Christ, assuming the form of the slave (*forma servi*) while remaining in the form of God (*forma Dei*), directly implicates the divine in human communion.[31] And the communion of the Church is the bearer of the divine presence,[32] as she is united to Christ. For Hilary, the Church is very literally Christ's body, united to Christ through his assumption of human flesh: the Church is *concorporeal* with Christ.[33] Owing to this, as Dupont-Fauville writes, 'the ecclesial communion is not only permitted by communion with God but it is the very *expression* of it'; it is 'where the presence of Christ is met and plainly *lived*, to the point that its members become participants in God made human'.[34]

Christ himself is the locative expression of the triune life in the world, the place where God's life is embodied as a lived reality in creation, and through the Church's union with and in him, she is as well. Hilary goes as far to say that the divine unity is co-inhabited by Christ and the Church. The Church's participation in Christ brings her into the divine life so that there is a 'cohabitation', a *communionem domicilii* where Christ and the Church reside together.[35] This *cohabitaturi cum Deo* is even expressed as *admisceri Deo* (literally to be mixed with God).[36] Christ communicates the triune communal life and that communion is lived, *practised*, in the human society of the Church.[37] It is important for Hilary that this is not a created union, something new, rather it is given and shared by Christ. This communion is a gift granted by and in the life of Christ, and it is continually received and shared in by the Church in the Eucharist.

In the Eucharist, the Church is constituted 'in the communion of the holy body' (*in communione sancti corporis*).[38] Such strong language can be used precisely because the triune life of God is *granted as gift*. In the Incarnation, Christ unites divinity and humanity, and therefore brings forth, inserts, the Trinitarian communion into human life. In Christ the divine communion is lived out in human terms – there is a temporal, historical deployment of the eternal reality of intra-Trinitarian relations.[39]

On Hilary's account, because the second person of the Trinity enters into the human condition, the intra-Trinitarian life takes humanity into itself, so that to participate in Trinitarian communion is simply to be incorporated in, assumed by, Christ. The person of Christ exists as divine–human unity so that humanity relates to the Father and the Spirit as Christ's humanity does, united to the divine Word.

Incarnation and Eucharistic Mediation

In *Tractatus mysteriorum* 1.3, Hilary reads the creation of Adam and Eve typologically in reference to Christ and the Church.[40] As Eve is created out of the side of Adam, so is the Church born from the blood and water flowing from Jesus' side on the cross, and as Eve came forth from Adam in his sleep, so does the Church rise out of Jesus' tomb. As Eve was the flesh of Adam's flesh, and they are called 'one flesh', so is the Church one flesh with Christ. For Hilary, as noted above, the 'one flesh' of Christ and the Church has its initial foundation in the Incarnation, but it is here sanctified (*sanctificatam esse*) after Christ's resurrection 'by the communion of his body' (*carnis suae communione*).[41] The argument of being united to Christ in the flesh through his body and blood and that he 'might remain in us by the sacrament' (*per sacramentum maneat in nobis*) is clearly connected to Hilary's discussion of the Eucharist based on John 6.56–57 ('Those who eat my flesh and drink my blood abide in me, and I in them . . . whoever eats me will live because of me') in *Trin.* 8.14–16.

This eucharistic image takes shape in *Trin.* 8.13. Natural union with the humanity of Christ unites humanity with the divine, as Christ is one with the Father:

> If indeed Christ has assumed the flesh of our body (*carnem corporis nostri*), if that man who was born from Mary is truly the Christ, and if we truly receive in a mystery the flesh of his body (*carnem corporis sui*), and by this we will be one, because the Father is in him and he in us, how is a unity of will maintained when the property of the nature through the mystery is the sacrament of a perfect unity (*perfectae sacramentum unitatis*)?[42]

Union with Christ is union with the triune God through Christ's mediation, and the *cause* of this unity is the 'sacrament of body and blood' (*sacramentum corporis et sanguinis*).[43]

Eucharist: From Trinitarian Polemic to Trinitarian Communion

Hilary sets out the unity of humanity with Christ and one another clearly in eucharistic terms. The Eucharist is 'a mirror image of the Incarnation'.[44] As Christ takes humanity into himself in the Incarnation, in the Eucharist humanity takes Christ into itself.[45] Therefore, the common life of the Church (being 'in Christ') finds its source in Christ's eucharistic presence. As human unity was utilized by Hilary as a tool in Trinitarian polemic, so does the Eucharist, the source of that human unity, take its own polemical place, and in the process becomes a focal point for Trinitarian doctrine.

In a theological engagement between John 6.56–57 ('Those who eat my flesh and drink my blood abide in me, and I in them . . . whoever eats me will live because of me') and John 17.21 (Jesus' prayer that the

Church 'may be one, even as you, Father, are in me and I in you'), the communion of humanity in the Eucharist is seen to emerge into the intimacy of the Trinity.[46] For Hilary, there is a movement from Eucharist to Trinity that does not only elevate the human understanding to confess the truth of the divine but elevates humanity itself, united as Christ's body, into the divine life.

In *Trin.* 8.17 the connection between the Christ–Church corporeal union and the Eucharist is made sharply, along with its Trinitarian context:

> The heretics maintain that the unity between the Father and the Son is only a unity of will, and our unity to God is used as an example; as if we were united to the Son, and by the Son to the Father, only by obedience and a pious will, and we are granted no property of a natural communion by the sacrament of the body and blood.[47]

Hilary argues, on the contrary, that 'by the Son remaining in us according to the flesh, we share an inseparable and corporeal union in him', and this requires the proclamation of 'the mystery of a true and natural union' of the Father and the Son.[48] In the Eucharist 'the communion which is established between us and Christ is founded on the gift of his body',[49] and this communion is clearly and distinctly Trinitarian for Hilary as by being united to the Son we are united to the Father.

In the Eucharist, this *gift* of divine communion given in the Incarnation continues to be given. This givenness is significant as it marks the unity of God with the Church and the Church with one another in the Eucharist as not a second or derivative communion,[50] not a unity 'modelled' after the divine unity but the triune unity itself *spilling out over into human existence*. This is what allows for the strict correlation of 'nature' language between human union and Trinitarian union. For Hilary: 'the communion introduces us into a divine reality . . . because it is a reality which exists in God. The mystery in which the Church is called to be nourished finds its source in the intimacy of the divine persons.'[51] As La Soujeole writes: 'Christ, by the sacrament of his body and his blood, introduces us into Trinitarian communion.'[52] *How* Hilary sees this participation in divine life worked out speaks particularly poignantly to contemporary discussions.

As already noted, this indwelling is, *through the mediation of Christ*, a Trinitarian indwelling. *Trin.* 8.15–16 connects John 14.19–20 (where Jesus says, 'I am in my Father, and you in me, and I in you') and John 6.57 ('As the living Father sent me, and I live because of the Father, so he who eats my flesh will live because of me') to show that Christ abided in humanity while also abiding in the Father, 'so that we might advance to the unity of the Father',[53] and that 'as he lives through the Father in like manner we live through his flesh'.[54] He adds here that this 'sacrament of perfect unity' (*perfectae unitatis sacramentum*), which is the source of this mutual union of Father and Son and Son in humanity, shapes our understanding, so that our knowledge might progress from the example proposed to the subject exemplified.[55] This, the 'cause of our life' that we 'have Christ remaining in our carnal selves through the flesh',[56] Hilary argues, acts also as an epistemological gateway into the triune unity. The natural unity we experience by the communion of his body (*carnis suae communione*) as the human embodiment of the triune communal life, functions to avail the finite restrictions of human knowing to grasp something of the divine life.[57]

The Eucharist stands as an impetus for Trinitarian theology. It is the sacrament of perfect unity not only owing to the unity it gives the Church, or to the Church with Christ, but because that unity is mediated by a mediator who condescends to share the gift of triune 'perfect union' with those who cannot even conceive of it. For Hilary, the Eucharist is the appropriation of the Incarnation-as-Trinitarian-communion embodied in the human condition, and as such is the point of access for humanity to the Trinitarian life of God. There is a movement of human knowing and experiencing from the Eucharist to the Trinity – a 'transforming vision', you might say, with the Eucharist as an epistemic foundation opening us up towards the knowledge of God. There is a eucharistic priority in Trinitarian theology because the Eucharist, as the mirror of the Incarnation, creates the space where the triune life touches down, where the triune communion of God is lived in human existence.

A 'Retrieval': Christ and the Practice of Trinitarian Communion

A 'retrieval'[58] of Hilary's eucharistic Trinitarianism allows the Trinitarian life, or 'relations', to have ecclesial and anthropological effectiveness without the anthropomorphizing projection so prevalent in contemporary discussions, and sustains Trinitarian theology's necessary distinction between Creator and creature. There is no epistemic 'gap' to be closed by Trinitarian relations being something like human ones but humanity is joined to Trinitarian relations through Christ; indeed, Christ *gifts* them to us, so that, as Kathryn Tanner contends, 'in Christ we are therefore shown what the Trinity looks like when it includes the human, and what humanity looks like when it is taken up within the trinity's own relationships.'[59]

Further, there are significant anthropological implications for this account. The more similar Trinitarian relations are to human relations (i.e. the more they are a model or can be imitated by humans), the less the Trinity can tell humanity anything it did not already know about those relations. When *difference* is recognized, when an assumed gap is not bridged by human projection but infinite Creator–creature distinction is upheld, Trinitarian doctrine is not only a practised reality but a *hopeful* one – as the triune life is not brought down to our level for our imitation but we are brought up into it as *invitation*.[60]

Humans as humans cannot genuinely inhabit the kind of union described on perichoretic social models. Humans in this view cannot be taken into union with the divine while remaining the creatures that they are, yet these models continue to demand human participation in that union. The only hope then for communion with the divine life in these models is to become something other than human. The God who looks a lot like human beings cannot transform them but leaves them where they are. Not only is this an abstract Trinitarian theology and one that therefore lacks true 'relevance', it is an anthropocentric one that lacks genuine *hope*.

On the contrary, if the mediation of Christ as the Trinitarian life lived out in the human condition is given its proper primacy, humans are understood to be united to and in the divine life through being incorporated into Christ: not becoming what they are not but becoming more fully what they truly are.[61]

My suggestion here is that by re-establishing eucharistic priority in Trinitarian thought, the question of 'relevance' is avoided entirely: the Eucharist *performs*[62] or *practises* Trinitarian communion in human society. As brought out in Hilary's eucharistic Trinitarianism, there is no 'model' of Trinitarian communion given that humanity is to follow; rather, in Christ, Trinitarian communion has entered human existence. Jesus Christ *is* Trinitarian communion as expressed in humanity. The mutual indwelling of Christ and the Church in the Incarnation and in the Eucharist therefore effectively performs the intra-Trinitarian life in the world – in the manner that corresponds to human knowing and being, not in ethereal abstractions or propositions concerning divine realities that are unapproachable from within the confines of historically conditioned, finitely restricted human life. The same theological problem of divine and human relations that Hilary and the Homoians faced remains present in contemporary Trinitarianism, so we must ask ourselves: 'Why is Homoian logic winning?'

Conclusion: Eucharistic Priority

If Trinitarian theology is to offer anything to discussions of ecclesiology and anthropology, if it is to 'say' anything to human ways of
being and relating, it cannot be through univocal speech and a process
of projection that not only humanizes God but threatens to dehuman-
ize humanity, but by the triune life itself entering into and inhabiting
human space. There is a eucharistic priority in Trinitarian theology
because there is Incarnational priority – because knowledge of God as
Trinity is *practised* knowledge, *performed* knowledge, expressed in the
unity of the Church united to Christ; and the stage for such a performance is the Altar.

The Church therefore lives out Trinitarian communal life in human
society not by following an unapproachable model but by existing in the
world as the continuation of Christ within it through eucharistic unity.
In Trinitarian theology we do not find a guide for national governance
or family relations, or a model for economic stability, whether through
capitalistic trade unions or communitarian ideals. We do not find a pattern for congregationalist or hierarchical Church polity. What we find
is a compassion that touches lepers, a mercy that embraces sinners, a
self-giving love that results in a Roman cross, and a love that continues
to be on offer for the life of the world *carnis suae communione*. The triune life is not offered as a 'model' for humanity, it is *gifted* to humanity.

The Church knows and experiences unity with the triune God and
one another not in the abstract outside of this eucharistic gift given to
her in the 'sacrament of perfect unity' (*sacramentum perfectae unitatis*).
The Eucharist is our Trinitarian 'social programme'[63] if ever there was
one.

Notes

1 Miroslav Volf, 'The Trinity and the Church', in Paul Metzger (ed.), *Trinitarian Soundings in Systematic Theology* (New York: T. & T. Clark, 2005), p. 153.

2 See Karen Kilby, 'Hans Urs von Balthasar on the Trinity', in Peter C. Phan (ed.), *Cambridge Companion to the Trinity* (Cambridge: Cambridge University Press, 2011), p. 213.

3 I have chosen this language of 'priority' and 'primacy' to demonstrate not a level of importance but a movement from Eucharist to Trinity. Eucharistic priority in Trinitarian theology admits epistemic priority to the Eucharist in Trinitarian discourse.

4 For Hilary's novelty in giving the Eucharist a place of choice in Trinitarian theology, see Boris Bobrinskoy, 'L'Eucharistie et mystère du salut chez saint Hilaire de Poitiers', in *Hilaire et son temps: Actes du colloque de Poitiers 19 septembre – 3 octobre 1968 à l'occasion du XVIe centenaire de la mort de saint Hilaire* (Paris: Études Augustiniennes, 1969), p. 237.

5 Kilby, 'Balthasar', p. 213.

6 Karen Kilby, 'Perichoresis and Projection: Problems with Social Doctrines of the Trinity', *New Blackfriars* 81 (2000), p. 433. For more on the dominance of social Trinitarianism in modern thought, see Stanley J. Grenz, *Rediscovering the Triune God: The Trinity in Contemporary Theology* (Minneapolis, MN: Fortress, 2004), pp. 117–18; Khaled Anatolios, *Retrieving Nicaea: The Development and Meaning of Trinitarian Doctrine* (Grand Rapids, MI: Baker Academic, 2011), p. 6; Stephen R. Holmes, *The Quest for the Trinity: The Doctrine of God in Scripture, History and Modernity* (Downers Grove, IL: IVP Academic, 2012), pp. 1–32; Miroslav Volf, *After our Likeness: The Church as the Image of the Trinity* (Grand Rapids, MI: Eerdmans, 1998), pp. 27, 191. Its prominence, with particular regard to 'reviving' Trinitarian doctrine, is present throughout Catholic and Protestant, Eastern and Western theologies (see Kilby, 'Perichoresis', p. 432). The need for revival and in many ways the turn to relationality begins with Karl Barth and Karl Rahner in the Protestant and Catholic traditions, respectively, but finds its most influential proponents in the 'social' arena of Trinitarian theology in Jürgen Moltmann (especially *The Trinity and the Kingdom of God*, trans. Margaret Kohl (London: SCM Press, 1981)), with Pannenberg as a major impetus. In the Orthodox tradition, John Zizioulas has been the most influential voice, though some would argue that he himself is not strictly a social Trinitarian, and his influence has extended far beyond Orthodox theology (e.g. Miroslav Volf, Catherine Mowry LaCugna, Colin Gunton).

7 Kilby, 'Balthasar', p. 213.

8 See Holmes, *Quest*, pp. 15–16, also for this critique.

9 See John Zizioulas, *Being as Communion: Studies in Personhood and the Church* (London: Darton, Longman & Todd, 2004), pp. 40–9.

10 See Holmes, *Quest*, p. 15.

11 Holmes, *Quest*, p. 29. See also Kathryn Tanner, *Christ the Key* (Cambridge: Cambridge University Press, 2010), p. 221: 'The persons of the Trinity become very much like human persons. And therefore the Trinity itself becomes a collection . . . of distinct persons on a very close – too close – analogy to a society of human persons.'

12 Catherine Mowry LaCugna, *God for Us: The Trinity and the Christian Life* (New York: HarperCollins, 1991), pp. 8–9, argues the 'defeat' in Trinitarian theology was the Nicene understanding of the doctrine, which she interprets as strictly dividing *oikonomia* and *theologia*.

13 LaCugna, *God for Us*, pp. 160–1.

14 See LaCugna, *God for Us*, p. 228: Trinitarian life is not something 'belonging to God apart from the creature'; *perichoresis* is not only God in God but 'God in us, we in God, all of us in each other'.

15 See Grenz, *Rediscovering*, p. 125. Holmes, *Quest*, p. 11, elaborates: LaCugna and Moltmann insisted that Rahner was not sufficiently radical enough in carrying

his 'rule' to its logical conclusion – to them, 'his position demanded an insistence that the life of God simply is the life of the world'.

16 Kilby, 'Perichoresis', p. 436.

17 Jean-Luc Marion, 'The Impossible for Man–God', in Kevin Hart (ed.), *The Essential Writings* (New York: Fordham, 2013), p. 343.

18 Volf, *After Our Likeness*, pp. 210–11: 'In a strict sense, there can be no correspondence to the interiority of the divine persons at the human level.'

19 See Kilby, 'Perichoresis', on projection.

20 *Ibid.*, p. 443.

21 This is not to say that any contemporary theologians are proverbial fourth-century anti-Nicenes, but that while their conclusions may be different, there is something strikingly parallel about the *way* these theologians are thinking towards God.

22 Hilary, *De Trinitate* 8.5.

23 *Ibid.*, 8.11, SC 448:392. All translations of non-English texts are my own.

24 For Hilary on the inadequacy of human knowing, see Hilary, *Trin.* 1.7, 8, 13, 15, 18–19, 37; 2.2, 5–7, 10, 11; 3.20, 24; 4.2, 14; 5.1; 6.12; 7.1, 28–30; 8.43; 9.37, 72; 11.45–46; 12.31–32, 53–4.

25 Hilary, *Trin.* 7.28; 8.12.

26 *Ibid.*, 7.14; 11.22.

27 *Ibid.*, 8.7, SC 448:388.

28 *Ibid.*, emphasis added.

29 *Ibid.*, 8.8, SC 448:388.

30 *Ibid.*, 8.13.

31 See *Trin.* 11.14.

32 Denis Dupont-Fauville, *Saint Hilaire de Poitiers: théologien de la communion* (Rome: Gregoriana, 2008), p. 103.

33 Hilary, *Contra Consatantius*, 11.

34 Dupont-Fauville, *Hilaire*, p. 118.

35 Hilary, *Tractatus super Psalmos*, 14.1.

36 *Ibid.* See discussion in Dupont-Fauville, *Hilaire*, pp. 119–20.

37 Dupont-Fauville, *Hilaire*, pp. 119–20.

38 Hilary, *Tractatus* 64,14, CCSL 61:231. See Dupont-Fauville, *Hilaire*, pp. 119–20 and 144–5.

39 See Dupont-Fauville, *Hilaire*, p. 169.

40 Hilary, *Tract. mys.* 1.3, SC 19bis:70, 80. See also *Tract. sup. Ps.* 64.14.

41 The connection of Christ's resurrection to the Church's union with his body is very significant in Hilary's overall thought. See Dupont-Fauville, *Hilaire*, pp. 142–6; Bobrinskoy, 'L'Eucharistie', pp. 238–40; Ellen Scully, 'The Assumption of All Humanity in Hilary of Poitiers' *Tractatus super Psalmos*' (Marquette: unpublished PhD dissertation, 2011), p. 189. See Philip Wild, *The Divinization of Man According to Saint Hilary of Poitiers* (Mundelein, IL: Saint Mary of the Lake Seminary, 1950), pp. 37–8 and 112–13 for the Eucharist as eschatological preparation in Hilary. For a discussion of Christ himself as the human destiny of salvation, and the progressive nature of this, see Jarred Mercer, 'Suffering for Our Sake: Christ and Human Destiny in Hilary of Poitiers' *De Trinitate*', *Journal of Early Christian Studies* 22:4 (2014), pp. 541–68.

42 Hilary, *Trin.* 8.13, *SC* 448:398.

43 *Ibid.*, 8.15, *SC* 448:400. See Scully, 'Assumption', pp. 191–2: 'The Church is defined by its participation in the body of Christ and, through this body, in the life of the Trinity.' See Hector Scerri, *Koinonia, Diokonia and Martyria: Interrelated Themes in Patristic Sacramental Theology as Expounded by Adalber-G. Hamman O.F.M.* (Malta: Foundation for Theological Studies, 1999), pp. 130–1, for how Hilary is the first to develop this theme in relation to the Eucharist and deification, and how it continues in the patristic tradition (notably in Gregory of Nyssa, John Chrysostom, Augustine and Cyril).

44 Scully, 'Assumption', p. 83. See also Wild, *Divinization*, p. 113.

45 *Ibid.* See Hilary, *Trin.* 8.13.

46 Bobrinskoy, 'L'Eucharistie', p. 239.

47 Hilary, *Trin.* 8.17, *SC* 448:402.

48 *Ibid.*

49 Dupont-Fauville, *Hilaire*, p. 264.

50 As Dupont-Fauville, *Hilaire*, p. 154, rightly observes: the communion 'n'est pas créée mais communiquée par le sacrement'.

51 *Ibid.*

52 Denoît-Dominique de La Soujeole, *Le sacrement de la communion: essai d'ecclésiologie fondamentale* (Paris: Cerf, 1998), p. 118.

53 Hilary, *Trin.* 8.15, *SC* 448:400: *ad unitatem Patris proficeremus.*

54 *Ibid.*, 8.16, *SC* 448:402: *eodem modo nos per carnem eius uiuemus.*

55 *Ibid.*

56 *Ibid.*

57 Even if in an infinitely insufficient way. For a brief examination of divine infinity and human knowledge in Hilary, see Jarred Mercer, 'The Life in the Word and the Light of Humanity: The Exegetical Foundation of Hilary of Poitiers' Doctrine of Divine Infinity', *SP* 14 (2013), pp. 273–82.

58 By retrieval I do not mean simply reading Hilary's argument into contemporary discussions but a recapitulation of Hilary's way of thinking toward God in a contemporary theological context.

59 Tanner, *Christ*, p. 235.

60 See *ibid.*, pp. 235–36. For this concept in Hilary, see, for example, *Trin.* 2.24–25.

61 Tanner, *Christ*, p. 236.

62 The language of 'performance' of Trinitarian doctrine is taken from Anatolios, *Retrieving Nicaea*, 7–8 (Anatolios is not referring this language specifically to the Eucharist, however, but to Christian life generally).

63 The language of 'social programme' comes from Miroslav Volf's famous article, '"The Trinity is our Social Program": The Doctrine of the Trinity and the Shape of Social Engagement', *Modern Theology* 14:3 (1998), pp. 403–23. Volf, however, argues *for* the (limited) modelling of the Trinity in human society.

2

'A Semblance more Lucid'?
An Exploration of Trinitarian Space

JEREMY BEGBIE

One of the most spectacular artefacts of the fifteenth century, the Van Eyck Altarpiece in Ghent, introduces us to a richly Trinitarian world (Figure 2.1).

The Van Eyck Altarpiece.

The imposing seated figure has been variously described as Christ or the Father. A diminutive dove, the Spirit, hovers over the enthroned Lamb. But rather more subtle Trinitarian elements are also present. A panel on the upper right shows an angel at a keyboard, delighting her colleagues (Figure 2.2).

Detail showing an angel at a keyboard.

As far as one can tell, she plays three keys (C, E and G). If we were to gather those within the span of an octave, they would form what today we would call a major triad.

This painting dates from 1432, and this triad had not yet become the basic building block of Western music. But by the late sixteenth century it is being talked about as a kind of ideal: the celebrated Italian theorist Gioseffo Zarlino (1517–90) calls it the 'perfect harmony' (*harmonia perfetta*).[1] Ignatius of Loyola (1491–1556) was profoundly impressed by its Trinitarian suggestiveness,[2] and in the early seventeenth century the German theorist Johannes Lippius (1585–1612) wrote:

> The triad is the image of that great mystery, the divine and solely adorable Unitrinity (I cannot think of a semblance more lucid). All the more, therefore, should theologians and philosophers direct their attention to it, since at present they know fundamentally little, and in the past they knew practically nothing about it.[3]

Lippius was by no means the last to exploit the triad in this way. For J. S. Bach, it was almost second nature to use three consonant tones in Trinitarian settings, and we could name many others since Bach who have employed the chord in this way.[4] The question I want to press in this chapter is: 'To what extent is there something especially appropriate about what was hinted at in Van Eyck's musical panel and has been developed by countless musicians and music theorists since?' Is there something unusually 'lucid' about the 'semblance' between three consonant musical tones and the Trinity?

I want to contend that there is, and that allowing music its voice in Trinitarian theology will do very much more than provide useful illustrations for anxious clergy on Trinity Sunday. Indeed, there is much to suggest that at least some of the West's protracted struggles with Trinitarian doctrine have been severely hampered by what might be called unmusical habits – patterns of thought and speech that muffle and distort the testimony of Scripture and the Church's confessions, but that could have readily been avoided if more attention had been paid to something as unassuming as a three-note chord. I hope to show that music can yield remarkable resources not only for exposing some of theology's most intractable aporias but also for circumventing them, allowing the Trinitarian 'pressure' of the New Testament to be conceived and articulated more fully and faithfully. Moreover, far from defusing the mysteriousness of the triunity of God, its ungraspable, uncapturable character will be made all the more evident. I aim to show this with respect to a theme in Trinitarian theology that has become the focus of intense discussion in recent years: divine space.

The Space of Visual Perception

To open up the distinctiveness of what music has to offer here, I begin by making some very basic observations about the contrast between aural and visual perception.[5] To take the visual first: objects in our visual field typically occupy bounded locations such that they cannot overlap without losing their integrity. We are unable to see a patch of blue and a patch of yellow in the same space *as* blue and yellow. The colours either hide each other or, if they are allowed to merge, become green. The spatiality perceptible here is one of juxtaposition and mutual exclusion: things can be next to each other but cannot be in the same place at the same time. Things take up circumscribed places – so space becomes, in effect, the aggregate of places. This is a space that encourages zero-sum games: the more of one thing, the less of another. Discrete objects are related to each other against the background of a spatial whole. We distinguish 'somewhere' from 'elsewhere'. We can measure intervals between things, and things have different magnitudes – objects can be larger than or smaller than others. And, we might add, this is the space afforded not only by the eye but also by our sense of touch.[6]

At the risk of overgeneralizing, conceiving space in this way is habitual for most of us, so much so that we probably never stop to think that other options might be available. However, a moment's thought shows that in the world of theology, if left unchecked it can spawn considerable difficulties. Take, for example, the way God's relation to the world is imagined. As long as we remain wedded to visualizable pictures of distinct quasi-physical objects in bounded domains, it requires a constant struggle *not* to suggest that the more active God is in the world, the less the world can be itself. 'Transcendence' will tend to be opposed to 'immanence'. It is hard to sidestep some form of univocity: where God and the created world are regarded as two objects belonging to the same *genus* or type of thing, each contending for the same space. Likewise, divine and human agency will tend to be imagined as ontologically comparable categories striving for the same territory. Contractual models of salvation will find a ready home in this kind of scheme: God occupies one share of the salvific space, and humans the other, making some kind of agreement necessary about how the available terrain is to be distributed. And, needless to say, human freedom will tend to be envisaged primarily as freedom *from* the 'other' (whether divine or human).

All this reaches acute form in Christology – when the deity and humanity of Christ are seen as properties on essentially the same plane, jostling for the same ground. Commonly, the two 'natures' are nervously sustained in static equilibrium – like a tightrope walker with a double-weighted bar, poised far above heresy. Or else a compromise is negotiated by attenuating one of the natures – so, for example, the eternal Son is said to engage in some form of pulling back, non-exercise or even abandonment of divine powers or attributes; or Jesus' humanity becomes a truncated version of the real thing, in order to cope with a potentially overpowering divine presence.[7]

Our main concern here is with Trinitarian theology, and it is readily apparent that similar struggles and dangers apply here also. If our theological imagination is (over-)determined by visualization, it becomes challenging, to say the least, to comprehend how there can be irreducible threeness and oneness. Again, some type of precarious equilibrium is commonly suggested: the divine *hypostases* are strongly affirmed as distinct and inseparable but left in a lifeless tension that seems to have little to do with, for example, the energetic Trinitarian testimony of John's Gospel. Or failing that, some kind of compromise is advanced – swerving dangerously towards an association of individuals on the one hand (tritheism) or a collapse of distinctiveness (modalism) on the other.

Musical Space

Things are strikingly different if we turn to the space perceptible through our ears. If I press a key on a piano, the tone I then hear fills the whole of my aural field, my heard space. It does not occupy a bounded location. It is not 'here' as opposed to 'there'. It is 'everywhere' in my aural space; there is no spatial zone where the sound is not present. If I play another note along with the first, that second tone fills the entirety of the *same* (heard) space; yet I hear it as distinct. In this aural environment, two distinct entities, it would seem, can occupy the same space at the same time and yet be perceived as irreducibly distinct.

In modern times no one has done more to expound this sonic spatiality, especially in relation to music, than the twentieth-century Austrian musicologist Victor Zuckerkandl (1896–1965).[8] He points to several features of musical space-as-heard that are relevant here. Perhaps most striking is the phenomenon of 'interpenetration'. As we have just noted, when one tone is heard along with another of a different pitch, the second does not drive the first away, nor is it in a different place, nor does it merge with the first. We are not dealing with the space of juxtaposition and mutual exclusion, or an aggregate of places, nor with magnitude of parts – one tone does not take up more space than the other. Zero-sum games are gone; there is no question of 'the more of one, the less of the other'. We do not set notes in relation to each other against the backdrop of a spatial whole. Both tones make up the one heard space. They sound 'through' one another. They can be *in* one another while being heard *as* two full and distinct tones.

No less significant, Zuckerkandl writes of musical space as 'coming from'/'coming towards'.[9] This sounds somewhat mysterious at first but only because of our tendency to over-rely on visualization. Zuckerkandl's point is that when we perceive a sound, we are not perceiving the object that produces it, and therefore we are not perceiving an object at a distance, in a particular place. Philosophers have long reflected on the way perceiving sounds need not involve perceiving the objects that produce them.[10] Roger Scruton describes sounds as 'pure events', by which he means that although they are happenings, they do not happen *to* the entities that caused them. They are not qualities of objects.[11] *Contra* John Locke, who spoke of sounds as 'secondary qualities' of objects, when we call a sound rough, we are ascribing a quality to the sound, not to the object that produced it nor to any physical alteration in the object. Yet it is an event; something happens. I perceive a depth of sorts but not the depth that enables me to distinguish some entity as 'near' or 'far'. A sound has the depth of 'coming from', 'coming towards'. What we hear is not *at* a distance, it comes *from* a distance. In this way we hear space not as an inert vessel or container through which things can move but as an intrinsic dimension of a living sound; a living space, we might say.

Zuckerkandl also highlights a phenomenon he calls 'the order of auditory space'.[12] Depending on its frequency, a vibrating string can provoke another to vibrate – a phenomenon known as 'sympathetic resonance'. This is because a single string vibrates in multiple ways, creating a series of tones (overtones) along with its basic tone. If I play middle C and open up the string an octave above by silently depressing the appropriate key, the upper C string will vibrate even though it has not been struck. And the more the lower string sounds, the more the upper string sounds in its distinctiveness. The strings are not in competition, nor do they simply allow each other room to vibrate. The lower string enhances, brings to life the upper string, frees it to be itself, compromising neither the integrity of the upper string nor its own. We hear the resonant order of musical space.

By this time, the phrase 'merely metaphorical' may well be coming to mind. It will be objected that this heard sonic space is not 'real space' at all, despite the inescapable investment in spatial metaphors when describing it. Music is essentially non-spatial, or a-spatial. This was the position taken in a celebrated article by the philosopher P. F. Strawson,[13] and it has been picked up and developed by a number since, including Roger Scruton: 'The essential feature of a spatial dimension', he writes, 'is that it contains places, which can be *occupied* by things, and between which things can move.'[14] In other words, authentic space is found not in the eyes-shut world of hearing music but the eyes-open world of visual and tangible perception.

But are things quite so simple? Obviously, musical space does not correspond in all respects to the spatial order of three-dimensional objects. And metaphor is certainly unavoidable in this context. But need we assume that all our spatial language is to be evaluated according to the degree to which it measures up to what we have determined in advance is 'essential' or 'real' space? More pointedly: need we suppose that the only possible existent spatial order is that which can be straightfor-wardly visualized? I hardly need point out that this is a latently theolog-ical question, or at least one that pushes us in that direction, provoking us to wonder: might there be a type of spatial order that underwrites and perhaps enfolds the space we like to call 'real' space, and might our aural experience of music be gesturing towards it, perhaps even to some degree embodying it?

The relevance of all this to Trinitarian reflection will be fast becoming clear. The very term 'interpenetration' may well call to mind the ancient concept of *perichoresis*. The theological associations of Zuckerkandl's 'coming towards' are also surely potent, as is the phenomenon of res-onance. On a wider front, we can begin to see how some of the West's most arduous theological struggles might be recast, and in some cases exposed as misdirected and unnecessary. I am thinking, for example, of the way the Church has conceived of God's transcendence, two-natures Christology, divine and human agency, and interpersonal freedom. Not least, the vexed notion of our 'participation' in God (or Christ) no lon-ger needs to be hampered by zero-sum schemes that try to coordinate divine and human agency in somewhat lifeless 'balances' ('the more of God, the less of us'). Through sonic or musical space, fresh languages and thought-patterns are released that are arguably far more appropri-ate to Scripture and the Church's conciliar confessions than many of the default options on which we habitually rely.[15]

In this chapter we have a particular focus in mind: God's triune life, with particular attention to that life *ad intra*. Before we delve into this, however, two caveats need to be entered. First, and most obviously, to show that the kind of spatiality opened up above is at least conceivable does not of itself say anything about the truth or falsity of this or that formulation of God's triunity. Such issues cannot be resolved without reference to weightier, indeed ultimate criteria. Second, we should be distinctly cautious about extending this spatial model without qualifi-cation to the relation between God and the created world. In the case of two strings vibrating, we are hearing two sounds that belong to the same ontological class, and when both are activated they are mutually constitutive. The Creator–creature relation is, most would argue, not amenable to any such pattern. To expand the point: we need to be wary of sliding into an indiscriminate reduction of all relations to a sin-gle type.[16] The intra-Trinitarian relations, the relation of Creator and creature, divine and human in the hypostatic union, Christ and Church, and the relations between persons in the Church – all these need to be assiduously differentiated. Unqualified appeals to 'relationality' are to be treated with suspicion.[17]

Bearing these caveats in mind, however, and with what I hope is a due apophatic reserve, I propose, with musical space in mind, to explore a question very much alive and a matter of pointed controversy in contemporary Trinitarian theology: 'In what sense, if any, is it appropriate to speak of God as possessing "space"?'

God's 'Space'?[18]

For good reasons a large part of the Christian tradition has found itself resisting any notion of space as applied to God. It is said that space is a dimension belonging to the created, contingent world, not to God. Creation is composite; God is without parts. Further, there can be no space antecedent to God, 'in' which God could reside. As with time, God creates all things *with* space not *in* space. Granted, we can and must affirm God's direct engagement with the space of this world, climaxing in the Incarnation: the Son comes among us as a spatially located, embodied human. And spatial metaphors are probably impossible to avoid when articulating the God–world relation, as Scripture makes clear: God is 'close' at hand, 'far off', 'high above all' and so forth. But none of this warrants predicating space of God's own self in anything other than an extremely stretched, metaphorical sense. Moreover, much vigilance is needed not to allow our spatial metaphors to trick us into imagining that God and world share some common type of being. The doctrine of God's 'immensity' – or non-spatiality – underlines the absolute qualitative distinction between divine and created reality and protects us from the huge risk of projecting what is proper to the creature onto the Creator.

Understandable as all this is, in its more extreme forms this kind of position is in considerable danger of succumbing to the very positions being opposed. If we construe God's non-spatiality purely or primarily in terms of the negation of this world's space – as if this divine 'non-space' could be thought of as created space without bounds (our space, but infinitely extended) – then whatever our good intentions, we are open to the charge of imposing creaturely categories onto the Creator. And arguably, these difficulties are exacerbated by visual-spatial conceptuality (models of space dependent on our visual perception), in which God and world are plotted as if against the background of a 'hyperspace' that embraces both.

At the other end of the spectrum we find schemes that liberally employ spatial language of the Trinity and of God's relation to the world, but in ways that also quickly invite the charge of projection. Some of the highly 'socialized' doctrines of the Trinity emerging in the late twentieth century are a case in point, where Father, Son and Spirit can come close to being imagined as discrete individual quasi-personalities, engaged in a sort of triadic drama.[19] Other examples can be found in varieties of panentheism, in which the world is said to be 'in' God but where God and world are in danger of being imagined against the backdrop of a prior 'super-space'.[20] Again we should note that whatever the investment in metaphysical technicalities, it is hard to avoid the impression that fuelling many such proposals are visual-spatial habits of mind, where God and creation are being mapped on to a larger, preconceived spatial whole.

Webster and Barth

It is to the great credit of the much-lamented John Webster (1955–2016) that he recognized the dangers of both extremes. His long-time allergy to even a whiff of social Trinitarianism – let alone panentheism – was legendary. But he was equally resistant to expounding God's non-spatiality simply by maximizing creaturely notions of spatiality. In a penetrating article on our theme he insists that we conceive God's immensity strictly through attention to the self-enactment of God as Father, Son and Spirit:

> To offer a dogmatic presentation of the attributes of God is, therefore, to indicate *this one* in the supreme radiance and completeness of his triune being and act in which he freely turns to his creatures, claiming them and directing them to himself.[21]

God's infinity with regard to space cannot be expressed by magnifying creaturely properties and thus making it an 'inverted image of the finite';[22] rather we are speaking of the immensity of God's goodness, the 'boundless plenitude of his being, in which he is unhindered by any spatial constraint, and so is sovereignly free for creative and saving presence to all limited creaturely reality'.[23] In this way immensity and omnipresence can be seen as twin doctrines: God's immeasurability enables God to be redeemingly present to all places.[24] Immensity is to be understood, therefore, not by positing an abstract contrast between created and uncreated being, for then we are thrown back on ourselves to construe it in creaturely terms, and certainly not as a property of the 'one God' anterior to God's triune life but only out of the fullness of the eternal Trinitarian relations.

However, despite a repeated and robust adherence to God's irreducible triunity, Webster does not appear to go as far as ascribing spatiality to God. This is perhaps not surprising given a particularly fervent commitment in his later work to an especially uncompromising doctrine of the simplicity of God (broadly, the belief that God is not a composite being, constituted of parts).[25] In fact, recent years have seen a significant stream of writing that has sought to recover and reinvigorate an affirmation of divine simplicity.[26] And in this environment one can meet a sharp suspicion of the notion that, for example, Father and Son are substantively present to each other in a relation of love, or that at Gethsemane the eternal *Son* prays (as man) to the Father. Social Trinitarianism of almost any shade is shunned. Stephen Holmes, for example, insists that the three divine *hypostases* are to be distinguished by relations of origin ('unbegotten', 'begotten' and 'proceeds') and in no other way, and that this articulates by far the most pervasive tradition in the history of Trinitarian doctrine.[27] Clearly, this makes the language of spatiality as applied to God especially problematic.

On these matters, Karl Barth (1886–1968) is a good deal bolder. Although acutely alert to the hazards of projecting individualistic notions of human personhood onto the members of the Trinity, he nonetheless wants to insist that in the light of God's activity *ad extra*, we can and should affirm that God possesses his own space *ad intra*, by virtue of his differentiation as Father, Son and Spirit. Space is a condition by which Father, Son and Spirit are distinguished from one another. There is 'proximity' and 'distance' within God, and the latter is the source of the ontological distinction between God and world.[28]

> The space everything [other than God] possesses is the space which is given it out of the fullness of God. The fact is that first of all *God has space for Himself* and . . . subsequently, because he is God and able to create, *He has* [space] *for everything else as well.*[29]

In other words, the differentiation-in-love of God's own being is the antecedent condition of the otherness to each other of God and world. Barth even goes so far as to say that the non-spatiality of God is a 'more than dangerous idea', for space is the a priori of otherness.[30] To insist on God's non-spatiality (i) threatens the qualitative distinction between Creator and creature (God without 'distance' implies God's identity with the world); and (ii) threatens to dissolve the differentiation of Father, Son and Spirit (without 'distance', the three collapse into absolute identity). Thus Barth can daringly claim that omnipresence belongs first of all to God *in se*: Father, Son and Spirit are present to and for one another in the eternity of Divine Love. To use more technical language, omnipresence does not merely belong to the 'relative' attributes of God – those exercised by God with regard to the created world – but in the first instance characterizes God's own being.[31]

On these matters my sympathies are decidedly with Barth over against Webster, and over against the more fervent advocates of divine simplicity. This is principally for biblical-exegetical reasons. On scriptural grounds it is hard to sustain the view, for example, that the only distinctions that can be made between the Persons are those between relations of origin. Many texts of the Apostle Paul are exceedingly hard to square with this outlook, not to mention Gethsemane or Golgotha or indeed large portions of the Gospel of John – a text conspicuous by its absence in many current discussions of divine simplicity.[32] Indeed, the witness of the Fourth Gospel to the mutual love of Father and Son would seem to be drastically distorted if it is held that the Father's love is directed only to the humanity assumed by the Son and not to the eternal Son from all eternity – a position that entails something close to Nestorianism.[33] Speaking of John 17.3 ('Now this is eternal life: that they know you, the only true God, and Jesus Christ, whom you have sent'), Andrew Lincoln writes:

> for the evangelist, Jesus in his relationship as Son to the Father is intrinsic to this one God's identity. As the second petition will make clear [i.e. as in v. 5] Jesus was always included in the identity and glory of the one God, even before the foundation of the world.[34]

More pointedly, commenting on John 17.26, C. K. Barrett writes:

> The love which inspires and rules the church, and is its life, is the essential inward love of the Godhead, the love with which the Father eternally loves the Son (the love which God *is*, 1 John 4.8, 16).[35]

If this Jesus, the one into whose filial relation of love and knowledge of the Father we are granted access by the Spirit, is authentically *God from God*, the eternal Son enfleshed as one of us, then it is hard to see how we can*not* speak of a relation or exchange of loving and knowing belonging to God's own being, and thus of a divine spatiality *in this sense*.[36] Whatever post-biblical metaphysical apparatus we employ, we can hardly forget that the theological stakes are extraordinarily high here: in what sense does love belong to who God actually *is*?

Having said all this, if Barth's account of divine space is taken out of its distinctive theological matrix in the *Dogmatics*, his audacious prose is liable to significant misunderstanding (and misuse), especially if approached through a visual-spatial mindset of the kind I have been questioning from the start of this chapter. Can we find a way forward here?

Rehearing Trinitarian Space

Assuming, then, that there are grounds for speaking of divine spatiality along the lines suggested by Barth, but at the same time bearing in mind the pitfalls of such language that we have been highlighting, we can ask: 'What would a biblically responsible account of divine spatiality require, and how might 'musical space' speak to those requirements?' Here I think we can identify one general desideratum, and three more particular desiderata.

To begin with, the general one. Clearly we are going to need habits of thought and speech that avoid construing space as an inert receptacle, a mere frame into which things and events are installed. As we saw earlier, this has often caused many a theological shipwreck. In debates about divine spatiality all parties in one way or another are struggling to extricate themselves from just this – the notion that there is a logically prior 'meta space' encompassing both God and world, or a logically prior (perhaps even ontologically prior) divine space into which the Trinitarian Persons fit. Here the aural perception of musical tones would seem to have much to offer, for it entails a kind space not bound to these schemes: space not as a container through which sounds travel but space as an intrinsic dimension of sounds-in-motion. Music can serve to remind us that space is always the space *of* this, the space *of* that, and that theologically we should be careful not to operate with a concept of 'space in general' but only with the distinctive space manifest in the self-presentation of the triune God.[37]

Now for three more particular desiderata: and here we can return to the features of musical spatiality outlined by Zuckerkandl highlighted above, and draw on some major currents in John's Gospel. First, we recall that Zuckerkandl wrote of the 'interpenetration' of sounds in our aural perception. This speaks to the need to do justice to the 'in-one-anotherness' of the divine Persons, a term coined by Richard Bauckham to speak of the mutual indwelling of Father and Son in the Gospel of John.[38] The interpenetration of heard musical tones offers a remarkably apt way of allowing this extraordinary language of the Fourth Gospel to be heard more fully and profoundly, releasing us from some of the more damaging snares associated with visual-spatial discourse. We avoid any suggestion of God possessing 'parts' (the three heard notes are not parts of a whole, they *are* the whole) and we avoid the pitfalls of terms like 'proximity', 'remoteness' and 'distance' that opponents of divine spatiality rightly warn us about.

Second, Zuckerkandl spoke of sounds 'coming from'/'coming towards'. This speaks to the need to do justice to what we can call the '*for*-one-anotherness' of the Persons. So, for example, if we are to describe the Father's love for the Son and the Son's love for the Father as a dynamic of self-giving or self-dispossession that reaches its epitome at the cross, this language must not be allowed to push us into imagining some kind of shift of content from one location to another, or a self-evacuation of one for the sake of the other. In John's Gospel, the Father gives life to the Son such that the Son 'has life in himself' *as he, the Father, has life in himself* (John 5.26) – in other words there is no diminishment of the Father's divinity in the process; quite the opposite – for this is who God *is*. And there is no hint of a diminishment of the Son's deity as the Son in turn gives life to, and for, others in the world. In hearing a musical tone, we do not perceive anything moving within a pre-existing space, still less do we perceive anything diminished; the life of the sound *is* the life of 'coming from'/'coming towards' (going to/going towards). Again, this evades the cruder visual-spatial assumptions that those who oppose divine spatiality quite properly suspect.

Third, Zuckerkandl identified a resonant 'order of auditory space' arising from the sympathetic resonance of strings. This addresses a double-need: to do justice to (i) the *mutual enlivening* of the Trinitarian Persons; and (ii) the *uncontainability* of this mutuality. By mutual enlivening, I have in mind the reciprocal activation of the sort we hear between two resonant tones. There is arguably something of this in the concept of 'glorification' in the Fourth Gospel; the mutual glorification of Son and Father, climaxing at the crucifixion (e.g. John 12.23, 28; 13.31–32; 17.1). And, as with love, we are told this has characterized the life of Son and Father from before the foundation of the world (John 17.4–5). Glory carries with it a sense of honour as well as splendour; to glorify is to honour and magnify the other *as other*.[39] If all this feels too dangerously 'social' or plural, undercutting divine unity, we need to recall what we have just said about in-one-anotherness. To repeat, this is not a space with different objects inside it; it is a space *constituted by* the differentiated life of the three. The three tones I hear do not each *have* a space (akin to *having* an essence); they *are* that space in action.

With mutual enlivening goes uncontainability. Resonance is abundant (another key concept in John's Gospel). In hearing two resonant strings we are being introduced to a space of liveliness that by its very nature far exceeds the giving and receiving between these two. Here it is difficult not to invoke a lively tradition that speaks of the Holy Spirit as the excess of the mutual love of Father and Son, the pressure towards outgoingness within God's life, the divine capaciousness that saves the Father and Son becoming, as it were, a private duet.[40]

In this chapter I have done no more than sketch possibilities, but ones that I believe have considerable bearing on contemporary debates in Trinitarian theology. I have not even begun to discuss melody, dissonance and numerous other musical phenomena. But I hope I have done enough to show that the phenomenology of the perception of musical sound yields conceptual tools that can clarify, expose and even correct some of theology's worst bad habits, and thus enable the theologian to discover in fresh ways something of the New Testament's Trinitarian 'pressure' and shape. Theologically, music helps realize there is far more in what the Church says than we think, and far more in what we think than we can ever say.

Notes

1 Gioseffo Zarlino, *Le Istitutioni Harmoniche* (Venice, 1558).

2 Ignatius, *The Autobiography of St. Ignatius Loyola, with Related Documents*, ed. John C. Olin, trans. Joseph F. O'Callaghan (New York: Harper & Row, 1974), pp. 37–8.

3 Johann Lippius, *Synopsis of New Music = Synopsis Musicae Novae*, Translations – Colorado College Music Press No 8 (Colorado Springs, CO: Colorado College Music Press, 1977), p. 41.

4 For an illuminating and detailed discussion, see Chiara Bertoglio, 'A Perfect Chord: Trinity in Music, Music in the Trinity', *Religions* 4:4 (2013), pp. 485–501.

5 For a much fuller treatment of what I adumbrate here, see Jeremy Begbie, *Music, Modernity, and God: Essays in Listening* (Oxford: Oxford University Press, 2013), ch. 6.

6 Here I am drawing especially on Victor Zuckerkandl, *Sound and Symbol: Music and the External World*, trans. Willard R. Trask (London: Routledge & Kegan Paul, 1956), esp. pp. 82–5, 93–4, 275–6.

7 Significantly, the New Testament passage from which such Christologies take their cue – Philippians 2.5–11 – does not seem to carry any of these connotations, even if it is maintained that Paul is here holding to the 'pre-existence' of Christ. See e.g. Gordon D. Fee, 'Exploring Kenotic Christology: The Self-Emptying of God', in C. Stephen Evans (ed.), *Exploring Kenotic Christology* (Oxford: Oxford University Press, 2006).

8 Zuckerkandl, *Sound and Symbol*, esp. chs. 14, 15 and 16.

9 *Ibid.*, ch. 16.

10 This is one of the differences between music and what we call 'noise'. When we hear a noise, we typically follow the sound through to its source. We hear a noise in the children's bedroom upstairs, so we take action with respect to the presumed cause of the noise. In the case of musical sounds, no such action is required. Music is not interesting to us because of what it tells us about the physical objects that cause it. We can enjoy the interplay of sounds without following them through to the objects that gave rise to them. Indeed, recognizing music as such seems to *depend* on our ability to do this.

11 Roger Scruton, *The Aesthetics of Music* (Oxford: Clarendon Press, 1997), pp. 6–13; 'Sounds as Secondary Objects and Pure Events', in Matthew Nudds and Casey O'Callaghan (eds), *Sounds and Perception: New Philosophical Essays* (Oxford: Oxford University Press, 2009), pp. 50–68.

12 Scruton, *Aesthetics of Music*, ch. 17.

13 P. F. Strawson, *Individuals: An Essay in Descriptive Metaphysics* (London: Methuen, 1959), pp. 59–86.

14 Roger Scruton, *Understanding Music: Philosophy and Interpretation* (London: Continuum, 2009), p. 14; emphasis in original.

15 Begbie, *Music, Modernity, and God*, ch. 6, *passim*.

16 For discussion of these matters, see John C. Polkinghorne (ed.), *The Trinity and an Entangled World: Relationality in Physical Science and Theology* (Grand Rapids, MI: Eerdmans, 2010).

17 For strong exhortations to caution regarding *perichoresis*, for example, see Oliver Crisp, 'Problems with Perichoresis', *Tyndale Bulletin* 56:1 (2005), pp. 119–40; Randall E. Otto and E. Randall, 'The Use and Abuse of Perichoresis in Recent Theology', *Scottish Journal of Theology* 54:3 (2001), pp. 366–84. On the hazards of applying Trinitarian relations to the Church, see Mark Husbands, 'The Trinity Is Not Our Social Program: Volf, Gregory and Barth', in Daniel J. Treier and David Lauber (eds), *Trinitarian Theology for the Church: Scripture, Community, Worship* (Downers Grove, IL: InterVarsity Press, 2009), pp. 120–41.

18 In this section I gratefully acknowledge my considerable debt to a highly lucid and perceptive article by Murray Rae: Murray Rae, 'The Spatiality of God', in Myk Habets and Phillip Tolliday (eds), *Trinitarian Theology after Barth* (Eugene, OR: Wipf & Stock, 2011), pp. 70–86.

19 To be fair, however, most of these theologies resist the idea that behind the three persons lies a more ultimate space, in the form of an undifferentiated substrate or essence.

20 The classic instance is Jürgen Moltmann, who memorably portrays God's creative act in terms of self-retraction, God vacating a space for what is not God. Jürgen Moltmann, *God in Creation: An Ecological Doctrine of Creation* (London: SCM Press, 1985), pp. 86–93.

21 J. B. Webster, 'The Immensity and Ubiquity of God', in *Confessing God: Essays in Christian Dogmatics II* (London: T. & T. Clark, 2005), pp. 87–108 (p. 88); emphasis in original.

22 *Ibid.*, p. 92.

23 *Ibid.*

24 *Ibid.*, p. 93.

25 '. . . the creator is radically incomposite. As the cause of finite being, God is not one term or agent in a set of interactions, not a "co-eval, co-finite being", but unqualifiedly simple and in himself replete.' David Braine quoted in John Webster, *God without Measure: Working Papers in Christian Theology*, vol. 1 (London and New York: Bloomsbury, T. & T. Clark, 2016), p. 107. See also *ibid.*, ch. 6, esp. pp. 86–9.

26 See, for example, James E. Dolezal, *God without Parts: Divine Simplicity and the Metaphysics of God's Absoluteness* (Eugene, OR: Pickwick Publications, 2011); Steven J. Duby, *Divine Simplicity: A Dogmatic Account* (London and New York: Bloomsbury, T. & T. Clark, 2016).

27 Stephen R. Holmes, *The Holy Trinity: Understanding God's Life* (Milton Keynes: Paternoster Press, 2012), p. 200; Holmes, 'Classical Trinity: Evangelical Perspective', in Jason S. Sexton (ed.), *Two Views on the Doctrine of the Trinity* (Grand Rapids, MI: Zondervan, 2014), esp. p. 43.

28 Karl Barth, *Church Dogmatics*, trans. Geoffrey W. Bromiley and Thomas F. Torrance, vol. II/1 (Edinburgh: T. & T. Clark, 1957), pp. 461–4.

29 *Ibid.*, p. 474; emphasis added.

30 *Ibid.*, p. 468.

31 *Ibid.*, pp. 461–78.

32 Chris Tilling, 'Paul, the Trinity, and Contemporary Trinitarian Debates', *The Pacific Journal of Baptist Research* 11:1 (2016), esp. pp. 36–42; Wesley Hill, *Paul and the Trinity: Persons, Relations, and the Pauline Letters* (Grand Rapids, MI: Eerdmans, 2015).

33 In other words, splitting up the divine and human in Christ. For the Trinity in John's Gospel, see Michael F. Bird, *Evangelical Theology: A Biblical and Systematic Introduction* (Grand Rapids, MI: Zondervan, 2013), pp. 98–113.

34 Andrew T. Lincoln, *The Gospel According to Saint John* (Peabody, MA: Hendrickson; London and New York: Continuum, 2005), p. 435.

35 C. K. Barrett, *The Gospel According to St. John: An Introduction with Commentary and Notes on the Greek Text*, 2nd edn (Philadelphia, PA: Westminster Press, 1978), p. 515; emphasis in original. For an exceptionally clear exposition of John 17 in relation to these issues, carrying the argument that we have in Jesus' so-called 'high-priestly' prayer a manifestation of 'an intersubjective relationship of love between the Father and the Son in eternity', see Richard Bauckham, 'The Trinity and the Gospel of John', in Brandon Crowe and Carl R. Trueman (eds), *The Essential Trinity: New Testament Foundations and Practical Relevance* (London: Apollos, 2016), pp. 92–3. (I am not convinced that 'intersubjective

relationship' is the best phrase in this context, given the connotations of enclosed mutuality that it is almost bound to evoke in late modernity, but the thrust of his exegesis here is surely very much to the point.)

36 Christoph Schwöbel writes: 'If the *homoousios* ['of one substance'] is simply taken to mean that Father, Son, and Spirit instantiate the same divine essence three times over, without rooting how God is in relation to the world in how God is in God's own being, one has effectively made the doctrine of the Trinity meaningless for understanding the divine economy.' Christoph Schwöbel, 'Where Do We Stand in Trinitarian Theology? Resources, Revisions, and Reappraisals', in Christophe Chalamet and Marc Vial (eds), *Recent Developments in Trinitarian Theology: An International Symposium* (Minneapolis, MN: Augsburg Fortress Press, 2014), pp. 9–72 (p. 23).

37 The work of T. F. Torrance is especially relevant here; see for example Thomas F. Torrance, *Space, Time and Incarnation* (London: Oxford University Press, 1969); and *Space, Time, and Resurrection* (Grand Rapids, MI: Eerdmans, 1976).

38 Richard Bauckham, *Gospel of Glory: Major Themes in Johannine Theology* (Grand Rapids, MI: Baker Academic, 2015), pp. 9–13.

39 *Ibid.*, ch. 3.

40 See Rowan Williams, 'The Deflections of Desire: Negative Theology in Trinitarian Disclosure', in Oliver Davies and Denys Turner (eds), *Silence and the Word: Negative Theology and Incarnation* (Cambridge: Cambridge University Press, 2002). Colin Gunton writes: 'God is no lonely monad or self-absorbed tyrant, but one whose orientation to the other is intrinsic to his eternal being as God . . . The Spirit, we might say, is the motor of that divine movement outwards.' Colin E. Gunton, *Father, Son, and Holy Spirit: Essays toward a Fully Trinitarian Theology* (London: T. & T. Clark, 2003), p. 86.

PART TWO

Foundations

3

Theophany as Divine Hospitality in Origen and Chrysostom

HANS BOERSMA

Interpretation as Hospitality

Human hospitality intertwines with divine hospitality.[1] In the account of God's appearing to Abraham and Lot in Genesis 18 and 19, their welcome of the three divine visitors is predicated on God first appearing to both of them. The famous theophany – the 'appearing of God', literally – near the oak of Mamre makes clear that human hospitality is based on divine initiative. When God manifests himself – or, as Genesis 18.1 puts it, when he 'is seen' (*ōphthē*)[2] – he comes in the form of strangers visiting ('three men [*treis andres*] had come and stood above him', the text tells us).

God's hospitality is rather unlike human hospitality. The Greek fathers marked this infinite difference between our hospitality to God and his hospitality to us by means of the distinction between *philoxenia* (hospitality) and *synkatabasis* (condescension). The term *philoxenia* – derived from *philos* (friend) and *xenos* (stranger) – describes the stranger turning into a friend. As the opposite of xenophobia (fear of foreigners), *philoxenia* is a virtue that counters our isolationist inclinations. *Philoxenia* enables us to open up our space to those who are different from ourselves. At a fairly obvious level, *philoxenia*, turning strangers into friends, is what we see described in the narratives of Genesis 18 and 19. Abraham extends hospitality to three men visiting him by the oak of Mamre; by means of a shared meal, he turns these strangers into friends. His nephew, Lot, extends hospitality to two angels (*angeloi* in 19.1) alone in dangerous city streets, thereby turning strangers into friends.

Both Origen and Chrysostom have a great deal to say about *philoxenia*; but they also use the term *synkatabasis*, which is a conglomeration of the elements *syn* (together), *kata* (down) and *basis* (going). *Synkatabasis*, then, literally means a 'going down together' – or to put it in the Latinized word we have already met, 'condescension'.[3] It is understandable, therefore, that *synkatabasis* should become the object of patristic praise. *Synkatabasis*, for Origen, St John Chrysostom and other early fathers, is not just a matter of ordinary *philoxenia*, as though we would know precisely what God's hospitality is like by comparing his to ours. We could say that *synkatabasis* is the principle by which God reaches out and adapts to human creatureliness and weakness; it is the way divine transcendence relates to the limitations of human existence and to the weaknesses of human sin. This means that our hospitality towards God (*philoxenia*) is predicated on his *synkatabasis* – his condescension – to us.

In what follows, then, I will deal with the Mamre theophany as it is discussed by the third-century theologian Origen (*c*.185–*c*.254), and by the fourth-century preacher John Chrysostom (*c*.349–407). The two emphasized different aspects of the paradox of divine descent, and we will see that their different approaches resulted in two rather different understandings of what the human response of hospitality should look like: Origen's vertical approach to hospitality goes hand in hand with allegorical interpretation, while Chrysostom's horizontal view of hospitality corresponds to greater interest in a literal reading of the text. Origen wants us to recognize that it is the transcendent God whose condescension enables us to see him; Chrysostom draws our attention to the fact that God's condescension renders him immanent to the interpersonal relationships where we can meet him. I will argue that the two approaches are not mutually exclusive but that instead a sacramental approach to interpretation recognizes the validity of both. Origen's focus on the reality (*res*) of the sacrament means that he discerns in Abraham's hospitality to God a face-to-face encounter with the transcendent Lord; Chrysostom's attention to the outward sacrament (*sacramentum*) means that he observes in Abraham's hospitality to the stranger a generosity rendered to the God who becomes immanent in time and space. Both approaches give expression to a basic truth of the Incarnation: Origen bowing to the divinity of our Lord, Chrysostom praising his humanity; the two are complementary expressions of the mystery of God's ultimate *synkatabasis* in Jesus Christ.

Since we come to know the triune God in and through Christ, the pre-Nicene theologians were convinced that one of Abraham's three visitors was the pre-incarnate Word of God. Unlike many theologians of the later tradition (beginning with St Augustine), the pre-Nicenes did not, therefore, identify the three visitors as the three persons of the Trinity.[4] The later pro-Nicene theologians increasingly abandoned the christological reading of the Mamre theophany for fear that it might support the Arian cause. After all, if, as the Homoians argued, Genesis 18 shows that only the Word (that is to say, *not* the Father) can become visible in time and space, this turns the Son into a (potentially visible) creature, lower in status than the invisible Father. To counter such a misreading of Genesis 18, Augustine was the first famously to insist on a Trinitarian identification of the three visitors, thereby showing that each of the three persons has the same substance. Origen's and Chrysostom's identification of the three visitors as the pre-incarnate Lord with two of his angels in no way implies, however, that their interpretation is devoid of Trinitarian implications. On the contrary, the pre-Nicene interpretative tradition of this chapter reminds us that Christology and Trinitarian theology are closely linked: it is in and through Christ that we come to know and love the triune God.

Origen: The Son of God at Mamre

Origen devotes two homilies to the passage in question: *Homilies 4* and *5* of his *Homilies on Genesis*. As he discusses the end of the Lord's visit to Abraham, with the Lord commenting on the impending doom for Sodom and Gomorrah – 'After going down, therefore, I will see if they are per-petrating according to their crying that is coming to me' (Gen. 18.21) – Origen notes the difference between the verbs of verses 2 and 21. At the outset of the narrative, when the three men visit 'righteous Abraham', the text says that they 'stood' (*heistēkeisan*) before him; but when the Lord is about to visit the evil cities of Sodom and Gomorrah, he com-ments that he is 'going down' or 'descending' (*katabas*) to them. Origen warns his hearers against taking the spatial metaphors literally. The rea-son Scripture depicts the Lord as 'descending' to Sodom and Gomorrah is that he is going to visit them in response to human sin – something that, in Origen's view, obviously does not apply to Abraham, whom he repeatedly calls 'the wise man'. Origen takes the opportunity to reflect on the Lord 'going down' in the Incarnation:

> Therefore, God is said to descend (*descendere*) when he deigns to have concern for human frailty. This should be discerned especially of our Lord and saviour who 'thought it not robbery to be equal with God, but emptied himself, taking the form of a servant' [Phil. 2.6–7]. Therefore he descended (*descendit*). For, 'No other has ascended (*ascendit*) into heaven, but he that descended (*descendit*) from

heaven, the Son of man who is in heaven' [John 3.13]. For the Lord descended (*descendit*) not only to care for us, but also to bear what things are ours. 'For he took the form of a servant,' and although he himself is invisible in nature, inasmuch as he is equal to the Father, nevertheless he took a visible appearance, 'and was found in appearance as a man' [Phil. 2.7].[5]

Both in the Lord's descent to Sodom and Gomorrah and in the later descent of the Incarnation, the Lord comes down for the sins of humanity. Origen's appeal to the famous Philippian hymn draws attention to God's *synkatabasis*, his condescension, which is necessary for him to be able to appear to sinful human beings. Descent, or *katabasis*, implies God taking on a 'visible appearance', the form of a servant.

The sermon contrasts this 'visible appearance' of the form of a servant with the Lord being 'invisible in nature, inasmuch as he is equal to the Father'. Though we can't be sure, it is quite possible that we're dealing here with an editorial gloss from Origen's fourth-century Latin translator, Rufinus of Aquileia.[6] The statement touches on a controversial point: Origen (or Rufinus) states explicitly that in his divine nature the Son is invisible, which makes him equal to the Father. The *synkatabasis* of the Son of God therefore implies that the eternal Logos *becomes* visible in the Incarnation, whereas he is not so in his own nature.

As we have already seen, Origen follows the pre-Nicene Christian tradition in identifying one of the three visitors as the Son of God – though Origen (or his translator) is keen to point out the equality of the Father and the Son, something that fits with various other allusions to the Trinity in the homily.[7] So while Origen's homily retains the christological reading of the received tradition, the sermon clarifies the Father–Son relationship by insisting that by nature the Son is invisible just as the Father is invisible. In other words, Origen's sermon aims to prevent people from drawing subordinationist conclusions from seeing Christ in the Mamre theophany, and so Origen (or Rufinus) explains that the *synkatabasis* of the Word in the Incarnation is genuinely a descent, one that renders the invisible visible.

Origen: Hospitality as Allegory

I have devoted a fair bit of space to Origen's christological reading of the passage. However, Origen himself doesn't dwell at any length on the identity of the visitors. His exegesis focuses on Abraham's hospitality to his three visitors, and one might think that, in line with this, he would turn Abraham into a model for how to care for strangers and the poor. But Origen consistently declines to do so. Despite his emphasis on hospitality, nowhere does he allude to Hebrews 13.2 ('Do not neglect to show hospitality to strangers, for thereby some have entertained angels unawares'). Terms such as 'example', 'imitation' and the like are almost entirely absent from both homilies. To be sure, in some sense Abraham does function as an example: it is hard to listen to the two sermons and not be awed by the stellar attitude of this perfectly wise character. Abraham's perfection is such that the Lord doesn't need to 'descend' to come and visit him. The three men simply 'stand' in front of him. After all, it is sin that would make one dwell in the valley and that would necessitate the Lord's *synkatabasis*. Abraham is a mountain-dweller; he lives 'in the heights'.[8] As such, he is a model for a life lived 'in the heights', in the presence of God. But Origen does not use the perfection of Abraham's hospitality to encourage his listeners to reach out to others around them.

This raises the question of what kind of hospitality it is that Origen discerns in Abraham in the Mamre theophany. A look back to the previous homily, on Genesis 17, may help us here. This homily makes clear that Abraham was not always as perfect as he appears in chapter 18. On Origen's understanding, Abraham was the recipient of God's gracious condescension or *synkatabasis* in chapter 17, where he receives the name-change from Abram to Abraham and also undergoes circumcision.[9] Origen explains in *Homily 3* how Abraham along with others in his household was circumcised, describing in turn his circumcision of the ears, of the lips, of the flesh and of the heart. Origen treats each of these expressions as allegorical descriptions of people who live pure lives. Regarding circumcision of the heart, Origen comments that it describes someone 'who guards the pure faith in sincerity of conscience, about whom it can be said, "Blessed are the pure in heart, for they shall see God"' (Matt. 5.8).[10] So Abraham encountered God's gracious *synkatabasis* back in chapter 17. By the time we arrive at the Mamre theophany, Abraham has reached such perfection that he is now able to see God: 'God was seen by him near the oak of Mamre while he was sitting at the door of his tent during midday' (Gen. 18.1). In Origen's telling of the story, Abraham's vision of God is the outcome of divine *synkatabasis*, which was accompanied by a name-change and circumcision. Abraham's act of hospitality at the oak of Mamre, therefore, is hospitality extended to God as a fitting response to God's gracious condescension in entering into a covenant relationship with Abraham in the previous chapter. None of this has anything to do with caring for the poor.

In this light, it is hardly surprising that Abraham is fully aware of his visitors' identity from the start: 'The wise man is not ignorant of whom he has received. He runs to three men and adores one, and speaks to the one saying, "Turn aside to your servant and refresh yourself under the tree."'[11] Abraham deliberately adores only one of the three visitors; there is no entertaining of angels unawares. Origen sees the divine–human interplay of God's *synkatabasis* and Abraham's hospitality at work in the text; horizontal, interpersonal practices of hospitality are out of the picture. We should, therefore, not mistake Origen's encomium on hospitality as a moral admonition to reach out to strangers. The two sermons are mystical reflections on the intimate engagement between Abraham and the Lord. Living in the heights, near the oak of Mamre, pure of heart – Abraham sees God. This is human hospitality of so exalted a character that divine condescension has become an outmoded style of interaction, something restricted to an earlier, inferior phase in the divine–human relationship. Origen, in effect, has allegorized Abraham's hospitality: it no longer speaks of welcome at a horizontal level from one person to another; instead, it refers to one's openness to and readiness for a face-to-face relationship with God.

Chrysostom: Divine Condescension at Mamre and in Scripture

With St John Chrysostom's *Homilies on Genesis*, we enter a rather different exegetical world from that of Origen. Chrysostom, as a student of Diodore of Tarsus, was perhaps the most famous preacher that the Antiochene exegetical tradition produced, while the Alexandrian exegetes typically looked to Origen as their main source of inspiration. John's preaching avoided allegorizing and was down to earth, often focusing on themes of poverty and stewardship, and it tended to use straightforward exposition, with careful attention to details. This is not to suggest that Origen failed to pay attention to the details of the text: as we have seen, he loved analysing the linguistic particularities of the text. But Origen was happy to move quickly from the surface meaning of the text to its higher, allegorical meaning. By contrast, Chrysostom warned against excessive allegorizing, which he believed ran the danger of imposing the reader's own notions on to the biblical text.[12] John followed his teacher, Diodore, who had tried to steer a middle path between what he regarded as unwarranted literalism and radical allegorizing:

> This method neither sets aside history nor repudiates *theōria*. Rather, as a realistic, middle-of-the-road approach which takes into account both history and *theōria*, it frees us, on the one hand, from a Hellenism which says one thing for another and introduces foreign subject matter; on the other hand, it does not yield to Judaism and choke us by forcing us to treat the literal reading of the text as the only one worthy of attention and honour, while not allowing the exploration of a higher sense beyond the letter also.[13]

John's Antiochene exegesis took seriously the divine *synkatabasis* into the vagaries of human history, and for Chrysostom this meant treating the human form (as well as the historical meaning) of the biblical text with due care and attention.

In one of his later sermons on Genesis, as he deals with Jacob's wrestling with God at the Jabbok River (Gen. 32.22–32), the Antiochene preacher returns briefly to the Mamre theophany and links it explicitly with God's gracious condescension to human weakness:

> Don't be surprised, dearly beloved, at the extent of his considerateness (*synkatabaseōs*); rather, remember that with the patriarch as well, when he was sitting by the oak tree, he came in human form (*anthrōpou schēmati*) as the good man's guest in the company of the angels, giving us a premonition from on high at the beginning that he would one day take human form to liberate all human nature (*anthrōpinēn morphēn*) by this means from the tyranny of the devil and lead us to salvation. At that time, however, since it was the very early stages, he appeared to each of them in the guise of an apparition (*schēmati phantasias*). As he says himself through the inspired author, 'I multiplied visions and took various likenesses in the works of the inspired authors' [Hosea 12.10]. But when he deigned to take on the form of a slave (*tēn tou doulou morphēn*) and receive our first fruits, he donned our flesh, not in appearance (*phantasia*) or in seeming, but in reality (*alētheia*).[14]

God's appearance to Abraham was condescension (*synkatabasis*) to the weakness of the patriarch's human condition. This divine condescension means that God took the form (*schēma*) of Abraham's humanity, albeit in a vision (*phantasia*). On John's understanding, this shows God's care, as he slowly but surely prepared humanity for the Incarnation itself, when he would appear not in the form of a vision but in reality (*alētheia*). In short, for Chrysostom, God's gracious condescension or *synkatabasis* takes into account human weakness (*astheneia*) as he steps down to the limitations of human beings – at first in the human form of the Mamre theophany, and then climactically in the Incarnation itself.

What is more, for Chrysostom the biblical narrative, as it takes the form of human words, participates in this same *synkatabasis* of God.[15] Divine *synkatabasis* characterizes all of God's dealings with humanity, according to Chrysostom. The result is a profound sense that the human form matters, whenever and wherever God meets up with human beings. This divine condescension, both to Abraham and to the reader of Scripture, comes to the fore particularly, according to Chrysostom, when Abraham leads the Lord and the two angels away from the oak of Mamre towards the city of Sodom and pleads with the Lord to spare the city. Chrysostom uses the noun *synkatabasis* no fewer than six times in *Homily* 42. 'Wonderful is God's considerateness (*synkatabasis*) and his regard for the good man surpassing all reckoning', writes Chrysostom. 'I mean, see how he converses with him, man to man, so to say, showing us how much regard the virtuous are accorded by God.'[16] God's condescension to Abraham is clear from the back-and-forth dialogue between the two.

God shows a similar kind of condescension also to the biblical reader, when he says that he is 'going down to see if their deeds correspond to the outcry reaching me, so as to know if it is true or not' (Gen. 18.21).[17] Chrysostom writes:

> What is meant by the considerateness (*synkatabasis*) of the expression, 'I am going down to see'? I mean, does the God of all move from place to place? No indeed! It doesn't mean this; instead, as I have often remarked, he wants to teach (*paideusai*) us by the concreteness of the expression that there is need to apply precision (*akribeia*), and that sinners are not condemned on hearsay nor is sentence pronounced without proof.[18]

Divine pedagogy, Chrysostom intimates, means that God graciously comes down to our level in the process of *synkatabasis*. The reader, in turn, must treat the text with precision (*akribeia*), so as to discern properly what it is that God conveys by means of this condescension. In this case, the point behind the concrete expression of God 'going down' to find out the true state of affairs in Sodom is to make clear that sin is not condemned on the basis of hearsay.

Chrysostom: Hospitality as Interpersonal Moral Virtue

John Chrysostom, much like Origen, places Abraham's hospitality at the centre of his homilies on Genesis 18 and 19. It is Abraham's virtuous behaviour that induces the Lord to appear to him by the oak of Mamre. This is clear from the patriarch's exemplary attitude in the previous chapter, when the Lord first appeared to him (17.1) and gave him the command of circumcision. Abraham – the 'just man' (ho dikaios), as Chrysostom customarily calls him – obeyed God 'without hesitating in the slightest'.[19] This ready obedience is the reason God again appears to him in the Mamre theophany: 'This, you see, is what our Lord is like: when he sees people grateful in the first instance, he lavishes further kindnesses on them and never desists from rewarding the gratitude of those obedient to him.'[20] For Chrysostom, there is a harmonious interplay between divine synkatabasis and human hospitality: Abraham responds to the divine appearance of Genesis 17.1 with obedience, which in turn triggers the Mamre theophany of the next chapter, which then again moves Abraham to extend hospitality to God.

Abraham, then, is emphatically a 'just man' for Chrysostom. But Chrysostom does not link this justice with any kind of intimate, mystical relationship between Abraham and the Lord. For Chrysostom, it is not the vertical relationship with God that is central, and it is not the visitor's divine identity that turns Abraham's act of hospitality into a just act. To be sure, like Origen, Chrysostom assumes that the identity of the three visitors is that of 'the Lord of all with his angels'.[21] The Antiochene preacher takes his cue from what he regards as allusions to the Mamre theophany in the Letter to the Hebrews and the Gospel of Matthew:

> Hence Paul too said, 'Do not neglect hospitality, for through it some people have entertained angels all unawares' [Heb. 13.2], referring precisely to the patriarch. Hence Christ too said, 'Whoever receives one of the least of these in my name, receives me' [Matt. 18.5; 25.40, 45].[22]

So, like Origen, Chrysostom follows the well-trodden pre-Nicene path of a christological reading of the Mamre theophany.

But it is not the identity of his visitor as the pre-incarnate Christ that turns Abraham into a 'just man'. Unlike Origen, Chrysostom is of the opinion that Abraham does *not* know who his visitors are, and it is precisely this lack of knowledge that makes his virtue stand out.[23] Abraham, explains Chrysostom, simply 'realized that people obliged to travel are in need of much service at that time particularly'.[24] The patriarch's hurry to assist his visitors is commendable not because he recognizes the Lord but precisely because he does *not* recognize him; Abraham assists someone he believes to be a needy stranger. In other words, Abraham's hospitality functions not at the vertical level, as something offered to God – though that is the serendipitous side effect – but it functions first and foremost at the horizontal level: it is rendered to unknown, needy strangers. In Chrysostom's theology, God condescends to the level of ordinary human relationships; it is at that level, therefore, that the Antiochene preacher believes human hospitality ought to be practised in the first place. Chrysostom's point throughout – quite in contrast to Origen's – is that we ought to 'imitate' or 'emulate' Abraham and Lot, by living hospitable lives: 'Since this just man's [i.e. Abraham's] virtue (*aretē*) is so wonderful, therefore, let us bestir ourselves to imitation (*zēlon*) of him, and at least at this late stage let us acknowledge our own nobility, emulate (*mimēsō-metha*) the patriarch.'[25] Hospitality demands that, regardless of the status of the person we encounter or of our own material condition, we freely share our possessions and extend liberal care towards the poor.

In line with this moral turn of the hospitality theme, Chrysostom sees the virtue of hospitality as intimately linked to other virtues. Sermons 41–43 constitute a lengthy exposition on the importance of virtue (*aretē*). St John makes the point at the beginning of *Homily* 42 that Abraham not only was hospitable but also displayed care and compassion. Abraham is also a model of endurance, humility and faith.[26] The inevitable upshot of this focus on virtue is a sharp challenge to the congregation: 'So what excuse remains for us, when, despite the example of one human being adorned with every virtue, we prove to be so bereft as to have no intention to practice any virtue?'[27]

Though amelioration of the hardship of strangers and of the poor is important to Chrysostom, this is not the only aim of the virtue of hospitality. The preacher does not hesitate to point out that hospitality has payoffs also for the benefactor. Throughout his life, Abraham 'exerted every effort of his own',[28] as a result of which he was judged 'worthy' (*ēxiouto*) of God's help.[29] We ought to follow Abraham in his virtue in 'consideration of our salvation',[30] to 'gain a reward for it in the age that never ends',[31] 'taking great care of our salvation'.[32]

Chrysostom's preaching is perhaps characterized by a somewhat one-sided focus on moral demands – along with the prospect of reward. To be sure, the three sermons do have an obvious christological centre: the theophany is that of Christ appearing as one of the three visitors, and God's gracious condescension in the theophany is part of a divine pedagogy that foreshadows his *synkatabasis* in the Incarnation itself. At the same time, however, the incentive for Christian living stems at least as much from the Abrahamic example as from God's *synkatabasis* in the pre-incarnate Christ. For Chrysostom, the life of transformation leads invariably to its fitting, eternal reward, and he regards it his task, as a preacher, to lead his listeners towards that end.

Conclusion

We should not exaggerate the differences either between Origen and Chrysostom or between the Antiochene and the Alexandrian inter-pretative approaches. The Alexandrian tradition was not indiffer-ent to the historical or literal meaning of the text; and it is also true that theologians in the Antiochene school were keenly interested in exploring deeper levels of meaning in the biblical text.[33] Diodore of Tarsus, Chrysostom's erstwhile teacher, writes in the prologue to his *Commentary on the Psalms* that 'we will not disparage anagogy and the higher *theōria*. For history is not opposed to *theōria*. On the con-trary, it proves to be the foundation and the basis of the higher senses.' Diodore did add a word of caution:

> One thing is to be watched, however: *theōria* must never be under-stood as doing away with the underlying sense; it would then be no longer *theōria* but allegory. For wherever anything is said apart from the foundational sense, we have not *theōria* but allegory.[34]

While Diodore obviously disliked allegory, neither he nor the Antiochene tradition as a whole restricted its exegesis to the literal sense. As Frances Young rightly observes in her book *Biblical Exegesis and the Formation of Christian Culture*:

> The traditional categories of 'literal', 'typological' and 'allegorical' are quite simply inadequate as descriptive tools, let alone analytical

tools. Nor is the Antiochene reaction against Alexandrian allegory correctly described as an appeal to the 'literal' or 'historical'
meaning.[35]

Young's observation holds true particularly for St John Chrysostom: he
was perhaps even more interested in spiritual exegesis than were some
of his Antiochene predecessors. Chrysostom often employed typology
in his interpretation of Scripture, something of which Diodore had
been rather wary.[36] Chrysostom, comments Ashish Naidu, 'reflects a
modification of the Antiochene hermeneutical tendencies in a direction
which is broadly consonant with the Alexandrian tradition'.[37] Origen
and Chrysostom are not nearly as far apart as unwarranted caricatures
may make us believe.

It is also evident that both preachers take seriously God's *synkatabasis*
in relating to human beings. Both use the term – though Chrysostom
does so much more pervasively than Origen, and Origen doesn't use it in
his sermons on the Mamre theophany. Both see God's self-revelation – in
theophany, in the Incarnation and in the biblical text – as involving divine
condescension. Both wish to do justice to the divine transcendence as
well as to the divine immanence implied in the theophany. *Synkatabasis*,
David Rylaarsdam points out, both reveals and conceals God:

> On the one hand, adapted revelation overcomes the dissimilarity
> between God and humans by forming a symbolic bridge between the
> two. Since a corporeal symbol has similarities to the spiritual reality
> it represents, some knowledge is possible. Yet, on the other hand,
> Chrysostom's understanding of the symbolic character of revelation
> does not compromise the incomprehensibility of God. For a symbol
> and the reality it signifies are not only similar but also different. God
> is always higher than the reach of any symbolic bridge. In revealing
> himself, he appears not as he is. Symbols are a limited means of com-
> munication, but adequate to lead humans to faith in God's plan of
> redemption and to a heavenly way of life.[38]

Rylaarsdam's comments hold true not only for Chrysostom but also
for Origen. Both preachers believed that God's *synkatabasis* at Mamre
reveals and conceals at the same time; similarly, both were convinced
that also the Incarnation and the inspired Scripture reveal and conceal
at the same time.

Yet it is not overly difficult to enumerate the differences between
Origen's and Chrysostom's approaches. They each have their own

distinct reading strategies and their own styles of preaching. These differences have to do with the fact that the two authors do represent two fairly distinct theological and interpretative traditions. The Alexandrian tradition of Origen treated the allegorizing of the Jewish philosopher and exegete Philo as something that, to a large extent, was transferable to the Christian tradition. The reason for this is that Origen and other Alexandrian exegetes believed that the apostle Paul himself had allegorized the biblical text. Origen was convinced, therefore, that one couldn't possibly avoid allegorizing if one wished to do justice to the newness of the Christ event.[39] The Antiochene tradition of Diodore of Tarsus and St John Chrysostom was much more reticent in the use of allegory: both exegetes were distrustful of the speculative turn that the practice of allegorizing might take, preferring the term *theōria* (contemplation) instead.

The differences in nuance between the Alexandrian and Antiochene traditions are reflected in the exegetical and homiletical choices that Origen and Chrysostom make. The object of Abraham's hospitality is, for Origen, the Lord himself; for Chrysostom, this is true only indirectly: Abraham in the first instance reaches out to a fellow human being in need of food and drink. As a result, Origen's sermon has a more mystical feel. He wants to explore how the biblical text describes the soul's growth in perfection in relationship with God; Chrysostom, by contrast, is interested in fostering particular embodied practices in his listeners. He wants their behaviour to be like that of the 'just man'. Although both exegetes pay detailed attention to the particulars of the text, Origen often does this so that he can determine the allegorical meaning of various textual details, while Chrysostom does it mostly to explore the numerous ways Scripture brings to the fore the moral virtues of the main characters of the narrative. Perhaps the difference between the two preachers can best be expressed by noting that for Origen divine theophany is inextricably bound up with transformed *vision* ('sharpness of sight'), whereas Chrysostom connects it with transformed *virtue* (reaching out with compassion). Origen is more vertical whereas Chrysostom is more horizontal in his reading of the Mamre theophany.

Finally, we can put the difference between the two approaches in sacramental terms. Origen is typically intrigued with the transcendent, hidden truth of the theophany, of the Incarnation and of the Scriptures: Abraham's spiritual vision at Mamre gives him access to the inner reality (*res*) of the sacrament. Chrysostom is much more at home with the immanent, revealed symbol of the theophany, of the Incarnation and of the Scriptures: Abraham's hospitality to strangers indicates that there is no way of bypassing the outward symbol of the sacrament (*sacramentum*). Both approaches have their strengths: Origen beautifully highlights the importance of the contemplative life, of the vision of God as the sacramental aim of Abraham's hospitality, and Chrysostom rightly emphasizes that we dare not circumvent the embodied, sacramental grounding of the active life. Both approaches also have their weaknesses: Origen can come across as ignoring the significance of the human form in which God reveals himself in history; Chrysostom may seem to be courting a moralism that reduces salvation to the emulation of human examples.

We need the complementarity of the two approaches. Both, after all, are sacramental in character, even if the one tends to emphasize the inward reality and the other the outward sacrament. The tension between the two exegetes is one that we should be hesitant to relinquish, because it is only by retaining the tension that we can give expression to the paradox of the Incarnation. When in the Incarnation the eternal Word stoops down in gracious love, he invites us to enter into him and so to join the triune life of God himself. This divine grace is the ultimate form of hospitality, of which human hospitality is a mere shadow. Or, to put it theologically, ordinary human hospitality (*philoxenia*) is merely an analogous participation in God's gracious condescension (*synkatabasis*) in Jesus Christ.

In the context of this volume's theme of the transforming vision of the saving knowledge of God, there is perhaps no better way to end than with the words that conclude Origen's fourth homily:

> Let us give attention to make our acts such, our manner of life such, that we may be held worthy of knowledge of God, that he may see fit to know us, that we may be held worthy of knowledge of his son Jesus Christ and knowledge of the Holy Spirit, that we, known by the Trinity, might also deserve to know the mystery of the Trinity fully, completely, and perfectly, the Lord Jesus Christ revealing it to us.[40]

Notes

1 I explore hospitality as a metaphor for divine grace in detail in *Violence, Hospitality, and the Cross: Reappropriating the Atonement Tradition* (Grand Rapids, MI: Baker Academic, 2004).

2 Throughout this chapter I will quote the Greek translation (the Septuagint) from Rick Brannan et al. (eds), *The Lexham English Septuagint* (Bellingham, WA: Lexham Press, 2012).

3 For a helpful overview of the use of *synkatabasis*, see François Dreyfus, 'Divine Condescendence (*synkatabasis*) as a Hermeneutic Principle of the Old Testament in Jewish and Christian Tradition', *Immanuel* 19 (1984/85), pp. 74–86.

4 Justin Martyr's christological exegesis of Genesis 18 (*Dialogue with Trypho* 56) is followed by Irenaeus, *Demonstration of the Apostolic Preaching* 43–46; Tertullian, *Against Marcion* 3.9; Novatian, *On the Trinity* 18; Eusebius, *The Book of the Gospel* 5.8–9; *Ecclesiastical History* 1.2; *Ecclesiastical Theology* 2.21; and Hilary of Poitiers, *On the Trinity* 4.24–31. For Augustine's interpretation of the Mamre theophany, see *The City of God* 16.29 and *On the Trinity* 2.4.

5 Origen, *Homilies on Genesis and Exodus*, trans. Ronald E. Heine, Fathers of the Church (FC) 71 (Washington, DC: Catholic University of America Press, 1982), 4.5 (p. 108).

6 Cf. Ronald E. Heine, Introduction to Origen, *Homilies on Genesis*, p. 38.

7 Cf. Marie E. Doerfler, 'Entertaining the Trinity Unawares: Genesis xviii in Western Christian Interpretation', *Journal of Ecclesiastical History* 65:3 (2014), pp. 485–503 (pp. 499–500).

8 Origen, *Homilies on Genesis*, 5.1 (FC 71:112).

9 *Ibid.*, 3.3 (FC 71:91–93).

10 *Ibid.*, 3.6 (FC 71:98).

11 *Ibid.*, 4.2 (FC 71:105).

12 David Rylaarsdam, *John Chrysostom on Divine Pedagogy: The Coherence of His Theology and Preaching* (Oxford: Oxford University Press, 2014), p. 127.

13 Diodore of Tarsus, prologue to the *Commentary on the Psalms*, as quoted in Karlfried Froehlich, *Biblical Interpretation in the early Church* (Philadelphia, PA: Fortress Press, 1984), p. 86. Cf. Rylaarsdam, *John Chrysostom*, p. 128.

14 John Chrysostom, *Homilies on Genesis 46–67*, trans. Robert C. Hill (Washington, DC: Catholic University of America Press, 1992), 58.12–13 (FC 87: 159–160).

15 See Ashish J. Naidu, *Transformed in Christ: Christology and the Christian Life in John Chrysostom*, Princeton Theological Monograph Series 188 (Eugene, OR: Pickwick, 2012), p. 82.

16 John Chrysostom, *Homilies on Genesis 18–45*, 42.7 (FC 82:421–22).

17 *Ibid.*, 42.12 (FC 82:424).

18 *Ibid.*, 42.12 (FC 82:424–25) (slightly altered for clarity).

19 *Ibid.*, 41.7 (FC 82:405–6).

20 *Ibid.*, 41.7 (FC 82:406).

21 *Ibid.*, 41.9 (FC 82:407).

22 *Ibid.*, 41.7 (FC 82:405). Cf. 43.32 (FC 82:453).

23 *Ibid.*, 41.10 (FC 82:407); 41.11 (FC 82:408).

24 *Ibid.*, 41.9 (FC 82:406).

25 *Ibid.*, 42.5 (FC 82:420).

26 *Ibid.*, 42.1 (FC 82:418).

27 *Ibid.*

28 *Ibid.*, 42.3 (FC 82:419).

29 *Ibid.*, 42.2 (FC 82:419).

30 *Ibid.*, 42.5 (FC 82:420).

31 *Ibid.*, 43.8 (FC 82:439).

32 *Ibid.*, 43.32 (FC 82:453). Cf. 41.25 (FC 82:416).

33 Naidu, *Transformed in Christ*, pp. 28, 47–51.

34 Diodore, prologue to the *Commentary on the Psalms*, as quoted in Froehlich, *Biblical Interpretation*, p. 85. Cf. Naidu, *Transformed in Christ*, pp. 52–3.

35 Frances M. Young, *Biblical Exegesis and the Formation of Christian Culture* (1997; repr.; Peabody, MA: Hendrickson, 2002), p. 2.

36 Naidu, *Transformed in Christ*, pp. 72–5.

37 *Ibid.*, p. 19.

38 Rylaarsdam, *John Chrysostom*, p. 103.

39 See Henri de Lubac, 'Hellenistic Allegory and Christian Allegory', in *Theological Fragments*, trans. Rebecca Howell Balinski (San Francisco: Ignatius Press, 1989), pp. 165–96.

40 Origen, *Homilies on Genesis* 4.6 (FC 71:111).

4

The Gospels on the Knowledge of God

MARKUS BOCKMUEHL

Scripture repeatedly urges the possibility of knowing God, and strongly encourages the quest for such knowledge. Old Testament examples abound, from Adam, Enoch and the patriarchs who walked and talked with God, via Moses whom the Lord knew face to face, to the prophets who encourage Israel to press on and know the Lord – indeed, anticipating the day when all God's people will know him and the earth shall be filled with the knowledge of God as the waters cover the sea.[1] To search for wisdom and her commandments like silver or hidden treasure carries the explicit promise of discovery: the seeker will 'understand the fear of the LORD, and find the knowledge of God'.[2]

The New Testament, too, seems at first sight to provide plenty of encouragement in its evident conviction that in the Incarnation, Cross and Resurrection God makes himself known as man to humanity. More specifically, the key scriptural texts of confession and dispute in the formulation of the Church's historic creeds tend to be concentrated in the writings of St John and St Paul. Since for these apostolic writers God is revealed more specifically as Father, Son and Holy Spirit, it seems only reasonable to expect the journey from Scripture to the knowledge of the Trinity to run along a road that is well prepared and signposted. Or at least one encounters plenty of well-meaning affirmations and reassurances to this effect in confessional theological literature!

The difficulty, as we will see in a moment, is that this journey from the textual jungle to that desired theological mountain top turns out on a closer reading of the texts to require turning off the exegetical cruise control and exiting the epistemological superhighway. The destination is real, to be sure, and absolutely worth pursuing. It is just that before long the required mode of travel involves more of a concatenation of twisting mountain footpaths, from many of which the destination is frustratingly invisible because it is hidden by clouds or intervening hills and forests.

This difficulty certainly pertains to all four Gospels – but also, as a subsequent chapter of this book will show, in the letters of Paul. After briefly considering the synoptic evangelists, the present chapter will focus on an exploration of the Gospel of John.

Knowledge of God in the Synoptic Gospels

New Testament scholarship is not trained or conditioned to discern much Trinitarian theology in the synoptic Gospels. Nevertheless there is considerable benefit in critical observation of how these texts speak explicitly of God's knowledge of us – or ours of him. As one does this, it proves remarkably difficult to find clear affirmations of human knowledge of God, of Jesus or of the Spirit.

This mystery is already clear in the Gospel of Mark: the demons know who Jesus is (1.24), which is perhaps not the same as knowing him; but human agents know neither. Strikingly, this is true not only of his enemies but even of his friends, who appear to have little faith and even less knowledge: Peter eventually denies *any* knowledge of Jesus (14.71), and escapes the narrative weeping bitterly until his implicit restoration on Easter morning (16.7). Perhaps Peter realizes that his speech-act of denial has served only to confirm the profound truth of his words: even though Peter was the first to identify Jesus as Messiah (8.29), the reality is that he does not know him.

Matthew is perhaps clearest on this subject. God knows believers and their needs intimately, before they even ask him (6.8, 32). Similarly, he alone knows the day and the hour of our destiny, as Matthew unlike Mark stresses repeatedly; and the only appropriate human response is watchfulness (24.36, 42; 25.13; cf. Mark 13.32–35).

When that day does arrive, being known by God is decidedly a function of responsive and alert discipleship, including especially care for the poor, the sick, the imprisoned and the homeless. In a stark warning, even disciples who fail to serve Christ in the least of his sisters and brothers will find that in the day of judgement he quite explicitly does *not* know them but instead disowns them (25.12–13).

As in the other Gospels, for Jesus' leading disciple Simon Peter his greatest crisis and failure comes when under challenge he not only abandons his Lord but denies that he even knows him – in Matthew explicitly not once but twice: 'I do not know the man.'[3] We may note too that in this Gospel, uniquely, this episode comes *after* Peter has already received from the Father the revelation of Jesus' messianic divine sonship, something that flesh and blood could not reveal (16.16–17).[4]

The precariousness of that divinely revealed knowledge is already evident earlier in the Gospel, in a famous statement anticipating Johannine perspectives: 'nobody knows the Son except the Father and no one knows the Father except the Son, and those to whom the Son wishes to reveal him' (Matt. 11.27; Luke 10.22). Yet even divine revelation apparently does not suffice to guarantee knowledge of God. As Peter's case illustrates, the disciples' tragedy is that seemingly they often do *not* know God, even when faced with his Incarnation as Messiah and Son of God. Peter recognizes his fateful impotence and exits 'weeping bitterly' (26.75). God, however, in fact knows the disciples in spite of this. Therein alone, it seems, lies their salvation, and in the risen Lord's promise of his uninterrupted daily presence to Peter and the eleven until the consummation of the world (28.20).

For Luke as for Mark, Jesus remains more emphatically unknown to humans: only the demons know who he is (4.34). Conversely, however, the Father does know the disciple's every need (12.30). This is in contrast to those who do not enter salvation through the narrow door: they will find that the owner of the house does *not* know them (13.25, 27). And again, as predicted, Peter denies that he knows Jesus (22.57), being in this case hauntingly convicted by the arresting gaze of 'the Lord' (22.61). Significantly, however, Luke's Jesus has already sown the seed preparing for Peter's conversion and call to strengthen his brothers (22.32). As for Jesus' executioners, they neither know him nor what they are doing in crucifying him (23.34) – proof at least that they are not among those to whom the Father has revealed the Son (10.22).[5]

Even aside from this handful of selected passages, the Synoptic Gospels markedly downplay the theme of knowledge. It is worth stressing the surprising extent to which on this subject they depart both from classic tropes of Greek philosophy and from contemporary Jewish texts, including the Dead Sea Scrolls.[6]

John's Gospel on Knowledge of the Triune God

Many of these questions find decidedly fuller development in the Gospel of John, whose theological significance for the early Church is difficult to exaggerate. Whatever one's approach to the theological diversity of the New Testament, evidence for the Fourth Gospel's decisive influence in the early Church's reflection about God as Father, Son and Holy Spirit is overwhelming – whether in the surviving manuscript tradition, commentary culture, or theological reflection leading up to the great creedal formulations of the fourth and fifth centuries.

In turning from the Synoptics to the Fourth Gospel it is as if one enters a narrative world of selective but turbocharged intensity. The story is recognizable to anyone familiar with Matthew, Mark and Luke: their basic building blocks of narrative, theology, Christology and even history are in my view not fundamentally at odds with those of John. But whereas in the Synoptics the messianic Son of God's divinity appears in some respects to unfold cumulatively over the narrative as a whole, here it is as if from the outset the whole is replete and radiant in every part. That experience of finding the whole from the start in each detail is a in sense precisely what the Prologue signifies.

As E. C. Hoskyns (1884–1937) famously noted in his landmark theological commentary, synoptic episodes like the transfiguration, the exorcisms, the agony of Christ are absent but in fact spread through every part of the story and therefore not narrated: the Son of God's life and death in the flesh is '*the place of understanding*', the *locus intelligentiae*,[7] while 'the truth which Jesus *is* and *was*' can be known only by the Holy Spirit of God.[8]

The quest for a dogmatic centre of New Testament theology has a long and disputed pedigree, and indeed some have always denied that any such thing could be legitimately pursued amid the sometimes dissonant polyphony of its authors.[9] In this connection I have long found persuasive an argument of Robert Morgan, one of my predecessors, about the topical relationship of the New Testament to Christian doctrine. John's Gospel makes relentlessly explicit what may elsewhere be present but implicit or presupposed; it stands on this question at the heart of the 'Vincentian' orthodox conviction 'that in knowing and relating to the crucified and risen Jesus through the Spirit we know and are in relationship with God'.[10]

Knowing and unknowing matters centrally in John, yet this Gospel is profoundly sceptical about the human ability to know either the Father, the Son or the Spirit – a point to which the next chapter will return in relation to Paul. When the Word's Incarnation made known the invisible God, the world and even his own people did not know or accept him (1.10–11, 26, 31, 33; 1.18). Human beings know, or think they know, *that* certain things are the case,[11] even to the point of knowing *that* Jesus is the Holy One of God (6.69; cf. 8.28). But to know this to be the case is not the same as knowing the triune God himself.

So what might it take to know God? C. H. Dodd (1884–1973), a giant of twentieth-century Johannine interpretation,[12] rightly recognized the importance of this theme underlying much of the rhetoric, especially in chapters 7—8 and the Farewell Discourses of 14—17.[13]

Jesus' Jewish opponents claim to know him, but in a rare ironic concession Jesus allows that while humanly they may 'know him' and where he is from, they wrongly assume this rules him out as a Messiah (7.28–29). Unlike him, however, they do not know the one who sent him and thus ironically they do not in fact know where he is from (Dodd 1953, p. 158): 'Jesus is a visitor from Galilee, well-known by sight and repute to the inhabitants of Jerusalem. But in a deeper sense their 'knowledge' is a true ignorance . . . Knowledge of God comes into the question.'

On that point Dodd is undoubtedly right; indeed he is one of remarkably few commentators to foreground this question. This is despite the fact that he tends to abstract the language of 'knowledge' from verbs of knowing, even where they concern the apprehension of facts *about*, knowing *that* something is the case, rather than the direct knowledge of God. In all this it is surely significant that John does not use the noun *gnosis* even once. One might think it possible to redress this by appealing to the supposedly synonymous term *phōs* ('light'); but while this theme is undoubtedly vital for John, it clearly denotes for him divine revelation rather than human knowledge.[14]

It is also true that Dodd, in the spirit of his day, allowed himself to be excessively impressed by the Fourth Gospel's 'Hellenistic' qualities. He would, one suspects, have thought better of it if he had had a chance to look in greater depth at the Dead Sea Scrolls on the one hand and the Nag Hammadi library on the other, both of which were only recently and very partially available as he was completing his work on the Fourth Gospel.

Instead, throughout his work Dodd follows the precedent of Rudolf Bultmann (1884–1976) and the earlier writers of the *religionsgeschichtliche Schule* in relying heavily on comparisons with the Hermetic corpus of writings, for which the idea of saving knowledge is, as for Gnosticism, fundamental. Dodd moreover thought that John felt no 'duality' between Jewish and Hellenistic mysticism and that in breaking with Old Testament conceptions of 'truth' he therefore shed much of its Jewish associations in favour of the Hellenistic conviction that *gnosis* brings freedom and allows the knower to be deified (Dodd 1953, p. 159).

This is a theory few Johannine scholars have been prepared to sustain in the wake of serious study of the Dead Sea Scrolls in contrast to the Platonizing mystics of Nag Hammadi.[15] Specifically in relation to the prominence Dodd gave to the Hermetic literature, the leading Johannine scholars like Raymond E. Brown before long definitively ruled out its relevance to the interpretation of John, given its Egyptian synthesis of Middle Platonic and Stoic cosmological ideas dating to the second through fifth centuries.[16]

That said, Dodd does proffer a number of valuable insights into the dynamic of knowing and unknowing God in the Fourth Gospel. One of these is its undeniably moral dimension. 'Failure to know God is a failure on the ethical plane. It is wilful rejection of God',[17] and this is the stark and distressing retort Jesus launches against his Jewish opponents:[18]

> It is my Father who glorifies me, he of whom you say, 'He is our God', though you do not know him. But I know him; if I were to say that I do not know him, I would be a liar like you. But I do know him and I keep his word. (8.54–55)

More important still, Dodd recognized, and at least to a limited extent allowed for, Scripture's marked reluctance to speak of human knowledge of God – and its frequent affirmation that people do *not* know God, particularly in the Old Testament: 'God's knowledge of man is the fundamental, permanent and certain thing, while man's knowledge of God is problematical.'[19] God knows Israel intimately, as he knows Moses and the prophets;[20] but people's ability to know God is rather more in question.

In the Gospel of John, however, there is clearly a strong case to be made for saying that while God is himself intrinsically invisible and unknowable, Jesus Christ has made him known – God the only Son has 'exegeted' him (1.18).[21] Or as Jesus puts it most evocatively in the Farewell Discourses, 'Whoever has seen me has seen the Father' (14.9). According to John 8, what Abraham saw at Mamre was not the Father but the Son and his day (8.56–58): to Justin Martyr and many later interpreters this seems a perfectly reasonable inference if one reads in Genesis 18 that Abraham lifted his eyes to see the κύριος and stood before him.[22] It matches John's assurance that the Lord whose glory Isaiah saw in the Temple is none other than Jesus (12.41).

However, it does not follow that the knowledge of God dilemma is therefore resolved. For Dodd, the task looks easy:

> The Jesus of the gospel has a double role: he is, as Logos or Son, the divine Object of man's knowledge, and at the same time the Subject of God's knowledge of man; but He is also (as man) both the Object of God's knowledge of man and the Subject of man's knowledge of God.[23]

Yet it remains the case that even this gospel remains acutely reserved about the possibility of knowing the Father or even the Son. Despite the apparent assurance just cited from the Farewell Discourses, this is prefaced with an important qualification (14.7–9). 'If you have come to know me (ἐγνώκατε),' Jesus explains to the disciples, 'you *will* also know (γνώσεσθε) my Father. And from now on you *do* know (γινώσκετε) him and *have* seen (ἑωράκατε) him.' Taken in isolation, that seems straightforwardly reassuring to the disciples. Yet a much-debated textual variant in Codex Vaticanus and other early manuscripts suggests a more doubtful and perhaps reproachful meaning: 'if you *knew* me, you *would* also know the Father.'[24] Immediately afterwards Philip, one of Jesus' closest companions, is told that in fact 'you do *not* know me' (καὶ οὐκ ἔγνωκάς με, v. 9) – a sobering assessment reminiscent of what Jesus previously said to the Pharisees: 'You know neither me nor my Father' (8.19).

In other words, the disciples' doubtful knowledge even of Christ entails questions about their knowledge of God. Once again we find that there is evidently nothing intrinsic or automatic about the Incarnation as granting guaranteed knowledge of either the Son or the Father. The eternal Word, even in 'becoming flesh' and 'tabernacling among us' in his glory made visible (1.14), is the divine gift that is never simply available to be owned or possessed. The world did not know him; his own did not accept him; his forerunner John attests that they do not know him even when he stands in their midst – indeed even John himself did not know him (1.10, 11, 26, 31).

Several mitigating considerations are in play. First, the important Shepherd discourse of John 10 affirms that the Shepherd knows the sheep, and that they know his voice (10.4). Unlike many other places in the Fourth Gospel, however, here we find the affirmation that 'I know my own and my own know (γινώσκουσιν) me' just as Father and Son know each other (10.14–15). This is significant, but the inner-Trinitarian analogy raises the question of quite how literally or extensively this can be taken. It seems true to the Fourth Gospel to say that the Son knows the Father and the Father knows the Son (cf. 7.28–29, 8.54–55), just as Father and Son are One and co-inhere one another 'perichoretically' (10.30, 38). At the same time, this is a distinctive and unique relationship whose analogies, if any, in human knowledge or love of the triune God are at best partial and derivative.[25] After all, only the Son in fact has seen the Father (6.46); human seeing is only ever seeing the Son (12.45; 14.9).[26] Interestingly, even Dodd acknowledges that in the overall context of this gospel the use of the present tense here seems to function in a way that is '"gnomic" and timeless rather than strictly present in the temporal sense'.[27]

Implicit confirmation comes in the fact that positive affirmations about human knowledge of God appear by and large to retain a more eschatological point of reference in this gospel. Examples abound. Still in chapter 8, Jesus says to the Jews who have believed in him, 'If you continue in my word, you *are* truly my disciples; and you *will know* (γνώσεσθε) the truth, and the truth will make you free.' A moment later, that liberating truth is, as elsewhere in the Gospel, unambiguously personified: 'if the Son makes you free, you will be free indeed' (8.31–32, 36; cf. 14.6). Knowing the truth, the way or the life who is the Son is a function of being liberated by that Son,[28] just as the Evangelist later links apprehension of the truth to being guided into it by the Spirit of truth (16.13).

In the same context the disciples' potential binitarian ignorance is matched *a fortiori* by the world's *Trinitarian* ignorance concerning not only the Father and the Son but in addition 'the Spirit of truth, whom the world cannot receive, because it neither sees him nor knows him' (14.17).[29] Pilate asks 'What is truth?' (18.38) not out of some postmodern political or epistemological ennui but because he is ignorant of the Father, the Son and the Spirit (though perhaps that is true of the late-modern condition too?). The disciples, by contrast, *do* know the Spirit of truth because he abides in them and will be in them (John 14.17).

C. H. Dodd's treatment of texts like this manifests his explicit penchant for realized eschatology, in which the tension between present and future verbs is resolved – or dissolved – in favour of a decisive turning point in the present moment.[30] Although admitting that 'the dramatic situation' of John's Gospel appears to be 'proleptic', in his view what John *really* means allows for no eschatological slippage: the Farewell Discourses intend an *ex post facto* perspective that takes for granted the full realization of Christ's finished work through the Incarnation, effectively fusing knowledge and vision of God. 'Here, in its "realized eschatology", the Fourth Gospel stands apart from its Jewish Hellenistic predecessors and analogues, and firmly within its Christian setting' (Dodd 1953, pp. 165–6).

But these discourses do in fact preserve a greater eschatological dialectic than Dodd allows. This is perhaps at its most pronounced in the so-called High Priestly Prayer of chapter 17, oscillating as it does between the Jesus who prays for the disciples as their leader about to be crucified and the eternal Son who looks back on his earthly work as finished and in the past (17.4 and *passim*), to the point that he is 'no longer in the world' (17.11). Jesus prays that his own present unity with the Father may come to be reflected in the disciples' unity with one another (17.21–22), culminating in their beatific vision in glory, that they 'may be with me where I am, to see my glory' (17.24). By taking this eschatological context of the chapter seriously we can make sense of what is perhaps the one Johannine text that ascribes a saving function to human knowledge of God: 'this is eternal life, that they may know you, the only true God, and Jesus Christ whom you have sent' (17.3). The subjunctive construction clarifies that this knowledge is still an anticipated, eschatological reality, the gift of the Incarnation but still to be fully realized even for the believer.

Synthesis

The Gospels' apparent ambivalence about human knowledge stands to this extent in significant contrast to the second century's valorizing of *gnosis* in Valentinianism and some other Christian movements, leading up to its critical but constructive appropriation in the third century by figures like Clement of Alexandria and Origen. Not altogether unreasonably, the Valentinian commentator Heracleon reads Jesus' conversation with the Samaritan woman in John 4 as showing 'The will of the Father is that human beings should *know* the Father and be saved'.[31] Justin Martyr may constitute something of a watershed in the proto-Orthodox appropriation of this idea: he is not shy to describe the Incarnation as 'the fountain of living water which gushed forth from God upon a land devoid of the knowledge of God (that is, the land of the Gentiles)' (*Dial.* 69, trans. Falls); in his polemic against the Jews, on the other hand, he will insist that Christian baptism is distinctively an ablution both of repentance and of the knowledge of God (διὰ τοῦ λουτροῦ οὖν τῆς μετανοίας καὶ τῆς γνώσεως τοῦ Θεοῦ, *Dial.* 14).

Within the narrative of the Gospels, however, the act of knowing is certainly preferred to the abstraction of knowledge, let alone to knowledge as intrinsically salvific. This seems significant in view of the later proto-Orthodox Church's focus on the narrative fourfold Gospel tradition in contrast to the sayings and discourse gospels of Nag Hammadi. The latter celebrate Jesus, his appearance and death as 'fruit' of the saving 'knowledge of the Father',[32] which the spiritual elite embrace like the dawn while casting off ignorance like a nightmare (28.32—30.27).[33]

The Gospels, however, characterize experience and perception of the triune God primarily through the language not of knowledge but of love, mediated by participation, union, transformation, discipleship and imitation of Christ. This relationship between knowing and loving God is particularly strongly developed in the Farewell Discourses of John 14—17. Yet significantly, as we saw, even John strikingly prefers verbs of 'knowing' to corresponding nouns or abstractions like *gnosis*, which is never used.

The Father knows the Son and the Son knows the Father; by extension the Father and the Son send the Spirit, whom the world does not know but the disciples do, since he abides in them and 'will teach them everything' (14.16–17, 26 etc.). Where human knowledge of Father, Son or Spirit is at issue, two key emphases in the Gospels seem to include the recursively self-involving character of such knowledge and its nature as at best partial, contingent and proleptic. The knower only knows as he or she is known. Therein lies the only ground of certainty, as the scriptural authors recognized in a way that you might say both anticipates and cuts through the Gordian knot of late modernity's epistemological self-doubt.

Contrary to prevailing trends in its cultural and theological environment, the New Testament remains notably sceptical about the aptitude of human knowing to apprehend or respond to God as Father, Son or Spirit. In grappling with such uncomfortable ambivalence, we have briefly surveyed the Synoptic evidence before foregrounding the Gospel of John's preferred characterization of believers' relationship with the triune God in a vulnerable but enduring mutuality of love, seeing and coinherence.

For the Fourth Evangelist, God is only fully known in the eschaton, even by those who have seen the incarnate Word. Knowledge of God crucially begins with an inversion of subject and object: knowledge of God saves above all where it denotes God's knowledge, the unknowing human knower being divinely known by the Father through the Son in the Spirit, a subjective genitive long before it can become an objective genitive. And as John's concluding chapter shows, what overcomes and savingly transforms a disciple's moral ignorance and unknowing denial is not his or her knowledge but loving, and being known, by the Lord.[34]

That conviction seems uncannily reminiscent of something St Paul proposed in his first letter to Corinth (1 Cor 13.12). But therein lies the subject for another chapter in the present volume.

Works Cited

Bockmuehl, Markus. 2006. *Seeing the Word: Refocusing New Testament Study*. Studies in Theological Interpretation. Grand Rapids, MI: Baker Academic.

Bockmuehl, Markus. 2008. 'Is there a New Testament Doctrine of the Church?' In *Scripture's Doctrine and Theology's Bible*, pp. 29–44. Ed. M. Bockmuehl. Grand Rapids, MI: Baker Academic.

Bockmuehl, Markus. 2012. 'Dodd, Charles Harold.' *Encyclopaedia of the Bible and its Reception* 6: pp. 1025–8.

Brown, Raymond E. and Francis J. Moloney. 2003. *An Introduction to the Gospel of John*. New York: Doubleday.

Bultmann, Rudolf. 1941. *Das Evangelium des Johannes*. KEKNT. Göttingen: Vandenhoeck & Ruprecht.

Bultmann, Rudolf. 1971. *The Gospel of John: A Commentary*. Trans. G. R. Beasley-Murray. Philadelphia, PA: Westminster.

Charlesworth, James H. and Raymond E. Brown (eds), 1990. *John and the Dead Sea Scrolls*. New York: Crossroad.

Coloe, Mary L. and Tom Thatcher (eds), 2011. *John, Qumran, and the Dead Sea Scrolls: Sixty Years of Discovery and Debate*. Early Judaism and its Literature 32. Atlanta, GA: Society of Biblical Literature.

Dietzfelbinger, Christian. 2001. *Das Evangelium nach Johannes*. Zürcher Bibelkommentare NT 4 2. Zürich: Theologischer Verlag.

Dodd, C. H. 1953. *The Interpretation of the Fourth Gospel*. Cambridge: Cambridge University Press.

Festugière, A. J. and Arthur Darby Nock. 1945–54. *Corpus Hermeticum*. Collection des universités de France 4. Paris: Belles Lettres.

Festugière, A. J., Arthur Darby Nock and Ilaria Ramelli. 2005. *Corpus Hermeticum*. Milano: Bompiani.

Frey, Jörg. 1997–2000. *Die Johanneische Eschatologie I-III*. Wissenschaftliche Untersuchungen zum Neuen Testament 96/110/117. Tübingen: Mohr.

Gundry, Robert H. 2015. *Peter: False Disciple and Apostate According to Saint Matthew*. Grand Rapids, MI: Eerdmans.

Heine, Ronald E. (ed.), 1993. *Commentary on the Gospel According to John. Books 13–32*. Washington, DC: Catholic University of America Press.

Hoskyns, Edwyn Clement. 1947. *The Fourth Gospel*. Ed. F. N. Davey. Rev. edn. London: Faber & Faber.

Hoskyns, Edwyn Clement and Noel Davey. 1931. *The Riddle of the New Testament*. London: Faber & Faber.

Kammler, Hans-Christian. 2000. *Christologie und Eschatologie: Joh 5, 17–30 als Schlüsseltext johanneischer Theologie*. Wissenschaftliche Untersuchungen zum Neuen Testament 2:126. Tübingen: Mohr Siebeck.

Käsemann, Ernst. 1964. 'The Canon of the New Testament and the Unity of the Church.' In *Essays on New Testament Themes*, pp. 95–107. Studies in Biblical Theology 1:41. London: SCM Press.

Keener, Craig S. 2003. *The Gospel of John: A Commentary*, 2 vols. Peabody, MA: Hendrickson.

Keener, Craig S. 2016. *The Mind of the Spirit: Paul's Approach to Transformed Thinking*. Grand Rapids, MI: Baker Academic.

Koester, Craig R. 2003. *Symbolism in the Fourth Gospel: Meaning, Mystery, Community*. 2nd edn. Minneapolis, MN: Fortress Press.

Metzger, Bruce Manning. 1994. *A Textual Commentary on the Greek New Testament*. 2nd edn. New York: American Bible Society.

Morgan, Robert. 1996a. 'Can the Critical Study of Scripture Provide a Doctrinal Norm?' *Journal of Religion* 76:2, pp. 206–32.

Morgan, Robert. 1996b. 'St John's Gospel, the Incarnation and Christian Orthodoxy.' In *Essentials of Christian Community: Essays for Daniel W. Hardy on His 65th Birthday*, pp. 146–59. Ed. D. F. Ford and D. L. Stamps. Edinburgh: T & T Clark.

Reitzenstein, Richard. 1904. *Poimandres: Studien zur griechisch-ägyptischen und frühchristlichen Literatur*. Leipzig: Teubner.

Thompson, Marianne Meye. 2015. *John: A Commentary*. The New Testament Library. Louisville, KY: Westminster John Knox Press.

Thompson, Marianne Meye. 2016. '"Light" (φῶς): The Philosophical Content of the Term and the Gospel of John.' In *The Prologue of the Gospel of John: Its Literary, Theological, and Philosophical Contexts: Papers Read at the Colloquium Ioanneum* 2013. Ed. J. G. Van der Watt et al. Wissenschaftliche Untersuchungen zum Neuen Testament 359. Tübingen: Mohr Siebeck.

Williams, Catrin H. 2016. '(Not) Seeing God in the Prologue.' In *The Prologue of the Gospel of John: Its Literary, Theological, and Philosophical Contexts: Papers Read at the Colloquium Ioanneum* 2013. Ed. J. G. Van der Watt et al. Wissenschaftliche Untersuchungen zum Neuen Testament 359. Tübingen: Mohr Siebeck.

Williams, Rowan. 2000. *On Christian Theology*. Oxford/Malden: Blackwell.

Notes

1 E.g. Gen. 3.9–21; 5.22–24; Deut. 34.10; Isa. 11.9 Jer. 31.34; Hos. 2.20; 6.3.

2 Prov. 2.3–5.

3 Matt. 26.70–74, esp. 72, 74; cf. Mark 13.71; Luke 22.57.

4 Scholars have occasionally advanced the idea that Matthew singles Peter out not for praise but for condemnation, indeed perhaps as the false disciple and apostate par excellence (so e.g. Gundry 2015). This is not a position that has gained widespread support: it requires the implausible presumption that Peter's denial sufficed to thwart both the Father's messianic revelation to Πέτρος and Jesus' determination to build his church 'upon this πέτρα' and to grant him the earthly authority of binding and loosing (16.16–19).

5 Even there, as we saw above, revelation does not of course guarantee knowledge of God.

6 1QpHab 10.14–11.2 on 2.14; similarly 1Q27 (1QMysteries) 1.7. The Rule of the Community promises that God will instruct the upright in knowledge of the Most High (1QS 4.22; cf. 10.12; 11.3); 1QHᵃ 7.8 (4QHᵃ frg 3 1.2, 5; cf. 4Q175 (4QTest) 10 quoting Num 24.16 about Balaam.

7 Hoskyns 1947, p. 117; similarly pp. 80–2. Hoskyns and Davey 1931, p. 30 use the Latin phrase *locus intelligentiae*, in evident christological allusion to Job 28.13 (Vulgate).

8 Hoskyns 1947, p. 129; cf. p. 131.

9 So famously Ernst Käsemann 1964; also cf. e.g. Williams 2000, pp. 44, 48 in a sharp critique of Brevard Childs and others. See my further remarks in Bockmuehl 2008; Bockmuehl 2006, pp. 81–7.

10 Morgan 1996b, p. 148; cf. Morgan 1996a, pp. 218–19.

11 John 3.2; 4.25; 5.32; 7.26–29; 8.52; 9.20, 24–25, 29–31 etc.

12 Cf. my introduction to Dodd in Bockmuehl 2012.

13 Although not the most recent treatment of the topic, it remains one of the more focused and influential. Cf. e.g. Keener 2003, vol. 1, pp. 234–47; also Keener 2016, pp. 6–8 for the theme in Paul's Mediterranean environment.

14 Bultmann 1971, p. 43, n. 2 considers that apparent synonymity but also allows that the Johannine eschatological dimension requires the word to mean 'revelation'. Cf. recently Thompson 2016; Thompson 2015, pp. 29–31.

15 See e.g. Charlesworth and Brown 1990; Coloe and Thatcher 2011.

16 Brown and Moloney 2003, pp. 130–1. For the texts see Festugière and Nock 1945–54, with subsequent editions incl. Festugière et al. 2005.
In fact even Dodd himself seems at times to step back from the most sharply Hellenizing interpretations of truth in John: thus he acknowledges that at 3.21 this is more akin to Hebrew and OT ideas that would constitute a stumbling block for the Greek reader (p. 168). In contemporary scholarship the entire notion of a sharp polarity between Greek and Hebrew ideas has long been deemed outdated and is no longer serviceable.

17 Dodd 1953, p. 159. By contrast, it now seems decidedly misguided to go on, as Dodd does, to understand this as entailing 'the idea of knowledge as pure apprehension of truth, or reality, as liberating power, and as a sharing of the

divine nature; an idea which is not properly Hebraic, but belongs rather to the main tendency of Hellenistic religion'.

18 Dietzfelbinger 2001, p. 268 wonders if the Johannine community really had no alternative to such polemic.

19 Dodd 1953, p. 161.

20 Dodd 1953, p. 161 cites a range of OT passages in support: e.g. Amos 3.2; Hos. 5.3 (Israel); Deut. 34.10 (Moses); Jer. 1.5; 12.3 (Jeremiah); Ps. 139.1–2, 5, 10, 13, 23; Nah. 1.7. Strikingly, however, in keeping with writers like Reitzenstein 1904 and Bultmann 1941 (English trans. Bultmann 1971) he also allows corroborating support from 'the Hermeticist' (the *Poimandres* and other literature concerned with self-knowledge as knowledge of the 'thrice-great' god; this Egyptian pagan mystical writing was also attested at Nag Hammadi and shows Septuagintal or Philonic influence).

21 Philo famously regards knowledge of God as mediated through the Logos, knowledge of God being humanity's highest goal of happiness and bliss (e.g. *Decal.* 81; cf. *Det.* 86; *Abr.* 58).

22 Gen. 18.2–3, 22; Justin, *Dialogue* 56.

23 Dodd 1953, p. 160.

24 Εἰ ἐγνώκειτέ με, καὶ τὸν πατέρα μου ἄν ἤδειτε. Kurt Aland regards this reading, more critical as it is of the apostles, as the *lectio difficilior* and therefore earlier (annotation in Metzger 1994, p. 207).

25 Dodd 1953, p. 166: 'knowledge of God in the Johannine sense either takes the form of a knowledge of Christ, or is dependent upon a knowledge of Christ. It is only between the Father and the Son that the relation of full mutual knowledge exists independently.'

26 See also Williams 2016 for this ambiguity in the Prologue.

27 Dodd 1953, p. 164.

28 Koester 2003, pp. 287–99 offers a useful exposition of 14.6 in relation to the question of knowledge of God.

29 John 14.17. What this means, as Dodd also realizes, is that 'knowledge and vision of the Father, of the Son, and of the Paraclete are equipollent' (p. 165).

30 This assumption is equally found in a range of other interpreters; see e.g. Frey 1997–2000, vol. 3, p. 399 and n. 318 for more recent German scholarship, including Kammler 2000.

31 Frag. 31 on John 4.34: in Origen, *Comm. On John* 248 (trans. adapted from Heine 1993, p. 119). Origen himself accepts a connection of this water with the knowledge of God.

32 *Gospel of Truth* 18.11–19.34 *passim*; indeed in this document Christ, the Son, is himself the 'knowledge of the Father' (87.17).

33 Cf. similarly *Revelation of Adam* 72.1-14; 82.22; 83.19; *Paraphrase of Shem* 13.23 (knowledge of the Spirit); the thinly Christianized philosophical tract *Allogenes the Stranger* revels in the 'Triple-Powered Invisible Spirit' that makes knowledge of the Spirit available (e.g. 47.9–49.38), even while God himself is the Unknowable One par excellence (61.1–22 and *passim*). Contrast the *Teaching of Silvanus* 100.13–31 and *passim*, which exhorts knowing God through Christ (and does not dwell on 'knowledge' per se).

34 21.15–17: 'Lord, you know (οἶδας) that I love you.'

5

Knowing and Loving the Triune God: The Pauline Epistles

JENNIFER STRAWBRIDGE

Within the last decade a number of texts on Paul and the triune God have emerged, offering encouragement for an endeavour such as this chapter and confirming assumptions about the interdependence of biblical exegesis and theological doctrine.[1] Nevertheless, scholars such as Francis Watson recount warnings to those who dare enter this theological minefield that 'modern biblical scholarship has no great love for the doctrine of the Trinity'.[2] Others are less cautious, boldly claiming that the Pauline corpus, and the whole New Testament for that matter, 'contains no doctrine of the Trinity'.[3]

Such conclusions allow scholars who are, rightly, wary of anachronistic inferences and proof-texting to avoid speaking of the triune God in Paul's letters altogether. No one wants to be the person who finds the Nicene Creed tucked into the writings of the Apostle. The few who do focus on God as Father, Christ and Spirit in the letters attributed to Paul offer the quick caveat that Paul gives us all the ingredients to speak of the triune God, but a Trinitarian recipe, as such, has not yet been devised. With a focus either on Paul's understanding of God or that of Christ, many of these studies lead to the conclusion that Paul was a binitarian, but Trinitarian language is nowhere to be found.[4]

The scene, however, is rapidly and thankfully shifting as scholars like Watson call on contemporaries to 'resist this scholarly anti-Trinitarianism' and to stop living in a world that is 'hermetically sealed against current theological trends'.[5] Speaking about Paul's God as a triune God is no longer a faux pas and thus two conclusions are increasingly accepted within Pauline scholarship: that Paul's Christ cannot be separated from the triune God and that Paul cannot be a binitarian since he has a strong and clear pneumatology or understanding of the Spirit. Consequently, a number of recent studies draw attention to Paul's understanding of God's triunity as Father, Christ and Spirit and to the central role that exegesis of Pauline texts have played in the Trinitarian formulas of the fourth and fifth centuries.[6]

Such a shift in scholarship is not only welcome but is also supported by Paul's own writings. Statements about God's triune nature can be found across the Pauline epistles. In 2 Corinthians, Paul concludes the letter with a statement that begins some of our liturgies still today: 'the grace of the Lord Jesus Christ, the love of God, and the *koinonia* of the Holy Spirit be with all of you' (13.13). In Galatians, we encounter the language of Father, Son and Spirit together as Paul writes pointedly to the community that 'God sent forth the Spirit of his Son into our hearts, crying, Abba, Father' (4.6). And in Romans we catch a glimpse of how this triune God and love are intimately connected when Paul writes encouragingly that 'God's love has been poured into our hearts through the Holy Spirit' (5.5).[7]

One of the gifts of recent scholarship on Paul and the triune God is not only the attempt to reclaim Trinitarian conceptualities and language in Paul's writings but also the tools and different approaches used to examine the language of God as Father, Christ and Spirit within Paul's writing and how these three relate to one another. For it is in the relationship between God, Christ and Spirit that a number of triadic formulas are found.[8] Some of these will be considered briefly to give a flavour of Paul's language and theology. This chapter will then turn its focus to the intimate connection between the triunity of God in Paul's writings and Paul's perception of God's knowledge, wisdom and ultimately love.

God's Triunity

God and Christ

One of the chief criticisms of God's triunity in letters attributed to Paul is that while the epistles are clear that there is one God – something explicitly stated in Ephesians 1 among other places[9] – they do not address the Father, Christ or the Spirit as persons. When compared to the language of later Trinitarian doctrine, some therefore conclude that this means Paul cannot actually be Trinitarian. For Fee, Watson and Frances Young, such conclusions are both anachronistic and short-sighted since God's triunity in Paul is not limited exclusively to the language of persons, hypostases and other later terms.[10] Rather, Paul's understanding of God as Father, Christ and Spirit is Trinitarian because this understanding is both relational and also reciprocal. God the Father is not the Father without the Son. A son cannot by definition be a son without a father.[11] And the Spirit cannot be the one by whom love is poured and knowledge bestowed without the love of God and knowledge of Christ, God's Son. God's triunity in Paul's letters depends both on the relationship between God as Father, Christ and Spirit and on the reciprocity latent within each of these relationships.

Thus, within Paul's letters God is 'the God and Father of our Lord Jesus Christ' (Rom. 15.6)[12] and the one who 'raised Jesus our Lord from the dead' (Rom. 4.24).[13] Jesus is the 'Son' (1 Cor. 15.28),[14] the 'image of the invisible God' (Col. 1.15), who 'in the form of God' (Phil. 2.5), 'did not regard equality with God as something to be exploited' (Phil. 2.6). God is absolutely essential to Jesus' identity and Jesus is absolutely essential to God's. These statements are not simply christological, declaring who Jesus is in relation to God, but they are theological statements about who God is in relation to Jesus.[15] Therefore Watson – focusing on the language of God as Father and Christ as Son – can conclude:

> If Jesus is Son of God, then God is the God and Father of our Lord Jesus Christ: the purpose of the father/son language is to indicate that God and Jesus are identified by their relation to each other, and have no existence apart from that relation.[16]

God's identity is established by God's relation to Christ and Christ's identity is established by his relation to God.[17] The relationship is one of 'mutuality and reciprocity'.[18]

As we will see when we consider knowing and loving this God, just as the relationship between Father and Son is not a static relationship, neither is the one we have with God. Paul is clear that 'we were reconciled to God through the death of his Son' and then 'saved by his life' (Rom. 5.10). Moreover, 'we even boast in God through our Lord Jesus Christ' (Rom. 5.11) and 'confess that Jesus Christ is Lord, to the glory of God the Father' (Phil. 2.11). We too are invited into the relationship between Father and Son that we might be reconciled, as well as boast in and confess Jesus Christ as Lord, the one raised from the dead. For Paul, this relationship between Father and Son provides not only the foundation for the triunity of God but also the foundation for how we are to know and love this same God.

God and Spirit

Paul does not limit the relational aspect of God to God and Christ. What makes God triune and not binary for Paul is his understanding of the Spirit in relation both to God and to Christ. Paul is clear at the start of Romans that Christ is not only 'appointed Son of God' but is also Son of God 'in power according to the Spirit of holiness by resurrection from the dead' (Rom. 1.4). This Spirit in Paul's letters is described as 'the Holy Spirit'[19] as well as 'the Spirit of God',[20] 'the Spirit of Christ'[21] and 'the Spirit of the one who raised Jesus from the dead'.[22] In other words, the ways Paul identifies the Spirit throughout his writings places this Spirit in a directly relational position with God and with Christ.[23]

Moreover, within Paul's letters this Spirit plays an active role. In 1 Corinthians the wisdom of God revealed to those who love God is disclosed 'through the Spirit', for the Spirit is the one both who 'searches everything, even the depths of God' (1 Cor. 2.10) and the one who teaches us (1 Cor. 2.13) because 'no one comprehends what is truly God's except the Spirit of God' (1 Cor. 2.11). Reacting to the Corinthians' misunderstanding of the Spirit and their triumphalistic claims to know all things spiritual, Paul credits the Spirit alone with knowing the things of God and being the one by whom the wisdom of God is known. Paul's argument is both ontological and epistemological, as he is clear that only like can know like, therefore 'only God can know God',[24] which leads to the conclusion that God can only be known by and through the Spirit of God. And although the wisdom of God is secret and hidden (1 Cor. 2.7), those who love God can have access to this wisdom, revealed through God's Spirit. Love of God is intertwined with God's wisdom and knowledge, as this wisdom and knowledge fall into the category of being unseeable, unhearable and inconceivable, and yet can be made known in and through the Spirit to those who love God. The love appears to be ours to give but true knowledge and wisdom belong only to God.

Paul approaches this relationship between God and Spirit from a different and reciprocal angle in Romans, where we find that the Spirit is not the one who knows the mind of God but now God is the one who knows the mind of the Spirit. Here the Spirit does not search 'all things' as in 1 Corinthians, but God 'searches the heart' and 'knows what is the mind of the Spirit' (Rom. 8.27) who 'intercedes with sighs too deep for words' (Rom. 8.26). Once again knowledge is reserved for God. Only the Spirit knows how to pray – as Paul writes, 'we do not know how to pray as we ought' (Rom. 8.26) – and only God knows the mind of the Spirit (Rom. 8.27), and these two work together 'for those who love God' (Rom. 8.28). But lest we think this love is simply ours to give, Paul is clear that, just like knowledge, it stems from 'the love of God in Christ Jesus our Lord' (Rom. 8.39) and is that which 'has been poured into our hearts through the Holy Spirit that has been given to us' (Rom. 5.5). Here Paul drives home the reality that while love and knowledge go together, neither belongs solely to us and neither can exist on its own. In other words, we can only love when we are loved, and that love is given to us by God, in Christ, from which we cannot be separated (Rom. 8.35).

This passage at the end of Romans 8 takes a clear triune tone when Paul writes that Jesus, 'who died . . . who was raised, who is at the right hand of God', also, like the Spirit, 'intercedes for us' (Rom. 8.34). Thus, within this section about love, knowledge and intercession, Paul sets forth the crucial relationship not only between God and Spirit but also between Christ and the Spirit, as both are engaged in the act of intercession with God the Father, one on earth and the other in heaven, but both experienced by Paul. Knowledge and love are intertwined at the very heart of the relationship between God, Christ and Spirit, as the Spirit knows the mind of God and God knows that of the Spirit and of the Son in prayer, which is so deep it is reduced to wordless sighing.[25]

Knowing and Loving

Knowledge for Paul, however, is a tricky thing and he is doubtful whether humans can know God sufficiently.[26] While God knows the mind of the Spirit who intercedes for us, and the Spirit knows the mind of God, and we have the mind of Christ, our ability to know God carries an eschatological tension. This tension is clear in Paul's claims that he has 'decided to know nothing among you except Jesus Christ, and him crucified' (1 Cor. 2.2), and yet with love it is possible to 'understand all mysteries and all knowledge' (1 Cor. 13.2). This tension is evident when Paul writes that 'knowledge . . . will come to an end' (1 Cor. 13.9) and yet is also clear that he '[knows] only in part' and later 'will know fully, even as [he, Paul, has] been fully known' (1 Cor. 13.12). Human partial knowledge even in the face of revelation stands in synchronous contrast with God's knowledge of human beings, and in an eschatological tension with the full knowledge that is yet to be.

Origen, a great lover of Paul's writings and one of the first biblical exegetes and commentators, grasps this tension when he makes the distinction in his own writings between knowledge and sight, just as Paul does in 1 Corinthians 13. For Paul, seeing and knowing are connected for now we only see dimly and know in part but later we will see 'face to face' and have full knowledge (13.12). Origen echoes Paul's language when he writes that 'It is one thing to see (*videre*) and another to know (*cognoscere*)', and 'to see and to be seen is a property of bodies' but 'to know and be known is an attribute' of God as Father and Son.[27] In other words, knowledge disconnected from God is not true knowledge. Furthermore, our ability to know is possible even and perhaps only as we are fully known by God. God alone knows and is known, but in God's capacity to be known, room exists for us to have knowledge of God. Knowledge in many of Paul's letters, therefore, is not about the content of what is known, nor is it objective; rather, the one who has knowledge is the person who is known by God.[28] Drawing directly on Paul's language, knowing that Christ died and was raised by God through the Spirit cannot be separated from knowing God as Christ and Spirit. Knowing the love of God, the grace of Christ and the community of the Spirit cannot be disconnected from the God who loves, the Christ who gives grace and peace and the Spirit who searches all things.[29]

The God who is known is, for Paul, triune in nature and this triunity is grounded not in fourth-century doctrinal statements as such but in what some scholars call 'experienced conviction'.[30] This experience, which is a well-worn and even troublesome word in theological dialogue, cannot be disconnected from pneumatology and thus cannot be detached from experience of the Holy Spirit.[31] The Spirit is the link that enables us to be drawn into the knowledge and love of God and thus we can see why the triunity of God is central to Paul's theology. Without the Spirit, who pours the love of God into our hearts? Without the Spirit and Christ, who intercedes with God for us? Without the Spirit who knows the mind of God, how can we have the mind of Christ (1 Cor. 2.16)?

Nevertheless, even with the Spirit, full knowledge of God as Father, Christ and Spirit is unattainable this side of the eschaton, and the hubris of claiming such knowledge lies at the root of many difficulties in the communities Paul addresses. Paul is furious with the Corinthians, adamant that they are 'arrogant' (1 Cor. 5.2) and their 'boasting is not a good thing' (5.6) as he takes them to task for their actions (or lack thereof) towards sexual immorality and the reality that they thought they knew better than him. 'Do you not know', asks Paul, 'that a little yeast leavens the whole batch of dough?' Clearly they do not know, is the answer, and by claiming knowledge they do not have, they are living in the ways of the 'old yeast . . . of malice and evil' rather than in the ways of 'sincerity and truth' (5.8).

Paul is also not happy with the Romans and their continued sinful behaviour post-baptism. 'By no means!' exclaims Paul, should one 'continue to sin in order that grace may abound' (Rom. 6.1–2). 'Do you not know', he asks, using a tactic similar to that in his Corinthian letter, 'that all of us who have been baptized into Christ Jesus were baptized into his death?' Once again, clearly they do not know or they would live differently based on the 'newness of life' given through Christ who was raised by the glory of the Father (6.4).

Though knowledge and true wisdom may be secret and hidden, available only to those endowed with the Spirit (1 Cor. 2.7–10), this does not mean that in this life one can know nothing. Rather, it means that we see through a glass darkly, only know in part and yet live in the hope and knowledge that we will have the capacity to know fully, as we have been fully known (1 Cor. 13.12). Knowledge is about relationship and is intimately connected with God's love and knowledge of us, and therefore just as the triunity of God is reciprocal and relational, so is knowledge and love of the triune God.

When Paul writes in 1 Corinthians that one 'does not yet know as he ought to know' (8.2), this is not because this person does not grasp the content of knowledge. Rather, it is because this person does not have true knowledge, *gnosis*, which for Paul cannot be detached from love.[32] Love achieves what knowledge cannot. And this relationship of love and knowledge, while reciprocal in one sense, is also not an evenly balanced synergy. This love in its fullest sense expands to subsume true knowledge, whereas the reverse, for Paul, is not the case, as knowledge is not adequate and cannot expand without love. Without love our words are simply noise (13.1), without love our understanding is nought (13.2), without love what we possess is worthless (13.3).

Ultimately, Paul is not speaking about knowing and loving the triune God as if these are one and the same but about loving God, not because we know God but because God knows us. The foundation for the love of God within Paul's writings is God already knowing the person who loves, or in the words of Romans, God already calling the one who loves (8.28).[33] God is the one who pours love into our hearts through the Spirit (Rom. 5.5). God is the one through whom we exist (1 Cor. 8.6). When, in 1 Corinthians, Paul accuses the community of not yet knowing, he does so in response to their poor behaviour regarding their love of the other when faced with the issue of idol meat. He is clear that 'an idol has no existence' and that this is not what is at stake. What is at stake is the issue of knowledge and the danger that it poses when it is detached from love. And this love comes directly from the 'one God, the Father from who are all things and for whom we exist, and one Lord, Jesus Christ, through whom are all things and through whom we exist' (1 Cor. 8.6). He admonishes the Corinthians to base their behaviour on this reality, on that of the triune God, for knowledge is not an end in itself but only the means to the love of the one God and one Lord, and to love of the other.[34] Here, as in Romans 8, the triunity of God forms the basis for love that in turn can only be enacted fully when the person is known by God and, reciprocally, knows God.

And as we have observed in Romans 8 and 1 Corinthians, the key to knowing God, to grasping God's wisdom and to being known by God is the Spirit. The Spirit who knows the mind of God is the Spirit who moves those who have the mind of Christ to love and to fuller knowledge. Such knowledge and love are available only to those who have, in Paul's words, 'received the Spirit of God' (1 Cor. 2.12). In Romans the Spirit is the one who sighs and intercedes within us alongside Christ, who intercedes on the right hand of God. In Galatians God sends the Spirit into our hearts, enabling us to cry out to God as newly adopted children of our Father. The wisdom of God is revealed only to those who love God, as Paul is clear at the start of his letter to the Corinthians, and such wisdom, such knowledge, is revealed through the Spirit (1 Cor. 2.10). Here we cannot neglect Paul's equation of Christ with wisdom in this same letter: Christ 'who became for us wisdom from God' (1.30). With Christ as God's wisdom, and God as the one who reveals this wisdom through the Spirit, Paul offers a rather neat triadic relation of God, Christ and Spirit. Through the Spirit, the love of God is given expression in Christ and the knowledge and wisdom of God as Christ and Spirit can be realized, but not apart from the eschatological tension inherent in such claims.

That the Spirit sighs and intercedes for us to God points to the reality that such deep sighing can only come from those who have seen the hope of salvation but do not yet have full knowledge of it. Such sighing even from the depths of creation itself derives from knowledge. Those who know God's promise, those who know God's love in Christ through the Spirit, sigh for its completion and fulfilment.[35] Central to this understanding of knowledge is Paul's conviction that those to whom he writes are not yet perfect (to use the language of 1 Cor. 2.6–7), are not yet complete, and do not yet have full knowledge, even as they grow in their love of God. And thus to know that one does not yet possess full knowledge, that one only sees dimly, only knows in part and does not yet know as one ought to know, leads to longing, sighing and the knowledge that only the Spirit and only Christ can fully know and intercede for us with God. Such knowledge, combined with God's love and our love of God, moves us with faith to embrace the hope of salvation. And in the most circular way imaginable, Paul's argument takes us back to one of our starting points, for as Paul writes in Romans, this hope cannot disappoint those whose hearts have had God's love poured into them through the Spirit (5.5).[36]

Knowing what we do about the centuries after Paul and his status as one of the favourites, alongside John's Gospel, of many early Christian writers,[37] we can harbour no doubts that Paul's understanding of God as Father, Christ and Spirit influenced and even formed the foundation for questions that led to the doctrine of God as Trinity. Building on the writings of Robert Morgan, Frances Young is clear that Paul plays a key role in Trinitarian theology, which is simply 'the product of exegesis of the biblical texts, refined by debate and argument, and rhetorically celebrated in liturgy'.[38] But it would be a mistake to think that what we have just encountered is the triune God in a primitive and simplified form from which highly complex theology will develop. On the contrary, what we have encountered is an understanding of God that goes to the very heart of Christian doctrine, with which exegetes through the centuries will grapple.[39] However, the words of Paul were not enough to defend and protect the unity of God or the triunity of God in the early Church. While ultimately extra-scriptural words needed to be incorporated into doctrinal statements, so did the words of their favourite Gospel, that of John. For knowing and loving the triune God in Paul pointed early Christians into the heart of the Gospel. Thus, just as Paul's understanding of God as Father, Christ and Spirit is relational and reciprocal, so too are the two chapters on the New Testament in this volume.

Notes

1 For example, Wesley Hill's, *Paul and the Trinity: Persons, Relations, and the Pauline Letters* (Grand Rapids, MI: Eerdmans, 2015); Kavin Rowe's chapter in Gilles Emery, OP and Matthew Levering (eds), *The Oxford Handbook of the Trinity* (New York: Oxford University Press, 2011); and Gordon Fee's contribution to Stephen T. Davis, Daniel Kendall and Gerald O'Collins (eds), *The Trinity: An Interdisciplinary Symposium on the Trinity* (Oxford: Oxford University Press, 1999).

2 Francis Watson, 'Trinity and Community: A Reading of John 17', *International Journal of Systematic Theology* 1:2 (1999), pp. 168–84 (p. 168). Note that this is not Watson's view but part of his summary of what he believes to be an assumption in some corners of NT scholarship.

3 Donald H. Juel, 'The Trinity and the New Testament', *Theology Today* 54 (1997), p. 313. An almost identical statement can be found in Edmund J. Fortman, *The Triune God: A Historical Study of the Doctrine of the Trinity* (London: Hutchinson, 1972), p. 32.

4 See, for example James D. G. Dunn, 'Was Christianity a Monotheistic Faith from the Beginning?' *Scottish Journal of Theology* 35:4 (1982), pp. 303–36 (p. 336, n. 89).

5 Watson, 'Trinity and Community', p. 169.

6 Hill, *Paul and the Trinity*, p. 1, n. 1. See also Davis, Kendall and O'Collins (eds), *The Trinity*, p. vii. O'Collins goes so far as to state that 'I want to avoid here any false dichotomy between what is "trinitarian" and "christological"' – Gerald O'Collins, 'The Holy Trinity: The State of the Questions', in Davis, Kendall and O'Collins (eds), *The Trinity*, pp. 1–28 (p. 3). Gordon Fee, in one of the more extreme views of the field, even claims a number of times that Paul is 'a latent Trinitarian' – Gordon D. Fee, 'Paul and the Trinity: The Experience of Christ and the Spirit for Paul's understanding of God', in Davis, Kendall and O'Collins (eds), *The Trinity*, pp. 49–72 (p. 51). However, Fee also recognizes that 'this language itself is anachronistic for Paul' but nevertheless is clear that Paul's language 'is part of the stuff out of which the later articulations and language arose' – Gordon D. Fee, *The First Epistle to the Corinthians*, rev. edn (Grand Rapids, MI: Eerdmans, 2014), p. 650, n. 81.

7 Other examples of triadic language include 1 Cor. 12.3–6 and Eph. 4.4–6.

8 Wesley Hill's recent book focuses predominantly on reclaiming relational language to describe God as Father, Christ and Spirit within Paul's letters, informed by and set alongside Trinitarian statements of the fourth and fifth centuries.

9 This chapter refers both to texts accepted as genuinely by Paul and two of those attributed to Paul but whose authenticity is questioned, namely Ephesians and Colossians. In his Ephesian commentary, for example, Hoehner addresses the assumption that scholars are primarily against Pauline authorship and demonstrates with an elaborate chart that scholars through the twentieth century are equally divided on the issue of Ephesian authorship – Harold W. Hoehner, *Ephesians: An Exegetical Commentary* (Grand Rapids, MI: Eerdmans, 2002), pp. 9–20. Moreover, because the earliest Christian writers attribute both texts to the Apostle (see Irenaeus, Tertullian, Clement of Alexandria, and Origen, for example), I refer to both as Pauline letters, recognizing that they were either written or strongly influenced by the Apostle.

10 See, for example, Fee, *First Epistle to the Corinthians*, pp. 271, 650–4. For contrast, see F. C. Baur, *Die christliche Lehre von der Dreieinigkeit und Menschwerdung Gottes in ihrer geschichtlichen Entwicklung* (Tübingen: Osiander, 1843).

11 See Hill, *Paul and the Trinity*, pp. 162–3; Francis Watson, 'The Triune Divine Identity: Reflections on Pauline God-Language, in Disagreement with J. D. G. Dunn', *Journal for the Study of the New Testament* 23:80 (2000), pp. 99–124 (pp. 113–14); C. Kavin Rowe, 'Biblical Pressure and Trinitarian Hermeneutics', *Pro Ecclesia* 11:3 (2002), pp. 295–312 (p. 304).

12 See also 2 Cor. 1.3 and Eph. 1.3; and Watson, 'Triune Divine Identity', pp. 111–13.

13 See also Rom. 10.9 and 8.11.

14 Paul uses the language of 'Son' to describe Jesus in at least 14 other places in his letters including: Rom. 1.3–4; 5.10; 8.3, 29, 32; 1 Thess. 1.10; 1 Cor. 1.9; 2 Cor. 1.19; Gal. 1.16; 2.20; 4.4, 6; Eph. 4.13.

15 Watson, 'Triune Divine Identity', p. 111 and Hill, *Paul and the Trinity*, pp. 29–30. Dunn is also clear that Paul's Christology and theology are intimately connected – see James D. G. Dunn, 'christology as an Aspect of Theology', in *The Christ and the Spirit, Volume 1: Christology* (Grand Rapids, MI: Eerdmans, 1998), pp. 377–87 (p. 382); though it must be noted that both Watson and Hill challenge Dunn's christological conclusions and his understanding of the development of 'trinitarian monotheism' and his 'distancing Pauline theology from trinitarian theology' – see Hill, *Paul and the Trinity*, pp. 19–21; Watson goes so far as to accuse Dunn of being an Arian – see Watson, 'Triune Divine Identity', p. 117. Dunn does elsewhere briefly concede that within Paul one can find 'what might be called a *'Trinitarian' element in the believer's experience*' (emphasis in original) – see James D. G. Dunn, *Jesus and the Spirit* (London: SCM Press, 1975), p. 326. As Thiselton notes, however, this is the only reference to the Trinity in Dunn's book on Jesus and the Spirit – see Anthony C. Thiselton, 'The Holy Spirit in 1 Corinthians: Exegesis and Reception History in the Patristic Era', in Graham N. Stanton, Bruce W. Longenecker and Stephen C. Barton (eds), *The Holy Spirit and Christian Origins: Essays in Honor of James D. G. Dunn* (Grand Rapids, MI: Eerdmans, 2004), pp. 207–28 (p. 208).

16 Watson, 'Triune Divine Identity', pp. 114–15.

17 See Watson, 'Triune Divine Identity', pp. 115–19.

18 Hill, *Paul and the Trinity*, p. 169.

19 See 1 Thess. 1.5; 1 Cor. 2.4; 6.11, 19; 12.3.

20 See 1 Cor. 2.11; 2.14.

21 Rom. 8.9; Gal. 4.6; Phil. 1.19.

22 Rom. 8.11; Watson, 'Triune Divine Identity', p. 121.

23 For Longenecker, this relationship between Spirit and Son is decisively reciprocal as well – see Richard Longenecker, *Galatians* (Dallas, TX: Word Books, 1990), p. 173.

24 Fee, *First Epistle to the Corinthians*, p. 118; see the whole discussion by Fee on pp. 118–20.

25 Fee, 'Paul and the Trinity', p. 65.

26 One is tempted to say that this is about whether one can know God *fully*, but Markus Bockmuehl has questioned whether in Paul, as in the Gospel of John, such language could be stronger since 'fully' could be understood as a Platonizing ideal of perfection, which would not necessarily matter if it could be attained.

27 Origen, *Princ.* 1.1.8 (GCS 22).

28 See Fee's discussion of knowing God and being known by God in his *First Epistle to the Corinthians*, pp. 406–7.

29 This statement is adapted from a question asked by Francis Watson about John 17. See Watson, 'Trinity and Community', p. 175.

30 Fee, 'Paul and the Trinity', p. 62.

31 Fee, 'Paul and the Trinity', p. 62. See also Dunn, *Jesus and the Spirit*, pp. 319–21.

32 See Fee, *First Epistle to the Corinthians*, p. 406 for a more detailed discussion of 1 Cor. 8.2–3.

33 See Fee, *First Epistle to the Corinthians*, p. 407.

34 See Fee, *First Epistle to the Corinthians*, pp. 406–8.

35 Wojciech Szypuła, *The Holy Spirit in the Eschatological Tension of Christian Life: An Exegetico-Theological Study of 2 Corinthians 5,1–5 and Romans 8,18–27* (Rome: Pontifical Gregorian University, 2007), pp. 391–2.

36 Szypuła, *Holy Spirit*, p. 392.

37 See Jennifer R. Strawbridge, *The Pauline Effect: The Use of the Pauline Epistles by Early Christian Writers* (Berlin: De Gruyter, 2015).

38 Frances Young, 'The Trinity and the New Testament', in Christopher Rowland and Christopher Tuckett (eds), *The Nature of New Testament Theology: Essays in Honour of Robert Morgan* (Oxford: Blackwell, 2006), pp. 287–305 (p. 288).

39 Even those such as the Cappadocian Fathers, to whom Trinitarian doctrine is attributed, are clear that God's triunity remains a mystery – see Watson, 'Trinity and Community', p. 183, who quotes Gregory of Nazianzus from *Theological Orations*, 5.12. See also Young, 'The Trinity', pp. 288–92, 297–98.

6

The Trinity in the Mystical Theology of the Christian East

KALLISTOS WARE

Some years ago a useful booklet appeared entitled *The Good Cuppa Guide*. The author, Jonathan Routh, described various places in London, from The Ritz to East End stalls in Stepney, where a refreshing cup of tea could be obtained. Among other places, he visited the Surrey Tea Rooms in Waterloo Station. In those days the Surrey Tea Rooms gave you a table with a linen table cloth, and tea served by a uniformed waitress. Today, alas, all has changed. The Surrey Tea Rooms were well patronized on the day when Routh went there and he had to queue. As he was talking to two people just behind him in the queue, the manageress came up to him and said, 'Are you one person, or three?' He confessed that he was one person, and he was conducted to a small table and given a small teapot and a piece of fruitcake. As he consumed these things he reflected, 'Did the Surrey Tea Rooms in Waterloo Station frequently have mysterious visitors who said they were three in one and one in three, and could they have a larger tea pot?'

That perhaps is the impression that some people gain from the Christian doctrine of the Trinity. They see it as an arcane conundrum: one in three, three in one, and little more than that. But what is the practical effect of the doctrine of the Trinity on our Christian life? Christians, according to their traditional confession of faith, are not merely monotheists as are the Jews and the Muslims, nor yet are they polytheists as was Homer; they see in God both total unity and true personal diversity. Yet what difference does this belief make in our daily existence? Surely, with regret, we must agree with the words of Karl Rahner:

Christians, for all their orthodox profession of faith in the Trinity, are in effect virtually monotheist in their actual religious experience. One might even dare to affirm that, if the doctrine of the Trinity were to be erased as false, most religious literature could be preserved almost unchanged in the process.[1]

Do we need a doctrine of the Trinity, and if so, why? As a challenge to the widespread view that the doctrine of the Trinity is no more than a conundrum, a piece of technical jargon, of interest only to specialists, let me quote the views of two modern Orthodox Russian writers. The first is Fr Pavel Florensky, who died probably in 1943 in one of Stalin's prison camps. He says: 'Between the Trinity and hell, there lies no other choice.'[2] And my second phrase is from a friend of Tolstoy's, Nikolai Fedorov: 'Our social programme is the Trinity.'[3]

Looking at the doctrine of the Trinity, the first thing to be said is that it is a mystery beyond our understanding. The Russian theologian Vladimir Lossky rightly says that the doctrine of the Trinity is a cross for human ways of thought.[4] Yes, the doctrine of the Trinity is revealed to us through Scripture and tradition, through the living experience of the Christian people over many centuries, but it cannot be proved logically. Some writers do indeed attempt to provide logical proofs why God is one in three, but their speculations are not very convincing. We believe in the Trinity because it is a mystery transmitted through divine revelation. This is something the Christian East has been very much concerned to emphasize. We appeal to the Church's mystical tradition rather than to logical and systematic arguments. That has to be our starting point: the reality of the Trinity is something beyond our understanding and yet not totally unintelligible. A mystery does not signify in the religious context merely an unsolved problem, a baffling enigma. A mystery is rather something that is revealed to our understanding but never exhaustively revealed, because it reaches into the profound depths of the living God.

In discussing the doctrine of the Trinity let us concentrate on the teaching of the three fourth-century Cappadocian Fathers, St Basil of Caesarea, St Gregory of Nazianzus and St Gregory of Nyssa, for it was they who expounded the Trinitarian faith of the Christian East in its classic form. Now, if we want to single out one particular word that sums up the Cappadocian approach to the doctrine of God, then that word should be *koinonia*: communion, fellowship, relationship. The words of the greatest living Orthodox theologian, John Zizioulas, Metropolitan of Pergamum, exactly express the Cappadocian standpoint and the view of the Christian East in general: 'The being of God is a relational being: without the concept of communion it would not be possible to speak of the being of God.'[5] The word *koinonia* is used significantly in the work by Basil on the Holy Spirit. He writes: 'It is in the communion (*koinonia*) of the Godhead that the divine unity is to be found.'[6] In God, unity (*henosis*) means community (*koinonia*).

If we adopt this Cappadocian approach it means that we should not start from an abstract philosophical notion of one God and then try to argue from that to a Trinitarian distinction of three hypostases. We should rather proceed in the opposite direction. We should start from the Bible, from salvation history. We should discover how in Scripture, God is gradually disclosed as a triad of Father, Son and Spirit. We should reflect on the unique interpersonal relationship of these three, and on the basis of their interrelation we should then come to an understanding of the unity that makes these three to constitute one God. Typically, Basil's friend, Gregory of Nazianzus, says: 'When I say God, I mean Father, Son and Holy Spirit.'[7] God is not an intellectual abstraction but a community of persons, known to us through revelation and through prayer. Note that the Creed adopts precisely the same approach as Gregory of Nazianzus. It is true that the Creed begins with an affirmation of divine unity, 'I believe in one God'; but it does not then continue in abstract terms, 'I believe in an unmoved mover, in an uncaused cause, in a primordial ground of being.' No, the Creed continues in specific interpersonal terms: 'I believe in one God, the Father, and in one Lord, Jesus Christ, and in the Holy Spirit, the giver of life.' That is to say, 'I believe in the *koinonia* of the three who are joined in mutual love.' To quote Basil's younger brother, St Gregory of Nyssa:

> In the life-creating nature of Father, Son and Holy Spirit there is no division, but only a continuous and inseparable communion (*koinonia*) between them . . . It is not possible to envisage any severance or division, such that one might think of the Son without the Father, or separate the Spirit from the Son. But there is between them an ineffable and inconceivable communion and distinction.[8]

The Cappadocians in this way envisage the Holy Trinity on the analogy of three human persons, relating to each other in mutual love. Theirs is a social, communitarian doctrine of the Trinity. But any such doctrine is surely open to the objection: 'Are we not in danger of undermining the unity of God, of lapsing into tritheism?' And such a criticism has in fact been advanced in the West against the Cappadocians. If, then, we adopt a social approach to the Trinity, must we not also say that the unity of the Godhead is a unique unity? The interrelationship of the three divine persons is incomparably closer and stronger than the interrelationship between three human persons can ever be.

The Cappadocians were by no means unaware of this problem, and in fact they have several ways of indicating the uniqueness of the divine unity. Let me mention three such ways. First, they employ the notion of the monarchy of the Father. The ground and basis of unity within the Trinity is, in the Cappadocian view, not simply the essence shared by the three; there is also a personal ground of unity within the Godhead, the hypostasis of the Father. In the words of Gregory of Nazianzus, 'The three have one nature – God. And the union is the Father, from whom and to whom the order of the persons runs its course.'[9] The Father is thus for the Cappadocians the sole *arche* or *principium*, the sole principle of ultimate origin within the Trinity. The Father is the unique cause within the Trinity, and the other two persons are caused by him. (Some modern theologians are not happy about applying the word 'cause' in this way to the Trinity, but the Cappadocians are not afraid to use this term.) The Father is the one and only source or fountainhead within the Trinity. The other two persons find their unity in him and are defined in terms of their relationship to him. There is one God because there is one Father.

Now there is surely a difficulty here. This concept of the Father as the source of the Godhead, if pressed to extremes, leads us to subordinationism; and, indeed, the Cappadocians have sometimes been charged precisely with subordinationist tendencies. However, they counterbalance this emphasis on the monarchy of the Father by insisting with equal emphasis that the three are coeternal and coequal. We encounter here something that constantly arises in the theology of the Trinity. We are always in danger of deviating on one side or the other, of overemphasizing sometimes the threeness and sometimes the unity. When we are doing Trinitarian theology it is as if we are walking along a ridgeway with precipices on either side. If we wander from the path to one side, we see opening up before us tritheism, and if we react too sharply against this, we find modalism opening up before us on the other side. Thus in the doctrine of the Trinity we have constantly to be counterbalancing our statements. Having made one affirmation, we have to qualify it by another altogether different affirmation. The doctrine of the Trinity is, as it were, a system of checks and balances. As Cardinal Newman said, 'Theology is saying and unsaying to a positive effect.'

That, then, is one way the Cappadocians seek to safeguard themselves against tritheism, by emphasizing the Father as the unique source within the Godhead. A second way they adopt is to speak of coinherence or mutual indwelling between the three persons. This clearly is a direct development of the concept of *koinonia*. Father, Son and Holy Spirit indwell one another in mutual love. Each is totally transparent to the other two, each is totally embraced and enfolded by the others. There is no opaqueness, no impermeability between them, but an unreserved openness, which yet in no way impairs the personal distinctiveness of each. Each is totally receptive of the other two, each contains the other two and moves within them. In the words of Gregory of Nyssa:

> All that is the Father's is seen in the Son, and all that is the Son's belongs to the Father also; for the whole Son abides in the Father and he has in his turn the whole Father abiding in himself.[10]

This idea of mutual indwelling is often described by the term *perichoresis*, although this is not a term used by the Cappadocians but only emerges later in Greek Trinitarian theology.

The scriptural basis for this reciprocity of Father, Son and Spirit is to be found particularly in the Fourth Gospel. And if we seek a visual expression of it, let us have in our mind the well-known icon by St Andrew Rublev, where the Trinity is shown in the form of the three angels who came to visit Abraham under the oak of Mamre (Gen. 18). Now it might well be felt that this icon is too tritheist, because it shows the Trinity as three distinct persons. Indeed, for this reason, in the year 1745 (an unhappy year in British history when unfortunately the rightful monarchy was not restored), the Pope forbade the representation of the Trinity in the form of the three angels visiting Abraham. None the less, if you go today into Roman Catholic churches, almost everywhere you will see copies of Rublev's Trinity, so the word of the Pope is evidently not always the end of the matter. But Rublev has in fact included in his icon certain features that correct the impression of tritheism. If you look carefully, you will find inscribed on the icon a great circle. As you trace out the lines of the shoulders and of the legs and feet, and observe at the same time the way the three are not just looking at us but looking at one another, then you will see within the icon that they are embraced by a huge circle – by the great 'O' of mutual love.

Alongside this second way of safeguarding the unity of the Trinity through the concept of coinherence, the Cappadocians also employ a third way; and this is particularly important. The three persons, so they aver, have only a single energy and single will. Here the difference between the Trinity and us humans is most clearly evident. The three divine persons, Father, Son and Holy Spirit, share a single energy (*energeia*), a single operation or activity, and they have likewise only one single will. In this respect, manifestly, the unity of the three divine persons stands on a radically different level from the unity of any human group. Humans may cooperate together but each retains her or his own energy and specific will. The point is well expressed by Gregory of Nyssa:

> In the case of human persons, even if many participate in the same operation (*energeia*), each one acts individually and by himself . . . With regard to the divine nature, on the other hand, it is different. We do not learn that the Father does something on his own in which the Son does not cooperate; or again that the Son acts on his own without the Spirit. Rather does every operation which extends from God to creation have its origin in the Father, proceeds through the Son, and reaches its completion in the Holy Spirit.

You notice here again the idea of monarchy, for the Trinitarian movement originates from the Father. 'The action of each', Gregory continues, 'in any matter is not separate and individualized. But there is one motion and disposition of the good will which proceeds from the Father, through the Son, to the Spirit.'[11] Elsewhere he says: 'The identity of operation (*energeia*) on the part of Father, Son and Holy Spirit, plainly indicates the complete unity of nature.'[12]

From this identity of *energeia* there follows a basic principle of Cappadocian theology. In all their actions towards the world, none of the three ever acts on his own apart from the other two. All the divine actions are shared. For example, in creation, God the Father creates through his Logos and in the Holy Spirit. Or take baptism and confirmation, which in the Christian East occur together and constitute virtually the same sacrament. Some people consider that in baptism we put on Christ, and then in chrismation or confirmation we are sealed with the Holy Spirit. That is not very good theology. It is true to say that in baptism we put on Christ but we could not put on Christ without also being clothed with the Holy Spirit; and equally we cannot say that confirmation is just receiving the gifts of the Spirit, because these gifts of the Spirit are conferred on us precisely by Christ.

Again, in the Eucharist the Father, Son and Spirit are all three working together. At the high point of the Divine Liturgy of St John Chrysostom, in the Epiclesis, we pray to the Father to send down the Holy Spirit on us and on the gifts set before us, and to make the bread and wine to be the Body and Blood of Christ. So we see how at this decisive moment in the Eucharist, Father, Son and Spirit are working together. St Irenaeus calls the Son and Spirit the two hands of God, and God is always using both his hands at once. In the Eucharist we do indeed receive the Body and Blood of Christ but at the same time we receive the Holy Spirit. We do not receive the Holy Spirit in exactly the same way, because the Spirit was not incarnate and therefore he has no body and blood. Yet we could not receive the one person without receiving the other.

If, however, all the divine actions are shared, does that not push us too far in the direction of modalism? Do we not then fail to make a proper distinction between the persons? To this we can answer: yes, all the actions are shared but each person contributes to the shared action in a different way. There is a real presence of Christ in the Eucharist but there is also a presence of the Holy Spirit, equally real but in a different mode.

In these three ways, then, the Cappadocians tried to safeguard the divine unity and indivisibility: by affirming that the Father is the sole source; by developing the notion of dynamic *perichoresis*; and by insisting on the single energy and the shared will of Father, Son and Holy Spirit. God is indeed a *koinonia* of persons but a *koinonia* of an altogether distinctive kind. The divine three are one in a way that no human community can ever be, however closely knit; yet though they are one they are not fused and merged together.

Now let us think about some of the practical implications of the doctrine of the Trinity. What consequences does it have, first, for our understanding of human personhood, and then for our understanding of human society and political life?

Our starting point here is 1 John 4.8, 'God is love.' In this context, let me say that we should be rather careful to give exact biblical references. A friend of mine, some years ago, wanted to send a telegram of congratulation to two of his acquaintances who were getting married, and he decided to send a biblical quotation. What he chose was not actually 1 John 4.8 but 1 John 4.18, 'There is no fear in love, but perfect love casts out fear.' Unfortunately, the post office omitted the number 1 before John, so that it was no longer a reference to the Epistle of John but a reference to the Gospel. And if you look up John 4.18 you will find that it consists in the words of Christ to the Samaritan woman: 'You have spoken the truth: for you have had five husbands already, and he whom you now have is not your husband.' That required some explanation as a wedding message!

'God is love.' Among all the human analogies that can help us to understand the divine being, the least inadequate is our experience of loving and being loved. Love is the perfection of human nature, the highest thing we humans know, and so it is in and through love that we approach most directly to God. Let us apply this to the doctrine of the

Trinity. God is love. But self-love, the love of one, isolated and turned inward, is not the fullness of love. Love implies the presence of another, of a Thou as well as an I. Love signifies gift and exchange, communion and relationship. God, then, as love, is not merely one single person loving himself, he is a community or communion of persons loving one another.

Thinking of God as mutual love, we arrive at the affirmation: the one God is Father and Son. But we need to advance further than that. The love of two, absorbed in one another, may sometimes be exclusive, a closed circle, shutting out others. The circle needs to be enlarged so as to include a third. Loving each other, each of the two wishes the other to have the added joy of loving a third and of being loved by that third. To exist in its fullness love needs to be not only mutual but shared. So we arrive at a Trinitarian understanding of the one God: he is not only Father and Son but Father, Son and Holy Spirit. The Holy Spirit, the third member of the Godhead, is the bond of love between Father and Son, as St Augustine insisted.[13]

I have taken this understanding of God as mutual love from the twelfth-century Victorine, Richard of St Victor. Richard did not imagine – nor do I – that this constitutes a proof of the doctrine of the Trinity; for this doctrine, as already emphasized, cannot be proved on a strictly logical basis. But while it is not a proof, it can serve as a persuasive illustration.

Let us explore further the implications of this understanding of God as shared love. In Karl Barth's words, 'The Christian God is not a lonely God.'[14] God is social: there is within him, although at an infinitely higher level, something that corresponds to our human notion of society. God is not just a unit but a union. He is not simply the transcendent monad but one in three, a triad of coeternal persons dwelling in one another through an unceasing movement of mutual love. God is not just personal but interpersonal. The being of God, as we have said already, is relational being. We are to think of God not primarily in static but in dynamic terms; not primarily in terms of essence or substance but in terms of life and love. God is dialogic: there is within his being an unending Trinitarian interchange. From all eternity the first person addresses the second: 'You are my beloved son.' From all eternity the second person responds to the first: 'Abba, Father; Abba, Father'. From all eternity the Holy Spirit seals and confirms the fatherly–filial exchange of love. As three in one and one in three, God is shared love, reciprocal self-giving, interpersonal response and solidarity.

If that is what the doctrine of the Trinity is saying to us, then manifestly it is no mere piece of abstract speculation, devoid of practical implications, but something that has or should have startling and revolutionary consequences for our understanding of our own personhood. It is not just a technicality, it is concerned quite literally with matters of life and death, eternal life and eternal death. That reminds me of the reply by a leading sportsman to the question put to him by an interviewer: 'Football is very important to you. Is it a matter of life and death?' 'Oh no,' he replied, 'it is much more important than that!' We can say the same of the doctrine of the Trinity: it is not only a matter of life and death but much more than that.

What then does faith in the Trinity tell us about ourselves? As humans we are created in the image and likeness of God. That means, on the one hand, created in the image of Christ the divine Logos. If we wish to understand our own personhood, we look at the person of Jesus as revealed to us in the Gospels. But it also means created in the image of God the Trinity. If that is so, everything that we have been saying concerning God as Trinity has to be said also, although on a different level, concerning us as human beings. 'God is love', says St John; and that great English prophet William Blake extends this by saying: 'Man is love.' God is not self-love but shared love; so also is the human person in the divine image. God is exchange, self-giving, solidarity; so also is the human person. The being of God is relational being; so also is our human being.

We need to explore our own inwardness but we need also to realize that the self exists only in dynamic relation with the other. As persons we are what we are only through our relationship with other persons. There is no true person unless there are at least two persons, or better still, three persons in communication with one another. I only become personal in an I-and-Thou relationship. Selfhood is social, or it is nothing. To refuse to engage with others is to deny the Trinity. And we can find a basis for all this in Christ's High Priestly prayer: 'May they all be one, even as you, Father, are in me, and I in you; so also may they be one in us . . . May they be one even as we are one, I in them and you in me: may they be perfectly one' (John 17.21–23). Such is our human vocation: to reproduce on earth the movement of shared love that exists eternally in the Trinity. As Charles Wesley says in one of his hymns: 'You whom he ordained to be transcripts of the Trinity.'

Now perhaps we begin to understand why Pavel Florensky said: 'Between the Trinity and hell, there lies no other choice.' Either we love others after the image of the Trinity or else in the end we lose all meaning and all joy. Sartre said: 'L'enfer c'est les autres' ('Hell is other people'); and certainly it often feels like that. But in the end hell is not other people; hell is myself cut off from the others and refusing to relate to them. T. S. Eliot comes closer than Sartre to the truth when he writes in *The Cocktail Party*: 'What is hell? Hell is one's self, hell is alone, the other figures in it merely projections.'

All of this is illustrated by a story recorded in the Sayings of the Desert Fathers. Once Abba Macarius the Egyptian was walking through the desert, and he saw lying beside the path a skull. So he tapped it with his stick and asked: 'Who are you?' The skull answered: 'I used to be the pagan priest in this region.' 'Where are you now?' asked Macarius. And the skull replied: 'I am in hell.' 'What's the nature of your torment,' inquired Macarius, 'and how can it be diminished?' The skull answered: 'This is the nature of our torment: we are bound back to back and we cannot see each other's faces. But when you pray for us, we begin to see the face of the other.'[15] Not to see the face of the other: that in the end is hell. And it is precisely a denial of the doctrine of the Trinity. In Greek the word for 'person' is *prosopon*, and that means literally 'face', 'countenance', 'looking towards the other'. The ultimate torment is to be incapable of seeing the face of the other, incapable of relationship, incapable of love. Hell, therefore, is not to be able to love, and heaven is to love after the image and likeness of the Trinity.

In this way faith in the Trinity is directly relevant to our understanding of the human person. It is directly relevant, indeed, not only to our view of personhood but likewise to our understanding of political and social life. 'Our social programme', says Nikolai Fedorov, 'is the Trinity.' Every social unit, the family, the factory, the parish, the school or college, is called to be, each in its own modality, a living icon of the Trinity. Faith in the Trinitarian God, the God of interrelationship, of shared love, places us under an obligation to struggle at every level against oppression, injustice and exploitation. Our combat for social righteousness is specifically in the name of the Trinity.

Let me end with a story from Dostoyevsky's masterwork, *The Brothers Karamazov*, which I use as my all-purpose anecdote.[16] It is the story of an old woman and an onion. You may know the story already but I shall tell it to you all the same. I remember, when I began lecturing, the great Henry Chadwick said to me: 'Always remember that people like to be told what they already know.' I shall follow his advice. Once upon a time, there was an old woman. She died, and woke up to find herself, much to her surprise, in a lake of fire. Looking out she saw her guardian angel walking on the bank, and so she called out to him: 'There has been some mistake, I am a very respectable old lady, I should not be here in this lake of fire.' 'Indeed', said the angel. 'Do you ever remember a time when you helped somebody else?' She thought for some time and then she said: 'Yes, once I was gardening and a beggar came by and I gave her an onion.' 'Excellent', said the angel. 'I happen to have that very onion with me now.' Reaching into his robes, he produced it. He hung on to one end of the onion and she hung on to the other. Perhaps it was a shallot rather than an onion. Gradually he began to pull her out of the lake of fire. But she was not the only person there, and when the others saw what was happening, they crowded around her in the hope of being pulled out as well. This did not please the old woman at all. She cried out: 'Let go! Let go! It's not you who's being pulled out, it's me. It's not your onion, it's mine.' And when she said, 'It's mine', the onion snapped in two and she fell back into the lake of fire, and there, so I am told, she still is.

That is Dostoyevsky's story, and here is my addition. If only the old woman had said 'It's *our* onion', might it not have been strong enough to pull them all out of the lake of fire? But in saying, 'It's mine', she was denying her essential humanity, her true personhood, after the image and likeness of the Trinity. Such then is the all-important consequence of believing in God as Trinity. It commits those who hold such belief to say always not 'I' but 'we', not 'my' but 'our'. Precisely because God is three in one, I need you in order to be myself.

Notes

1 *Theological Investigations*, vol. 4 (London: Darton, Longman & Todd, 1966), p. 79 (translation modified).

2 See Vladimir Lossky, *The Mystical Theology of the Eastern Church* (London: James Clarke, 1957), p. 66.

3 Quoted in Olivier Clément, *L'Eglise orthodoxe* (Paris: Presses Universitaires de France, 1961), p. 63.

4 Lossky, *Mystical Theology*, p. 66.

5 *Being as Communion: Studies in Personhood and the Church* (London: Darton, Longman & Todd, 1985), p. 17.

6 *On the Holy Spirit* 18 [45].

7 *Oration* 45.4.

8 *On the Difference between Essence and Hypostasis* [Basil, *Letter* 38] (*P.G.* 32:332 A–D).

9 *Oration* 42.15.

10 *On the Difference between Essence and Hypostasis* [Basil, *Letter* 38] (*P.G.* 32:340C).

11 *To Ablabius: That there are not three Gods*, ed. W. Jaeger and F. Mueller (Leiden: Brill, 1958), pp. 47–8.

12 [Basil], *Letter* 189.7 (*P.G.* 32:693C).

13 *On the Trinity* 15.10 (6); 15: 27 (17).

14 *Dogmatics in Outline*, trans. G. T. Thompson (New York: Harper, 1959), p. 42.

15 Macarius the Great (the Egyptian) 38; trans. Benedicta Ward, *The Sayings of the Desert Fathers: The Alphabetical Collection* (London/Oxford: Mowbray, 1981), pp. 136–7.

16 *The Brothers Karamazov*, III. vi.3.

7

Wisdom as True Worship: From Augustine's *De Vera Religione* to *De Trinitate*

PAIGE E. HOCHSCHILD

The 'early' Augustine is often represented as having a dual conversion: the first, inspired by Cicero and the 'books of the Platonists', being a conversion to a philosophical culture, and the second, inspired by the sacramental demands of Christian initiation and, eventually, public, ecclesial life, being a conversion to a fully Christian *religio*.[1] Augustine often speaks with regret, in the *Retractationes* and elsewhere, about his early optimism that philosophical wisdom might be too easily reconciled with the wisdom of Christ. Nevertheless, a substantive form of a reconciliation is consistently present in later writings, certainly as late as Books 8−10 of *De civitate Dei*, completed by 417. If Augustine seems to offer a vague 'wisdom Christology' in his early writings, by contrast to a more mature 'salvation-historical Christology' in later writings, this chapter argues that a clear thread linking these is the idea of wisdom as true worship or right *religio*. In *De Trinitate*, Augustine continues to converse with Cicero on the topic of wisdom, rejecting the scepticism of the New Academy but not its broader philosophical aspirations. He also reserves wisdom to the person of Christ, 'in whom are hidden all the treasures of wisdom and knowledge'. Finally, he suggests a fuller understanding of wisdom as true worship.[2] Articulating the coherence of wisdom in *trin.*, especially in Book 14, reveals significant theological consistency between *trin.* and the earliest dialogues. The key text proves to be another relatively early work, written just before Augustine's ordination, *De vera religione*.

Wisdom in *De Trinitate* 14

At certain points, Augustine strongly differentiates the wisdom of God from merely human wisdom. The wisdom of God is God himself, specifically 'the only-begotten Son' (*trin.* 14.1.1). 'Wisdom' is a personal and relational Trinitarian name; it is also a substantial attribute of the divine nature (*trin.* 7.2.4–6; 15.2.8). Human wisdom is initially defined in Book 14 as a relational state: it is the 'true worship' (*verus cultus*) of God, a properly human activity that is 'true' only insofar as it orders a person to the right end. In Books 12–13, Augustine appears to have rejected the idea of a properly human wisdom in the order of history and nature, by relegating wisdom to the eternal contemplation of eternal things, chiefly God. This is defended on the basis of scriptural texts differentiating wisdom from knowledge (cf. Col. 2.3 and 1 Cor. 12.7, cited at *trin.* 13.19.24), and on the basis of other texts associating Christian life – as progress in faith, and avoidance of moral evil – with practical knowledge (cf. Job 28.28, cited at *trin.* 12.14.22). Wisdom, however, is given an accessible human form in Book 14 in the idea of 'true worship'. We might reasonably ask where this new definition comes from. Augustine notes that Latin employs two words to describe worship that is true: *Dei* and *cultus*, translating the Greek *theosebeia*. The lexical binding of the words 'God' and 'worship' limits the definitional reach of religion, clearly excluding idolatry; it also parallels the binding together of knowledge and wisdom in the person of Christ, as argued in Books 12 and 13. There, knowledge, especially in the form of the *scientia* of faith, describes the intentional subject ordered to truth through temporal means, while wisdom describes possession of the truth as end. The dynamic unity of knowledge and wisdom, however, is only realized in the person of Christ; he alone is the truly wise man because he is the Truth (*trin.* 13.19.24). Again, the *scientia–sapientia* distinction seems to have made a clear treatment of the nature of wisdom, as a truly human wisdom, almost impossible.

In Book 13, Augustine characterizes wisdom in strongly non-philosophical terms; the central chapters of Romans guide the whole book. The personal unity of knowledge and wisdom in Christ is accomplished through *humility*. If 'knowledge' pertains to things in time, the summit of knowledge is the recognition of providence at work in history, especially in the Incarnation of the Word (*trin.* 13.19.24). The 'conjunction' of human and divine, *in unitate personae*, entails a singular divine humility, evidence of the willingness of God to adapt to the human condition (cf. *trin.* 4.2.4: *coaptatio, consonantia, congruentia, convenientia*). Humility is further demonstrated by Christ's *exemplum* of victory over sin, which is not a work of power (*potentia Dei*) but first a work of the greater justice (*iustitia*) of humility (*trin.* 13.13.17; 14.18; 17.22; 18.23).

God appears to the eyes of faith in the form of a servant (*forma servi*), and through this form Christ completes the work of reconciliation by obedience to God's will, and by shedding of blood (13.17.22). Far more than an *exemplum*, Christ becomes the *sacramentum* of piety (1 Tim. 3.16, cited at *trin.* 4.20.27); through this sacrament, the weakness of God triumphs over concupiscence and pride, to make the will into a good will, and direct the affections to higher things (*trin.* 1.1.2).

The christological form of wisdom is announced in the opening chapters of *trin.*, where it is linked to true worship just as in Book 14. Augustine identifies the justice (*iustitia*) or right order of faith with the right observance of piety in the Church (*observata pietas, trin.* 1.2.4). Augustine promises to offer his readers reasons for the 'one, only and true God' being a Trinity; reasons (*ratio*) nourish knowledge but should above all move his readers to return to the 'justice of faith' as necessary for the purification of wisdom.[3] Reasons may nourish but the justice of faith actually heals. The appeal to reasons promises to incorporate the philosophical aspiration for wisdom into the logic of faith as a kind of *scientia*. The correlation of the 'justice of faith' with the very practical language of healing suggests that the ancient and universal desire for happiness might be fulfilled through true worship.

According to Augustine, Books 12 and 13 do not relegate wisdom to an exclusively eschatological vision; rather, they argue that the *scientia* of faith is a kind of wisdom, by being a temporal but true knowledge of eternal things. Temporal knowledge, in the form of history, teaching or exemplary virtue, may become wisdom insofar as it is 'referred' to faith in Christ, by directing one to truly eternal things (14.1.3). On the basis of the unity of natures in Christ, Augustine appears to relativize the distinction between wisdom and other modes of knowing; in fact, the *scientia–sapientia* distinction is not useful for exegetical purposes, since even eternal mysteries, such as the identity of the Word with God, must be reported by witnesses: 'there was a man sent from God, whose name was John' (cited at *trin.* 13.1.2). This makes the appeal to Cicero's definition of wisdom as the 'knowledge of things human and things divine' (*trin.* 14.1.3) seem like an unhelpful reversion to the framework of the Cassiciacum dialogues.[4] More puzzling is the account in Book 14 of how access to eternal verities is a necessary condition for *scientia*. 'True knowledge' presupposes the presence of 'true standards of justice' to the mind. These standards are inscribed 'in the book of light which is called truth, from which every just law is copied and transferred into the heart of the man who does justice' (14.15.21).[5] This 'transferral' is explained by a strikingly Aristotelian image, whereby an impression is made in wax by a signet ring, yet remains when it is removed. Where Aristotle uses this image to describe how sense-organs receive impressions, Augustine insists that this 'presence' is not a physical event, involving actual movement (*non migrando, sed tanquam inprimendo*). Moreover, while the verbs are passive in form, the veritable 'touching' (*tangitur*) that occurs is neither contingent nor occasional: the presence of true principles to the mind makes the rational soul to be what it is in the order of nature, possessing a defining capacity for *scientia*. The presence of these principles explains the soul's desire for the happy life, even when it is miserable, and the soul's desire for justice, even when it acts unjustly. They transcend the mind because they are unchangeable, whereas the soul, in time, is changeable. The changeable character of soul, however, together with its innate access to transcending principles, is not enough for even Cicero to hope to attain a wisdom that is human, beatifying and truly a *sapientia contemplativa* (14.19.26). A brief look at two early texts, then *De vera religione*, will help to show that the suggestion that wisdom is 'true worship' in *trin.* 14 is not a digression but an essential apologetic realignment, in preparation for the defence of Trinitarian participation in *trin.* 15. The foundation of human wisdom is laid in the order of creation, in the natural capacity of persons (*duntaxat hominis*, 14.19.25); but it must be received as a gift and a *participatio*, given through the blood of Christ, which alone establishes the justice of faith.

Conversing with Cicero on Ancient Wisdom: *Contra Academicos* and *De Beata Vita*

In the first book of *c. acad.*, written in 386–7, Cicero's definition of wisdom as the knowledge of things human and divine is expanded to include two further elements: wisdom is the *diligens inquisitio*, the 'loving inquiry' into things human and divine; moreover, it is an inquiry that orders a person to happiness.[6] Augustine tries to clarify the distinction between things human and divine. Licentius considers at length the difference between *happiness* in human affairs and happiness in God. The divine life, Augustine says, is marked by the happiness of possession; human life is, at best, marked by the happiness of 'loving inquiry'. The necessity of seeking (as *inquisitio*) implies non-possession; this is nevertheless a happy state, because the one seeking 'collects himself' within himself and 'turns himself toward God'.[7] The re-collecting of oneself, which is immediately also directed to God as end, is not a state of restless and anxious poverty; rather, directing oneself to God, who alone possesses full and stable happiness, ensures that 'loving inquiry' is experienced as a kind of peace (*tranquillus*).

The second dedication that opens Book 2 of *c. acad.* makes clear that Augustine has a twofold concern for his patron, Romanianus: he may still be a Manichean, and resting in the stability of Manichean religious 'truths', he might experience the peace of a search brought to its end. If Romanianus has abandoned 'loving inquiry' after truth for this reason, Augustine reminds his patron that he left them with many doubts, and he warns him against the error of presumption. Alternatively, Augustine appeals to Romanianus' 'love of truth' as a remedy against the error of despair (2.3.8). Augustine offers a twofold exhortation in response: first, do not abandon the search, by making the criterion of certitude impossibly narrow; second, seek after the one who says 'search, and you will find' (Matt. 7.7, cited at 2.3.9). Augustine adds to this oblique reference to Christ as truth a promise that he will send Romanianus a text on *religio*, arguing for truth in religion and dispelling the errors of *superstitio*.[8] The truth of philosophical wisdom, and the truth of Christ who promises a certain end to 'loving inquiry', coincide. Nevertheless, in this early text Augustine signals the necessity of articulating the coincidence in terms of the opposition of right *religio* and *superstitio*.

In Book 3 of *c. acad.*, Augustine returns indirectly to the distinction between things human and divine, through a critique of sceptical models of certitude and assent (3.2.3; *assentiri*, 3.14.32). The New Academy strongly differentiates what is true from what is probable, suggesting that the former is exclusive to divine wisdom and the latter to human wisdom. Augustine asks why anyone would undertake the pursuit of wisdom if the only available outcomes are the ignorance of non-possession – since human wisdom remains merely probable – or a divine life so eschatological as to be foreign to human life in its present state of loving inquiry.[9] Augustine solves the dilemma on the basis of the assumed unicity of both truth and happiness, which in turn necessitates collapsing the human–divine distinction: if the fullness of happiness is found only in God, and if human wisdom appears to be a legitimate and natural desire, then the completion of the search for wisdom will be one and the same with the happiness of the divine life.

Is this really a solution? Has Augustine convincingly shown that the non-possession of truth, albeit with 'loving inquiry' after truth, will generate a godlike felicity? The occasional references in this dialogue to divine grace at work, the 'power and wisdom of God himself' (cf.

2.1.1, where this is identified as 'the son of God'), are surely significant. The striving of the Academicians' philosophical search is clearly
marred by their refusal to give *assent* to wisdom. Refusing assent, even
under the influence of a credible teacher, makes something to be nothing (*nihil*). Augustine implies that Cicero is limited by his sense of the
greatness of (his) opinion (*magnum esse opinatorem*, 3.14.31). Platonic
dialectic, which links methodologically the world of sense experience
to the veracity of intelligible truths, seems to have the last word in *c.
acad.* However, this 'true' philosophy must itself be humbled, purified by the Incarnation, which extends 'divine compassion' to bodily
life, 'submitting' all things to its authority and wisdom, and recalling
all souls by *both* teachings and deeds. The language of 'submission'
implies the strong language of order, the mark of true *religio*. This
should be contrasted with the weakness of Cicero's 'great opinion',
and the implication that non-assent gets the order of things wrong: by
making something to be nothing, and by problematizing the reach of
the divine into the creaturely – something articulated much better by
dialectic. However, wisdom is clearly more than dialectic: the emphasis
on deeds as well as words points the reader back to a further, neglected
definition of wisdom at 1.5.13: wisdom is a right way of life (*recta via
vitae*). Incorporating this definition, the 'loving inquiry' after wisdom
is most fully understood in *c. acad.* as willingness to seek what is true
with assent, and a submission of the whole of life to this truth as an
architectonic end.

The form of wisdom is both contemplative-philosophical (with truth
as its end) and practical (with its execution being an ordered 'right way
of life'). The practical, visible dimension of wisdom suggests a way wisdom might be truly universal, because truly human. To summarize the
elements of wisdom from *c. acad.*:

1 It presupposes an ordering to the right end (*intenditur . . . in se/in
   Deum*).
2 It is an activity (note verbs related to action, e.g. *satis exercueris*,
   3.9.20):
   a) marked by non-possession, it is *diligens*;
   b) marked by certainty of the end (1) it makes one *tranquillus*.
3 It is practical-moral, truly perfecting of the human person, re the end
   of happiness:
   a) eschatologically, promising the fullness of the *beata vita*;
   b) in present life, as a right way, and a way that purifies (*atque mun-
      daveris*, 3.9.20).

In *b. vita*, written in the same, early period of Augustine's career, wisdom is immediately identified with happiness (*esse beatum*).[10] Happiness is understood as a mean between fullness and poverty – comparable to absence and possession in *c. acad.* but subtly different. A principle of mediation between the fullness of the divine life and the poverty of human desire is given, in the identification of the 'divine Son' with the moral virtue of temperance, or *frugalitas* (2.8; 4.32), which is later subsumed under Cicero's 'highest virtue' of *modestia* – significant as an etymological basis for *modus*, said to be the measure of all virtues (4.31). Temperance is 'most useful' in life because its exercise reveals the presence of *modus* (measure) in the soul. True *modus* is in turn identified with the 'truth' that comes into being 'through and from the *summus modus*' (4.34). The 'highest measure' mediates by: (a) being *true*, because it is self-identical (*per seipsum*); and (b) because it *is* through the 'highest measure' that it – as *truth* – proceeds from the 'highest measure' (*veritas autem ut sit, fit per aliquem summum modum, a quo procedit*), and is converted thereto (*et in quem se perfecta convertit*). The Trinitarian dynamic of truth 'proceeding' and 'converting' accounts for the presence of *modus* in the soul as truth. In *b. vita*, this is made explicit by the reference to Ambrose's hymn '*Deus Creator*' and Monica's invocation of the Trinitarian faith of the Church. Augustine, on the other hand, cites John 14.6: 'I am the truth' (4.34). Although he does not give the complete verse, he clearly implies what he does not bother to cite: 'I am the way', in the dynamic of return 'through the truth', by which one comes to the Father (*venerit . . . ad summum modum*); 'I am the life', in the conclusion of this return, since 'arrival' at the Father, the 'highest measure', through the truth, is the 'happy life' (*beata vita*). It is a veritable possession of God in the soul (*hoc est, animo Deum habere, id est, Deo frui*). This is certainly a cryptic representation of the work of the Trinity in salvation; however, the cryptic approach is consonant with the underdeveloped role of temperance in this work, as the 'mother' and unifying principle of all the virtues, particularly in a dialogue that involves a great deal of eating.

In *Retractationes* (1.1.2), Augustine expresses regret that he considered happiness in *b. vita* as a good determined by what is 'best in man', namely reason; reason, he says, must be subordinated to God. In fairness, Augustine repeats this same idea at *trin.* 14.4.6, where he says that the greatness of the soul is found in its *capax* for the 'highest nature' (*summa natura*); the capacity for God is one and the same as the capacity for corruption. Although he walks 'in the image of God', the human soul is changeable (*mutabilis, trin.* 14.15.21). Without undermining

Augustine's concerns about *b. vita* articulated in *Retractationes*, one can observe within the relatively playful genre of that dialogue that non-fulfilment is a happy state because mediation does not depend on individual genius. It is a divine work. For this reason, the Trinitarian 'proceeding' (*procedit*) of truth from the Father immediately follows the conclusion: 'whoever is happy is wise, that is, he has his *own* measure' (*modum suum, b. vita* 4.33). Measure is found only in the truth, and it is sought after thanks to divine *admonitio* and the illuminating brightness of the 'unseen sun', which restores the weak gaze of the soul (*convertit*, 4.35). From the side of human agency, receiving, possessing and acting on divine mediation becomes visible as lived holiness. Being 'propitious' to God – or not in hostility to God – includes all three options offered at *b. vita* 2.12 as possible definitions for a happy life: living rightly (*bene vivit*), doing the will of God (*facit quae Deus vult fieri*) and not having an unclean spirit; that is, a spirit of vice and falsehood (*spiritum immundum non habet*). Such a comprehensive definition of the happy life takes up the architectonic sense of wisdom from *c. acad.* and points ahead to the fully practical form of right religion, as will be articulated most clearly in *De vera religione*.

To conclude on *c. acad.* and *b. vita*, one might reasonably observe the absence of elements of Augustine's mature soteriology from his teaching on the primacy of grace in the pursuit of wisdom. Nevertheless, the position of Olivier Du Roy remains untenable, namely that Augustine's understanding of wisdom in his earliest works lacks any 'Trinitarian-economic' aspect or that Augustine lacks a sense of human wisdom as a practical-ethical participation in divine wisdom.[11] The abstract language of 'measure' is surely Ciceronian in its literary genealogy; however, the personification of measure by Christ, and its work of mediation and conversion, is obviously Augustine's unique Trinitarian appropriation. Mediation by measure is developed christologically in the role of *harmonia* in *trin.* 4, where 'human wisdom' is located in the worship of God who, in his 'supreme wisdom', reconciles by harmony the opposition of the 'double death' of sinful humanity through the 'single death' of Christ's sacrifice (4.1.1). Even in the earliest works, human wisdom is only true wisdom if it is somehow a sharing or participation in God's wisdom. If it is merely human, it is hollow (*vana est, trin.* 14.4.5), offering a false resting place, a 'mountain of pride' with no real solidity under foot or within the soul (*superbum stadium inanissimae gloriae, quod ita nihil intus plenum atque solidum habet, b. vita* 1.3). If wisdom is both human and divine, it must be a work of divine grace in the soul, and one that is not merely *intus* but possessed and realized visibly through a *recta via vitae* – a life ordered to God as end, a life formed according to true worship.

De vera religione

The approximation of wisdom and true worship is given its most complete form in *De vera religione*. While the content and intention of this work was laid out during the time of writing the Cassiciacum dialogues, its execution was delayed to the years immediately preceding Augustine's ordination to the priesthood (390–1).[12] In *vera rel.* the economy of salvation is articulated in light of the coincident ends of philosophical wisdom and *religio* – the 'true worship of the true God'.[13] This text is anti-Manichean, while reasonably including a broader intended audience. The crucial added element, in the near identification of wisdom with true worship (at 5.8 they are 'one and the same'), is Augustine's developing understanding of *historia*. From the writing of *Gn. adv. Man.* in 388–9, to the next attempt at Genesis in *Gn. litt. imp.* in 393–4, Augustine expands the hermeneutic burden from the enigmatic signs of the text itself, to include the broader canvas of history. The things narrated in the 'sacred history' of Scripture become a lens through which the events (*gesta*) of history are interpreted under the providence of God, with the unique historical event of the Incarnation of God as the theological centre.

Isabelle Bochet rightly describes *vera rel.* as soteriological at its core.[14] The name of Christ that dominates this work is *truth*: as truth, Christ is the wisdom of God, and through this wisdom the one God creates (*artifex*, 39.72). Another name for Christ is implied: the divine physician. God is the provident source of creation and salvation, and through a historical pedagogy he applies the *ars medicinae* (17.34) that has its complete form in Christ, in whom the truth, beauty and *forma* of all things is seen (55.113). Reminiscent of the *summum modus* of *b. vita*, Christ the truth is identified in *vera rel.* with the *summa convenientia*, to which the soul desiring truth must be conformed (*ipse conveni cum ea*, 39.72). The historical veracity of the Incarnation makes this conformity less abstract, and puts the question and modality of effective mediation at the forefront. Christ mediates in the *forma servi*: through his human works and teaching, he is the *exemplum* – victorious over the threefold condition of sin, according to 1 John 2.16 (cf. *vera rel.* 38.70–71; 55.107) – and he is the *sacramentum* – enacting purification in the soul (through faith; 12.25) and liberation of the whole person (through right understanding and moral self-mastery; 16.31–32; 48.93). By mediating effectively the human and divine, Christ reconciles in his person the divergence between 'things human' and 'things divine' that has occurred in historical time. Christ fulfils the ordering of ancient wisdom to a divine end, through the attainment of truly human goods. He thus reveals the form of true religion because he is the truly wise and good man; he is truly wise and good, because his life is an act of perfect worship. Three brief sections show how history, revelation and wisdom offer parallel insights into the form of true worship or true religion; the fourth section shows how Christ's effective mediation is truly perfecting of the human person.

1   History as teacher of true religion

Augustine clearly differentiates (on the Trinitarian terms, above) God as creator from God as provident governor (*gubernante ille pro vera salute generis humani, vera rel.* 3.3). History, or the 'temporal dispensation of providence', provides evidence for this differentiation even as it argues for the unity of God, given the singular aim of creation and salvation. History is therefore a source for 'the true religion' (7.13; 8.14; 25.46). As a subject for study, history begins with things taken on authority, since they are witnessed and recorded; then the student progresses by understanding from things merely probable or fitting to things more certain (26.49). Analogous in form to special revelation, history consists of *verba visibilia*, sensible manifestations of the divine will extending to meet the human condition. Finding humankind under slavery to sin, providence adapts pedagogically to human weakness through appropriate modes of teaching and exhortation (50.98). Piety has its birth in this state of suffering and fear: in entreaty and response, the prophets articulate a universal longing for liberation through divine grace (17.33).

Augustine articulates human maturation in terms of historical stages: the ages of man are seven, moving from infancy to old age. Interpreting this natural progress 'not by years' but by 'spiritual ages' (*spiritales aetates suas*, 26.49), Augustine describes an intellectual pedagogy reminiscent of the seven steps of the soul (*gradus*) concluding De quantitate animae (~388; 33.70–6).[15] In *vera rel.* the 'new man' begins with *exempla* drawn from 'useful history' and then extends himself, by forgetting things human, to things divine; this is a process of moving from understanding on the basis of authority to understanding things on the basis of the 'unchanging law' of reason. The third stage establishes a lived unity in a person, a moral life resulting from a harmony of appetite and mind: this seems to be the crucial stage, and it is worth noting that, in *quant. an.*, the third stage is that of memory, and *religio* comes in explicitly at that point as essential to 'leading' and 'forming' the memory rightly in relation to things human and divine, and in transition to the fourth *gradus*, in which the providence of God is seen to govern the whole of life (33.72–3; 34.77). In *vera rel.* the central distinction is between the Pauline 'new man' versus the 'old': these establish the 'two cities' from the start, suggesting that two historical narratives run parallel one to another. One treats the human race as a whole, regulated under divine providence; the other concerns a people 'dedicated to God' but which remains a mere image of a people to come, established with clarity at the advent in time of 'the Lord in humility' (27.50). Nevertheless, the 'old man' is the universal foundation of history, shared by all and entered into by the 'Wisdom of God' who subjected himself to its logic (16.30).

The advent of the Wisdom of God initiates the historical progress of the 'new man': Christ acts as pedagogue and moral exemplar. As the truth manifest in the fullness of time, he is the best pedagogue, demanding progress from the relative infancy of simple faith to the right use of reason in understanding divine mysteries (24.55). As the perfect man of justice, he is the best moral exemplar, making his whole life into a *disciplina morum* standing in opposition to and correction of the 'old man' of sin (16.31):

> Whole peoples, to their own ruin, were setting their hearts on riches, the escort required by pleasures of all sorts; he made up his mind to be poor. They were greedy for honors and political power; he refused to be made a king . . . (they) in their pride and self-esteem couldn't stand insults; he put up with insults of every kind. They considered it intolerable to be treated unjustly; what greater injustice than for a just and innocent man to be condemned? They shrank from physical pain; he was scourged and crucified.[16]

Christ teaches and exemplifies on the basis of his divine authority but with 'inexpressible kindness', adapting to the human condition and applying healing to the soul 'step by step' (*gradatim*, 24.45). Christ never does this by force but instead by admonition and persuasion (16.31). Starting with visible *exempla*, the student of Christ passes through *disciplina* to *sacramenta*, strengthened at each point in maturity of spiritual sight. Christ is the central historical *gestum* teaching and revealing the form of 'true religion'. Augustine says that this providential work is not only kind but 'most beautiful', because a christological pedagogy unites, preserves, and makes good use of the distinctness of things human (the *initium* of faith, through authority) and things divine (the 'Truth itself', to which understanding tends). If the form of true religion is seen in the architectonic and dynamic unity of the human and divine in the historical man, Christ, the glue that unites them is the 'low door' of divine humility.

2 Scripture as teacher of true religion

De vera religione intimates the mature scriptural methodology of *De civitate Dei*, especially Books 15—18, in the subordination of its pedagogy to that of history. Scripture is the lens through which divine providence in *history* comes into focus, just as it is the only lens through which the spiritual struggle associated with intellectual purification, or wisdom, is seen to attain victory. The anti-Manichean dimension of *vera rel.* is evident in the basic requirement that Scripture be read correctly: Augustine argues that it violates sound reason to separate the Old and New Testaments, as though giving an account of different divine beings working at different times in history. Dividing the revealed text divides the nature of God and therefore the unity of divine providence in history. He appeals to the image of God as a divine physician who, like any good doctor, would administer the appropriate cure at one time and a different cure at another time (17.34), with the consistent end of health in view. The internal unity of Scripture is secured on the foundational logic of promise and fulfilment: as the 'old man' is an integral image of the 'new man', so also does the Old Testament promise in an earthly kingdom an image of the New Testament, in turn a promise of the kingdom of heaven (27.50). Teachings received in the age of spiritual infancy are appropriate to the servility of that age. The revealed signs given through the patriarchs and prophets are more ambiguous than the clear signs of Christ's words and deeds; they require greater care and piety to be interpreted well.[17] Augustine dwells at 50.98 on the inevitable limits of special revelation. Since Scripture employs words, apprehension and understanding will always require corporeal phantasms. This is a concession to human nature, even to a 'carnal way of thinking': God uses humble means to signify 'things ineffable' precisely because humans are captive to the 'fanciful products of the imagination'. Comparing words in general to the more obscure sacraments of the Old Testament, Augustine says that from an inexpressible mercy, God 'did not disdain to play with us in our child-hood, through sounds and letters, smoke, a column of fire and cloud, as it were visible words . . . curing our inner eyes with the mud of parables and similes'. What the divine physician enacts on the broad canvas of history, he also enacts at the individual and ecclesial level, assisting the student of wisdom in a 'good use' of revealed signs.

Error in interpretation is an ever-present concern: this occurs when the student of Scripture fails to differentiate between temporal and eternal realities, and the degree of certitude appropriate to each. Interpretation must be disciplined by the same dynamic pedagogy as that of history: beginning with faith in temporal realities, the student passes to under-standing by a process of spiritual 'return' to eternal realities, which are less ambiguous by their nature but also by virtue of the help of 'the true light' that enlightens understanding conformed to wisdom (52.101). The ambiguity of signs is intrinsically pedagogically useful, because it stimulates the desire for clarity and the 'yearning for Wisdom itself' (51.100). On the other hand, clarity comes only with the rigorous pur-gation of 'carnal conceptions' that have been heretofore permitted by the biblical text. Augustine is outlining the Christological pedagogy (or *exercitatio*) of *Gn. litt. imp.*, the execution of which began about two years after the completion of *vera rel.*: in *Gn. litt. imp.* the biblical text is said to direct the reader to move through the temporal to the eternal, passing from the faith vested in the historical humanity and resurrection of Christ to the piety of 'spiritual understanding' vested in the divine nature of Christ, one God with the Trinitarian persons.[18] The alignment of historical ages with the stages of growth in wisdom in *vera rel.* is not as strongly christological as the *scientia–sapientia* alignment with the natures of Christ in *De Trinitate*. However, the crucial idea in *vera rel.* is the theological as well as hermeneutic dominance of the Incarnation as a historical event. The historical irruption of divine providence permits a new discipline of interpretation, moving one confidently from faith in the historical Christ towards 'more solid foods, with the few who are wise' (28.51).

Faith in the historical event – associated with the humanity of Christ as *exemplum* – is never abandoned in the dynamic of progress; it is preserved in the Church, which contains in a visible, social unity those who are variously arrayed on the one *via*. Scripture teaches true religion by offering, in the hermeneutic and sociological reality of the Church, an architectonic ordering of interpreters to a single end. This partially addresses the problem of universality raised by the alignment of phil-osophical wisdom with scriptural interpretation, a matter Augustine addresses constructively in the first two books of *doctr. Chr.* and critically in the ninth book of *civ. Dei.* The unity of Scripture and the necessary authority of the Church – the central themes of *De utilitate credendi* – make humility to be the central christological and anthropological principle, linking faith in revelation to the form of true worship.

3 Wisdom itself as teacher of true religion

De vera religione argues that wisdom, as understanding (*intellectus*) and as true 'philosophy', reveals the form of true worship. The dynamic character of the ways of useful history and revelation suggest that wisdom, in this sense, is not simply an eschatological state but a veritable sharing in the way that God sees.

God the *artifex* creates through the 'Wisdom of the Word'; accordingly, creation is a 'weaving together of divine' working and a 'portrait of truth' (39.72). Augustine attributes the formal distinction of species, both intelligible and corporeal, to the Wisdom of God: this is not because the Wisdom of God is the form of all things but because things have being because they have their proper forms. The being of things is their unity, even if particular things do not have unity *simpliciter* (30.55). Things are knowable because they have the unity of formality: considering creation as a whole, distinctions are made not by the immediacy of perception but by judgement that presupposes first principles such as likeness/unlikeness or sameness/inequality. The order of creation and the order of judgement coincide in making correct distinctions; even more, they coincide in making right valuations within the whole, discerning the superior character of living things over non-living and so on. Augustine concludes that all things are equally good, insofar as they have being and their being is dependent on a single divine source. Nevertheless, some things are greater than others because they possess their unity, form and beauty (*species*) in a greater mode. As creation reveals more or less sophisticated ontology, so also does human judgement reveal, passing by *gradus* from perception to judgement, a capacity to discern the very principles that make creation to be intelligible. Augustine identifies these principles as 'the law of judgement' and in turn as 'primary Wisdom' (31.57).

Augustine does not dwell here on the potential problems of identifying the principles of human reason with the person of the Word of God. His concern is to establish right judgement as the basis for right use and correct love of created goods. Only Christ judges all things rightly, and therefore uses all things with 'total charity' (31.58). Sin is not a matter of knowing or loving lesser things; it is rather the tendency to get the whole order of goods wrong, by 'seeking the highest among the lowest' and the 'lowest among the highest'. This wilful deceit amounts to seeking the true while abandoning 'the Truth' (34.63; 36.67). The necessary correction is, of course, to see all of creation as much as possible as it *is*, in the Word as from a single source (given the unity of *forma*) and ordered to God as a single end (through the beauty of *convenientia*). The idea of creation *through* the Wisdom of God allows Augustine to boldly equate idolatry with impiety – at least insofar as one is the origin of the other (37.68). Worship is only a true and 'just service' when it has the one God as its object and end, *and* when all human loves reflect a right ordering of creation to God, under God. Impiety cannot be corrected by good judgement alone but only by a heart that is purified, made capable of truly enjoying things in their relation to God. This is a work of grace, a re-formation of the person accomplished by the 'same Wisdom' who gives form to all things, together with the 'gift of the Holy Spirit' who brings the work of creation to its full perfection (*ipsum donum Dei*, 12.24; 55.113). Wisdom, in sum, teaches true religion by ordering the ancient desire to *know* to Christ who alone is the fullness of 'Truth'.

4   How this teaching is effective: mediation as re-formation

The second half, roughly speaking, of *vera rel.* shows *how* grace restores understanding and love, and therefore how Christ who is Wisdom actually applies the *ars divinae medicinae*, in order to restore true worship. These chapters are structured around the triple form of sin from 1 John 2.15–16 – concupiscence of the flesh, pride of life and curiosity of the eyes – which in turn correspond to the temptations of Christ in the wilderness (cf. Matt. 4.3–4, at *vera rel.* 39.71).[19]

To correct **concupiscentia carnis**, Christ applies the beauty and harmony of the created order, especially as seen in lesser things, given that even these reveal divine handiwork. One must observe, Augustine says, that these goods offer real pleasure and satisfaction; however, this pleasure passes quickly, just as hunger returns again and again. Spiritual pleasures (*spiritalis voluptas*) offer a more lasting fullness, comparable to the *convenientia* of bodily pleasures but more stable. Augustine's study of St Paul during the 390s bears fruit in *vera rel.*, particularly in the opposition of temperance – a virtue only poorly developed in

De beata vita – as an observance of divine order, to the foolishness (*stultitia*) of 'fleshly desire', particularly greed and lust (41.77). A rich sense of the order and beauty in things gives rise to a sense of the order of goods in the whole of creation. Augustine exhorts his readers to observe and love in accordance with order at the systemic level, and on this basis to conquer what is 'lesser within ourselves' through the *modus* of temperance, so that the higher might 'lead the lower' and all things be subject to 'Christ the head' (41.78).

To correct *superbia*, the pride of life by which one 'seeks to be the one and only . . . to whom all things are subject', Augustine offers a gentle provocation: What does one seek in this? Surely it is freedom (*libertas*), the freedom of a good life and the peace we associate with ease and non-slavery to the passions (45.84; 48.93; 52.101). Christ's *exemplum* shows that moral freedom cannot be attained with ease: pride is corrected most of all by the hard labour of moral victory. Christ's own sonship is completed through his trials and suffering. The correction of pride particularly reflects the architectonic character of true religion, since pride is the vice that imitates most clearly the singular primacy of God. Humble submission to God and the order within creation is never a private or interior work. Moral progress is summed up in the commandment of charity, which can only be fulfilled in the coincidence of loving God as this is due to him, and loving others as this is due to them – specifically, not with 'respect to what belongs to oneself' but with 'respect to how others belong to God' (46.86–8). When things or persons are loved apart from the order of right religion, they are loved 'for oneself' and not in themselves (or as they are 'for God'); this is to love things as 'private goods' rather than as 'common goods' (*non commune sed privatam rem diliget*, 46.88). Against the self-assertiveness of pride (*pervicacia posita*, 52.103), the generosity of divine adoption as a child of God is the prime example of the 'justice of Christ'. The effect of Christ's establishing this justice is the enjoyment of peace through reconciliation with God (55.113).

Finally, to correct *curiositas*, Augustine offers the contemplation of intelligible realities. Curiosity is here, as it is in other texts, associated with 'spectacles and other vanities' (54.104); however, it is also associated with the ambiguity of the corporeal forms through which all learning occurs. Christ addresses this problem through his lived dissonance with respect to worldly expectations (cf. 16.31, cited above). Christ's whole life is a *disciplina morum*. Christ's final work, the 'liberation of mankind' through the Resurrection, also demands a radical re-reading of history and Scripture in light of a higher spiritual vision. The historical event of the Incarnation becomes a sacramental and not only a hermeneutic lens through which the providence of God comes into clear focus. The end of resurrection demands a daily 'transferal of loves' from temporal things to eternal things, from visible to invisible, on the *via* of Christ that restores all things to God through a right order.

To conclude, wisdom in *vera rel.* is seen to be both fully human and fully divine, by its dual identification with the person of the Word of God and the order, form and measure of creation. Moreover, human wisdom is not simply a kind of intellectual correctness, a mere philosophical acuity; it requires a right ordering and restoration of loves. The duality of wisdom as divine and human is preserved in the dual character of the commandment of charity. However, the unicity of wisdom is more fundamental, since this reflects the oneness of God: to love God well is to love creation well; to love creation rightly is to love the order of the God who creates and recreates all things. History, Scripture and wisdom itself are offered as ways to discern the primacy of the Wisdom through which all things are created. The temperance of *modus*, the humility and hard work of moral progress, and the 'daily transferal of loves' are offered as christological corrections to the desire, pride and curiosity that oppose the wisdom of charity. The role of justice in *vera rel.* confirms that this wisdom fulfils the form of true worship. Justice is the only truly architectonic virtue, describing an objective order of goods with appropriate obligations, as well as a subjective order of moral valuation. Perfect justice, Augustine says, is to 'love better things more and lesser things less' (48.93). The goal of effective mediation is the re-formation of the human person, described throughout the text as the Pauline 'new man' and the 'man of justice' (26.45; 27.50; 40.76; 47.91). At the same time, the only perfectly just man is the eschatological Christ. Justice is the virtue spanning ontological, moral and eschatological orders. For this reason Augustine suggests at *trin.* 14.9.12 that the other three cardinal virtues need not abide in the state of perfect happiness, except analogically, since they pertain to temporal goods alone. However, justice will abide because it is one and the same, in the order of time as in the state of immortality, since justice is nothing other than 'to be subject to the nature . . . which created and established all other natures'.[20]

Wisdom in *De Trinitate* 14: Conclusion

Trin. incorporates the thematic approaches to 'true worship' from *vera rel.* History has a more serious, literal importance because of the temporal

character of the object of faith, and the appropriately temporal character of faith as a *scientia* (4.18.24). Scripture is closely aligned with the
person of Christ at key points in *trin.*, as a pedagogical tool for nurturing and purification, since Scripture offers 'all the treasures of wisdom
and knowledge' to the weakness of human understanding (e.g. 1.1.2).
Wisdom in *trin.* is perhaps best understood *not* in terms of the polarity
of *scientia* and *sapientia* from the later books but rather through the
soteriological dynamic of Christ as *forma Dei* and *forma servi*: according to the 'form of God', Christ is 'the Truth'; according to the 'form
of a servant', Christ is 'the way' (1.12.14). These aspects of Christ are
linked by the virtue of justice. The fourth book of *trin.* considers the
restoration of creation through the *harmonia* of Christ's single-death,
which submits to and reconciles the double-death of sin (or mortality)
and separation from God by uniting a perfected humanity with the
power proper to divinity. The virtue essential to effective mediation is
justice; power is secondary even if necessary, because justice is the subordination and right ordering of all things in relation to God. Justice is
literally harmonic because it requires many things so as to reduce them
to the unity of order. Augustine emphasizes the 'multiplicity' of division from God, the 'crashing discord' of sin (*dissonantes defluxeramus*,
4.7.11), as well as the historical plurality of testimonies and imperfect
rites.[21] Christ unites what is many, what is temporal and what is disor-
dered by 'being the one' principle of harmony. Through the humility of
sacrifice he unites many persons in himself simply by being 'the one just
man' (*in uno iusto facti unum*); in turn, being made one in him, Christ
unites many with God the Father in an 'identity of will' and 'fellowship
of love' (4.8.12).

Wisdom appears to have the form of true worship in *trin.* 4 as in *vera
rel.*, albeit with a more developed Trinitarian soteriology and a sense
of *iustitia* more deeply grounded in Pauline Christology. In addition to
the central role of justice as the architectonic virtue, we must note that
wisdom takes on a practical, moral character, linked to effective mediation in *trin.* as it is in *vera rel.* The evidence for mediation – by contrast
to the false promises of the devil or the 'man of pride' (4.15.20) – is
found in purification and death to self: the 'old man is crucified' with
Christ in the 'sorrows of repentance and a kind of salutary torment
of self-discipline, a kind of death' (4.3.6). The harmony of Christ is
applied as a medicine, which sacramentally heals the inner man and
morally corrects the outer man. In Book 14 this is described as a grad-
ual progress in stages of post-baptismal conversion: it is a recollection
(as in *c. acad.*), a turning to God (as being 'propitious' to God in *b. vita*)

and a re-formation of the person according to the 'justice and holiness of truth' (the 'right way of life' in *c. acad.* and 'living rightly' in *b. vita*; cf. *trin.* 14.16.22). Healing the wound of sin takes time, even daily progress (*de die in diem*, 14.17.23; cf. 2 Cor. 4.16), in the form of 'transferal of love' (*transfert amorem*) from earthly to spiritual goods. The completion of worship is presence (*perducendus ad Deum quem coluit*, 14.17.23). While full presence with God is eschatological, it is already enjoyed 'in part' through true worship, which is an ordering of the whole person to God as end, through participation in the justice of Christ (as *forma servi*). 'Eternal life with God', Augustine says, is true 'contemplative wisdom'; but it is a properly human kind of wisdom not only because it perfects the human desire for truth and happiness but because it extends by the grace of divine initiative into the daily life of faith, through history, revelation and justification through the blood of Christ (*trin.* 13.11.15). *De consensu evangelistarum*, written around the time Augustine began work on *trin.*, identifies wisdom more clearly with Trinitarian participation: since Christ is the wisdom of God, by whom 'all things are created', no *mens rationalis* 'becomes wise unless by participation in this wisdom, to which we cling by the Holy Spirit, who is charity spread abroad in our hearts'.[22] In the unity of the person of Christ, two things 'are reduced' (*reducuntur*) to unity through the middle term of a 'temporal justice' (*iustitia temporalis*): that which is above (the eternal; the truth itself) and that which is below (e.g. things with a beginning in time; faith) are then truly reconciled one to another. The logic of Trinitarian renewal as kind of participation in the justice of Christ is clearly the central theme of the final book of *trin.* (cf. 15.11.20; 17.31—18.32), completing the picture of wisdom as 'true worship' put forward in Book 14.[23]

Augustine closes *trin.* 14 with amazement that Cicero should have sought after this wisdom, given its exclusively eschatological character but also given the basic scepticism of the New Academy, which refused assent to the veritable goods of the created order, such as the unique dignity of the rational soul. However, this insight would not have sufficed, Augustine says, because if the labour of philosophy in 'love and investigation of truth' hopes rightly for contemplative wisdom, it would still fail the test of 'true religion' by lacking the degree of universality appropriate to the unicity of divine providence in history. All people do not have 'faith in the mediator', Augustine says; but all people are 'truly wretched' (14.19—25.26). True wisdom begins from a sense of this universal human condition, and a *timor Dei*, a fear of God, appropriate to this condition.[24]

Notes

1 H. I. Marrou, *Saint Augustin et La Fin de La Culture Antique* (Paris: E. de Boccard, 1949), pp. 161f.

2 Col. 2.3, cited at *trin.* 13.19.24 (CCL 50 and 50a). See G. Madec, '*Christus, Scientia et sapientia nostra*. Le principe de cohérence de la doctrine augustinienne', *Recherches Augustiniennes* 10 (1975), pp. 77–85.

3 On the audience for *trin.* and the appeal to the 'seeds of reason present in pagan culture', according to Justin Martyr, see J. Cavadini, 'Trinity and Apologetics in the Theology of St. Augustine', *Modern Theology* 29:1 (2013), pp. 49–54; M. R. Barnes, 'Exegesis and Polemic in Augustine's *De Trinitate* I', *Augustinian Studies* 30:1 (1999), pp. 43–59.

4 Cicero's *De officiis* 2 adds to this definition of wisdom, knowledge 'of the causes of things'. On the *Hortensius*, see G. Madec and I. Bochet, 'Augustin et l'Hortensius de Cicéron', in I. Bochet (ed.), *Augustin Philosophe et Prédicateur* (Paris: Institut d'Études Augustiniennes, 2012), pp. 197–294.

5 14.4.21, according to the numbering in Edmund Hill's translation in *The Trinity* (New York: New City Press, 1991). Lewis Ayres describes this passage as 'Augustine's consciously non-technical celebration of the presence of truth to the mind', in *Augustine and the Trinity* (Cambridge: Cambridge University Press, 2010), p. 130.

6 *C. acad.* 1.3.9; 1.8.23 (CCL 29).

7 *C. acad.* 1.8.23: '*Nam hoc ipso quo quaerit, sapiens est; et quo sapiens, eo beatus: cum ab omnibus involucris corporis mentem quantum potest, evolvit, et seipsum in semetipsum colligit; cum se non permittit cupiditatibus laniandum, sed in se atque in Deum semper tranquillus intenditur.*'

8 M. Sachot, '*Religio/superstitio*: historique d'une subversion et d'un retournement', *Revue de l'histoire des religions* 208:4 (1991), pp. 355–94.

9 *C. acad.* 3.9.20: '*Sed videamus per quem potius a philosophia deterreantur. Per eumne qui dixerit: Audi, amice; philosophia non ipsa sapientia, sed studium sapientiae vocatur, ad quam te si contuleris, non quidem dum hic vivis sapiens eris (est enim apud Deum sapientia, nec provenire homini potest), sed cum te tali studio satis exercueris atque mundaveris, animus tuus ea post hanc vitam, id est, cum homo esse desieris, facile perfruetur? An per eum qui dixerit: Venite, mortales, ad philosophiam; magnus hic fructus est: quid enim homini sapientia carius? venite igitur ut sapientes sitis, et sapientiam nesciatis?*'

10 *De beata vita* 4.33 (CCL 29). Initially, wisdom is identified with *plenitudo*; Augustine checks this, saying that, if in 'fullness, we find measure', then in that same fullness, we find the 'measure of the soul'.

11 O. Du Roy, *L'intelligence de la Foie en la Trinité selon Saint Augustin: Genèse de sa Théologie Trinitaire jusqu'en 391* (Paris: Études Augustiniennes, 1966), pp. 414–20; cf. G. Madec, 'Notes sur L'intelligence Augustinienne de la Foi', *Revue des Études Augustiniennes* 17:1–2 (1971), pp. 119–42.

12 Cf. *ep.* 15. Shifting to *vera rel.* bypasses the highly relevant aspects of *De quantitate animae* (~ 388), in which the right order of creation is linked to right worship through what is implied by gradations in valuation. Whatever the soul worships, it deems de facto more excellent than itself; at the same time,

getting worship right requires acknowledging that valuing (or judging) things rightly is a divine work (34.77–78, *ita ut hoc ipsum cum bene agitur, Deum per nos agree intellegamus*). On valuation as 'good use', see *De diversis quaestionibus LXXXIII* 30.

13 *De vera religione* 2.2 (CCL 32).

14 I. Bochet, *'Le Firmament de l'Écriture': l'Herméneutique Augustinienne* (Paris: Institut d'Études Augustiniennes, 2004), pp. 334–40; see also the analysis of *vera rel.*, with a potential link to the Christology of *trin.* 4, in J. Lössl, 'The One: A Guiding Concept in *De Vera Religione*', *Revue des Études Augustiniennes* 40:1 (1994), pp. 79–103.

15 CSEL 89; compare *Gn. adv. Man.* (388–9), 1.25.43, where the historical stages are linked to the days of creation, and a spiritual interpretation is briefly offered, moving from faith in visible things, to eternal rest in God.

16 *Vera rel.* 16.31, trans. E. Hill, *On Christian Belief* (New York: New City Press, 2005), p. 48.

17 Cf. *Contra Faustum* 6.2, comparing 'shadows' to clarity of witness. The ambiguity of biblical signs does not compromise the historical veracity of the biblical account. Therefore, as an example, Augustine says that circumcision is a 'signifying precept' and not a moral precept; it is a true sign because it is valid in its historical context, while it also signifies (as a 'witness') what will become more clear at a later time (6.3). See K. Kloos, 'History as Witness: Augustine's Interpretation of the History of Israel in *Contra Faustum* and *De Trinitate*', in C. T. Daly, J. Doody and K. Paffenroth (eds), *Augustine and History* (Lanham, MD: Lexington Books, 2008), pp. 31–51; P. Fredericksen, 'Augustine and Israel: *Interpretatio ad litteram*, Jews and Judaism', in D. Patte and E. TeSelle (eds), *Engaging Augustine on Romans: Self, Context and Theology in Interpretation* (Harrisburg, PA: Trinity Press International, 2002), pp. 91–110.

18 Cf. *Gn. litt. imp.* 5.19 (CSEL 28.1): *'nec carnalis imago subrepat in animam, et intellectum pium spiritalem conturbet'*.

19 Pars. 70 and 107 use terminology closer to the text of the Vulgate, *concupiscentia carnis-concupiscentia oculorum-ambitio saeculi*; pars. 71 and 101 use *voluptas* (or, *cupiditas voluptatis*)-*superbia-curiositas*.

20 G. van Riel implies a parallel move in Plato, from *Gorgias* 507a–c to *Republic*, Book 4. In the first, temperance implies the other virtues and in the second, justice includes and presupposes the other virtues: 'La sagesse chez Augustin', in I. Bochet (ed.), *Augustin Philosophe et Prédicateur* (Paris: Institut d'Études Augustiniennes, 2012), p. 392.

21 On the centrality of *unum/unus* in *trin.* 4, see I. Bochet, 'The Hymn to the One in Augustine's *De Trinitate IV*', *Augustinian Studies* 38:1 (2007), pp. 41–60. Note that a new historical schema is offered to support the *harmonia* of Christ's death at 4.6.10.

22 1.35.53, CSEL 43.

23 R. Williams, *'Sapientia* and the Trinity: Reflections on the *De Trinitate*', in B. Bruning, M. Lamberigts and J. Van Houtem (eds), *Collectanea Augustiniana: Mélanges T. J. Van Bavel* (Leuven: Peeters, 1990), pp. 317–32; B. Studer, 'History and Faith in Augustine's *De Trinitate*', *Augustinian Studies* 28.1 (1997), pp. 7–50; L. Ayres, 'The Christological Context of *De Trinitate* XIII: Towards

Relocating Books VIII–XV', *Augustinian Studies* 29.1 (1998), pp. 111–39; M. R. Barnes, '*De Trinitate* VI and VII: Augustine and the Limits of Nicene Orthodoxy', *Augustinian Studies* 38:1 (2007), pp. 189–202; 'The Visible Christ and the Invisible Trinity: Mt. 5:8 in Augustine's Trinitarian Theology of 400', *Modern Theology* 19:3 (2003), pp. 329–55.

24 Cf. S. 347.3; *De serm. Dom.* 1.4.11.

PART THREE

Explorations

Sermon

Caught in the Divine Net

Jonathan Goodall

Eucharist, Thursday 30 June
Lectionary: Psalm 84.8–end; 1 Peter 3.8–15; Luke 5.1–11

'At your word I will let down the nets.' (Luke 5.5)

It appears that alongside our conference on the Holy Trinity we are also being asked to keep at least an eye on St Peter, or as we encounter him this morning, Simon. Yesterday we celebrated his feast, along with St Paul. And our readings this morning and tomorrow, from the Fifth Sunday after Trinity in the Book of Common Prayer, the old common lectionary of the Western Church, describe the miraculous draft of fish.

It occurs twice in the Gospels, here in Luke and in John 21. In each case we are on the sea of Galilee. In Luke the incident forms part of the first calling of the disciples; in John it takes place after the Resurrection. In both cases (or perhaps they are the same story?), although James and John (the other members of the inner band of three disciples) also feature, it is Simon Peter whom Jesus engages in dialogues that will mark his whole life.

In both cases also the image of the fish refers to the Church's mission. In this connection, St Augustine says:

> Twice the disciples went out to fish at the Lord's command: once before the Passion and the other time after the Resurrection. In the two scenes of fishing, the entire Church is depicted: the Church as it is now and as it will be after the resurrection of the dead. Now it gathers together a multitude, impossible to number, comprising the good and the bad; after the resurrection, it will include only the good. (*Homily 248*, 1)

This must be an allusion to the fact that in Luke the nets begin to break; and in John we're specifically told they did not.

But let's dwell on Luke. Unlike Matthew and Mark, where Jesus' invitation to follow him is met with an immediate response, Luke's story is a much slower burn, reaching back into events in the last paragraphs of chapter 4. The climax of the sequence of events arrives when Jesus, after preaching to the crowds from the vantage point of Simon's boat, tells Peter: 'Put out into the deep waters and let your nets down.' It appears to Simon to be a senseless idea (if you have static nets you fish at night when the fish are nearer the surface – this is not a north sea trawler!), but Simon agrees: 'On your word I will let down the nets.'

It's an extraordinary statement, which expresses the essence of Christian faith: a trusting and profound obedience to Christ's word. The result we know: a miraculous haul, followed by a stark moment of humility and acceptance that have been slowly growing in Peter since he first heard of Jesus' arrival in his home town. It is an *apokálypsis*, a revelation, and not the last in Peter's life; an experience similar to Isaiah's when he was confronted by the holiness of God, and cried out: 'Alas! I'm an unclean man; yet my eyes have seen the King, the Lord of hosts!' (Isa. 6.5).

It is Peter's first deep perception of the divine life and energy – mysteriously at one with Jesus – that was now irresistibly drawing his life towards a profoundly more fruitful end: 'Do not be afraid!' reassures Jesus, 'But from now on it is people, not fish, that you will be catching.' Peter had begun, and he would continue – through many moments of falling away and 'turning back' (cf. Luke 22.32) – to give his life into the hands of his Master. May God give us the same trust and faith.

8

Humanity Created for Communion with the Trinity in Aquinas

RICHARD CONRAD

Introduction: The Need to Vindicate St Thomas

In the last few decades of the twentieth century, St Thomas Aquinas' rather Augustinian Trinitarian theology suffered something of a bad press. Rahner claimed that, as a result of the 'Augustinian-Western' doctrine of the Holy Trinity, Western Christians had lost much sense of the Trinity as a Mystery of Salvation. He suggested that the way Thomas arranged the treatises in the *Summa Theologiae* caused the Mystery of the Trinity 'to lock itself up in ever more splendid isolation'.[1] It is well known that Rahner wanted to reconnect the 'Immanent Trinity' with 'the Economy'. I suspect a deeper concern was to make the divine self-communication the most fundamental of all realities.[2] I take issue not with this laudable concern but only with Rahner's reading of theological history, since I hope to demonstrate that this concern is one he *shared with* Augustine and Thomas.[3]

'The Answer is 43'

Thomas' treatise on the Holy Trinity in the *Prima Pars* is normally seen as running from Questions 27 to 43. Is this correct? Is this treatise as 'self-contained' as Rahner held? Rowan Williams has argued that earlier Questions deliberately prepare for the explicit discussion of the Trinity;[4] in addition to this, I propose that Question 43 has a distinct status.[5] It is not a begrudging nod towards the Economic Trinity tacked on to a severely abstract treatise on the Immanent Trinity, but a pivot that engineers the transition from the treatise on the Holy Trinity to the remainder of the *Summa*.

The pattern – better, one of the patterns – of the *Summa* is *exitus-reditus*. The account of the *exitus*, the coming of creatures from God, commences in *Prima Pars* 44. *Secunda Pars* explores what is involved in the *reditus*, the journey home, of a rational animal (a fallen rational animal): we need the Holy Spirit's divinizing presence to craft us in Charity and Wisdom, by which, respectively, we desire to be in God, and can 'feel' the way towards him. *Tertia Pars* covers how in historical particularity God made the *reditus* possible: the Father sent the Son to take flesh, so as to be our Way, and so as to impart, by his Passion and Resurrection, and through the sacraments, 'the Grace of the Holy Spirit'.[6] Before detailing the *exitus*, Thomas speaks of the God from whom all things come and to whom they are drawn. This treatise, *Prima Pars* 2–42 (*sic*), repeatedly points forward to the Economy of Salvation. In 1a 8, 3 we find that God dwells 'as in a temple' in those empowered to know and love him. In 1a 12 Thomas explains that we can, indeed, come to rest in knowing God, in the Beatific Vision.[7] 1a 34, 3 says that the Father knows himself in his Word, and creatively knows things; 1a 37, 2 ad 3 says that Father and Son eternally love *us* in the Spirit.

It is *Prima Pars* 43 that explains the *exitus*. Here is the pivot that tells us *why* the triune God goes out in Creation and in the great deeds of Salvation: God does so precisely for the sake of the *reditus*, so that the rational creature may come to its fulfilment in God. *Prima Pars* 43 tells us that *each of Father, Son and Spirit wills to give himself to us, to be known, loved, possessed and enjoyed, now and for ever.*

Missions and Self-Giving

The introduction to 1a 43 says: 'Now we must consider the missions of the Divine Persons.' Much of this Question is indeed on the missions of the Son and the Spirit, anticipating how the heart of the *Secunda Pars* is the Spirit's invisible mission, and the *Tertia Pars* is about the Son's visible mission.

Augustine had explored the missions in *De Trinitate* Book IV, partly in order to demonstrate that the Son's and the Spirit's being sent does not imply they are less divine than the Father. Thomas chiefly develops the soteriological aspect of Augustine's concept. 1a 43, 1 says that a Divine Person is sent if: (a) he becomes present in the world in a new way; and (b) he is from another Person who can 'send' him. It is as if the intra-Trinitarian Procession[8] is 'projected' into the world. Both Son and Spirit are sent visibly: the Son to become incarnate; the Spirit when his presence is symbolized by dove, wind and fire. Both Son and Spirit are sent invisibly, *when they dwell in us by grace.*[9]

Of course, the Divine Persons indwell inseparably, just as they exist inseparably. If Son and Spirit dwell in us, so does the Father. 1a 43, 4 explains that he is not sent, since there is no other to send him or give him. But he does *give himself* in the sense that: 'He liberally bestows himself on the creature for her to enjoy.' So Son and Spirit are given to us as sent by the Father; but *each* of the Three *gives himself* to us to be known and loved, possessed and enjoyed. This suggests that, besides the Missions, there is a related, and perhaps deeper, theme in 1a 43: the *giving* of the Divine Persons, and their being *possessed* by creatures. Article 2 introduces these concepts: 'A [Divine Person] is given so as to be possessed (*ad hoc quod habeatur*).' Article 3 picks up a theme introduced in 1a 8, 3, to which 1a2ae 110, 1 will return, namely the radically new mode of presence by which a Divine Person is in someone who, by grace, knows and loves him. God is in all things as giving them their own being and goodness; God is present in a higher and nobler way when he bestows on us *his own being and goodness*!

To quote 1a 43, 3, God is in the graced rational creature 'as the Known in the knower and the Beloved in the lover'. This hints at a *reciprocity* between us and God: 'by knowing and loving, the rational creature, by her own operation, comes into contact with (*attingit*) God himself.' It is possible for us, who are creatively known and loved by God, to know and love him! – to 'act' on God, to seize, to embrace God! Thomas has already hinted (1a 20, 2 ad 3) that there can be *amicitia*, friendship, between us and God, because of the possibility of 'loving in return'; in 2a2ae 23, 1 he will define Charity as friendship between us and God. This is striking, given how aware Thomas is of the *difference* between God and creature, and how he takes from Aristotle that a note of equality must attend true friendship. But so it is: 1a 43, 3 says that by *gratia gratum faciens*, which could be paraphrased as 'the gift that makes us gracious, graceful and grateful',[10] we are empowered to *possess* and *freely to enjoy* the Divine Persons! Of course, God's absolute priority is not compromised: *gratia gratum faciens* is God's pure gift.

Conformity to the Divine Persons

God gives *gratia gratum faciens* so that we may receive the divine self-gift. 1a2ae 110 presents *gratia gratum faciens* as 'deploying itself' into the God-given strengths of Faith, Hope and Charity that empower us to hold to God by knowledge and love. So by a work of the divine power, which is common to Father, Son and Spirit, we are crafted into God's children (3a 23, 2). But there are hints in *Prima Pars* 43, 5 ad 2 that the presence of each Divine Person 'evokes' these gifts: Thomas says we are necessarily *likened* to a Divine Person who is sent to us, by means of some gift of grace. It is tempting to read him as saying that, precisely in coming to us, each Divine Person *assimilates* us to himself so that we are able personally to welcome him.[11]

1a 43, 5 ad 2 says our conformity to the Holy Spirit is by Charity, which is a created participation in the Holy Spirit, who is 'uncreated Charity'.[12] We are conformed to God the Son, the Divine Wisdom Begotten, by the Gift of Wisdom. The Son is the-Word-who-breathes-forth-the-Divine-Love, and of the various graces seated in the intellect, Wisdom is the one that erupts into love.[13]

This leaves a question: If the Father, too, gives himself to us, are we conformed to *him* by some gift? Thomas does not give an answer but I suggest the gift is *gratia gratum faciens* itself. This participation in the Divine Nature is 'seated in the soul's essence'; that is, it 'moulds' what we are. From the soul's essence flow its powers;[14] in a parallel way, from the 'higher nature' that is *gratia gratum faciens* flow the Theological Virtues that perfect those powers, and the Gifts of the Holy Spirit.[15] Of these Gifts, Wisdom is the chief, and of these Virtues, Charity is the chief. Now, the Divine Nature belongs in a prior way to the Father, who imparts it to the Son who is Wisdom, and to the Spirit who is Love. I propose that we envisage our participation in the Divine Nature as, principally, a participation in *the Father's* Nature.[16] This would let us see the 'structure of grace', in which Wisdom and Charity flow from *gratia gratum faciens*, as a reflection of the Holy Trinity, in which the Word and the Spirit proceed from the Father.

The Human 'Model' of the Holy Trinity

Questions 43 and 93 of *Prima Pars* are correlative, but before we examine 1a 93 it will be helpful to see what Thomas does with the 'psychological analogies' found in the second part of Augustine's *De Trinitate*. In Books I—VII Augustine defended the orthodox Faith in the Trinity by a careful analysis of Scripture in the light of Tradition. Thus the way *De Trinitate* develops suggests that only in the light of revelation, authentically interpreted, can we see the human psyche for what it is, so as to recognize in whose image we are made, and for whom we are made. Augustine heralds a new stage in *De Trinitate* by saying we will approach the Trinity by *a more interior route*,[17] and it may well be his conviction that in an unfallen world our clear knowledge of our own nature *would* have pointed us towards the Trinitarian Creator. But as things stand, the image of the Trinity that we are has been fractured by sin; further, our mind is weighed down, making it difficult for us to know (or value) ourselves truly. Only in the light of Christ, and through the incarnate Word's healing work, can we see a *Trinitarian* structure to our psyche, and realize our vocation to rise from sin towards communion with our Divine Archetype.

Two analogies are explored in *De Trinitate* Books IX and X: first, the mind, its knowledge and its love; second, memory, intellect and will.[18] Though the second may be adapted from Cicero's 'memory, intellect and providence',[19] Augustine is making an invaluable and original contribution. For Athanasius, for example, we are in the image of the Logos (who is *the* Image of the Father) because we are *logikoi*, rational[20] – just as for Plato and Aristotle, *logos* is the highest part of the soul. For Augustine, we are in the image of the *whole* Trinity, and are so not only because we can think (have *intellectus*) but also because we can *love* (have *voluntas*). In connection with according this nobility to our power to love, Augustine is able to picture the Holy Spirit as the Divine Love.

Rather than speaking of 'memory, intellect and will', as if Augustine had identified three faculties, it would be more accurate to speak of 'remembering, understanding and loving': three *activities* that necessarily go on in the 'core' of the human psyche.[21] Each has its own distinct dynamic, hence the three are irreducible. Especially when the soul remembers (possesses), understands and loves (values) *itself*, and above all when, being healed, it does this aright, the three activities work on the same 'object', which they grasp equally well. Here we have a 'model' for how the Divine Persons possess, equally, the one, single Divine Nature but in irreducibly distinct manners. Augustine's analogy may not be intended to *prove* the Divine Trinity; but it does serve to indicate that irreducible distinction and intense unity are compatible.

In both of Augustine's analogies, the will, or love (mirroring the Holy Spirit), is a *uniting force* that joins understanding to remembering – basically, if we love something that is in the memory, we 'bring it forth' so as to contemplate it. Hence the 'birth' of knowledge from the mind or from memory takes place 'within' love. Just as the birth of knowledge in our mind is a created analogy for the eternal Birth of the Divine Word, so the unitive character of love reflects the Holy Spirit as the one 'by whom the Begotten is loved by the Begetter, and loves his Begetter' (*De Trinitate* VI, 5). This picture of the Holy Spirit as the Bond of Love between Father and Son seems to be in some tension with Augustine's teaching that the Holy Spirit proceeds from the Father and the Son.

In his presentation of Trinitarian doctrine that starts in 1a 27, Thomas chiefly draws on Augustine's first model, the mind, its knowledge and its love. He does not identify three activities that mirror the Divine Persons. We have two spiritual faculties, intellect and will, and their 'movements' of knowing and loving are created analogies for the two Divine Processions, the 'comings' of Word and Spirit from the Father. Memory is not a third faculty, for at the spiritual level to remember something simply is to know it.[22]

It is tempting to summarize or paraphrase Thomas' Trinitarian doctrine robustly:

1 By knowing himself perfectly, the Father conceives a Perfect Image of himself: his Word and Son;
2 'Then' by loving himself-as-known he breathes forth a coequal *Spiritus*, Impulse of Love.
3 'In uttering his Word, the Father expresses both himself *and creatures*' (1a, 34, 3); 'He spoke, and they were made' (Ps. 32.9) – we can picture God the Father as an artist who conceives beforehand what he will craft; we are creatively foreknown in the Word.
4 'The Father loves not only the Son, but also himself and us, by the Holy Spirit' (1a 37, 2 ad 3); we can picture God the Father as an artist who not only conceives beforehand what he will craft but delights in it and so fashions it. We are fore-loved in the Spirit.

While this summary is true, it is noteworthy that Thomas does not proceed 'robustly'; he does call on the human psyche as a model for the Trinity, but reticently and step-by-step; he seems very wary of seeing the Divine Processions as merely bigger and better versions of what goes on in us. That would risk making the Trinity provable by reason. The closest he gets to picturing the Word as the Father's self-knowledge, and the Spirit as his self-love, and indeed to Augustine's remembering-of-self, understanding-of-self, and loving-of-self, is in 1a 37, 1: 'If someone understands and loves himself, he is in himself by identity, and as the known in the knower, and as the beloved in the lover.'

Thomas also rejects whatever might compromise the Trinitarian 'order' in which the Son proceeds from the Father, the Spirit from the Father and (or through) the Son. In 1a, 37, 2, while appearing to defend Augustine's saying that the Holy Spirit is the one 'by whom the Begotten is loved by the Begetter, and loves his Begetter', Thomas in fact denies that the Spirit is the principle of the Father's and the Son's loving; he is *not* the Bond of Love between them. Thomas is willing to say that *by loving each other*, Father and Son breathe forth the Spirit as Love Proceeding; as a rule he prefers to see love as a delight that *proceeds from* the known truth, this pattern dimly reflecting the Spirit's procession from the Father through the Son.

I have used the word 'models' as well as 'analogies', since science uses complementary, limited *models* to gain us some purchase on realities we cannot grasp fully. Augustine seems to use the human psyche in this way, as well as to defuse objections to the Faith; perhaps the apparent tension in *De Trinitate* is due to his offering complementary models. While Thomas is unhappy with the model of the Spirit as Bond of Love, and prioritizes the model of 'the mind, its knowing and its loving', he too employs 'psychological models' to help us move towards a deeper understanding of the triune God.[23]

Our movement towards God is always *re*-active; it is evoked by originating movements from God to us: creation, revelation, redemption and grace. Augustine's and Thomas' exploration of our being created in the *image* of God needs to be distinguished from the use of models. Models may help our minds move towards God; but to discover, in the light of revelation, that we have been made in the *image* of the Holy Trinity, is to discover that God has moved towards us so as to build into us a project and a goal: the triune God has made us for himself. A dynamism towards our Archetype is built into us; we are attracted to God the Trinity because we are in the image of God the Trinity. Augustine is clear that we can only reach fulfilment by journeying into communion with the Creator:

> This trinity, then, of the mind is not therefore the image of God, because the mind remembers itself, and understands and loves itself; but because it can also remember, understand, and love him by whom it was made. And in so doing it is made wise itself . . . Let it then remember its God, after whose image it is made, and let it understand and love him. (*De Trinitate* XIV, xii, 15)

This aspect of Augustine's thought is taken up by Thomas in *Prima Pars* 93, to which we now turn.

The Goal of the Creation of the Human Being: *Prima Pars* 93

Prima Pars 43 launches Thomas' account of how the Trinity creates and governs the cosmos, and how Christ's saving work and the Spirit's guidance gently and powerfully lead us home. *Prima Pars* 93 is correlative to 43. Thomas introduces it by saying we are to consider the goal (*finis, terminum*) of God's production of the human being, insofar as we are made to God's image and likeness.[24]

Thomas begins by expounding Genesis 1.26 with Augustine's help: we are in God's image because we are both *like* God (in a very imperfect way) and *derived from* him. In creatures below the human being, and in those elements of human nature we share with them, we find *vestigia Trinitatis*, traces of the Trinity. In the human (and angelic) mind we find a real *image* of God. The journey on which Thomas takes us in this Question really commences in Article 4, where we find that the image is capable of varying degrees, since God knows and loves *himself*, and we can imitate him in this:

1 by nature all human beings have an aptitude towards knowing and loving God;
2 by grace, we habitually or actually love God, but imperfectly;
3 when we are likened to God in glory, we shall know and love him perfectly.

Given his Augustinian background, and given the way his treatise on the Trinity developed, we might expect Thomas to say that by knowing and loving *ourselves* we mirror God who knows and loves himself. Instead, he goes straight to how at our natural level we are *capax Dei*, open to *God*, made for *God*. The God who wants to give himself to creatures to be known and loved, possessed and enjoyed, calls into being creatures naturally apt to come to their fulfilment in knowing and loving him; and by grace perfecting nature he brings them to the goal that consists in active communion with the One in whose image they are made.

By mentioning God knowing and loving himself, Article 4 reminds us of the Trinity, since in God the Word proceeds by way of knowledge, and the Spirit by way of love. It is therefore not surprising that Article 5 says we are made in the image of the Trinity of Divine Persons. This is stated fairly baldly but fleshed out in the next three articles.

Article 6 ostensibly argues that we are properly in the *image* of God according to our *mind* (which includes will as well as intellect), not according to our bodily nature. But it recalls how, in the Divine Trinity, the Persons are distinct because of the procession of the Word from the Speaker and the Love from Both; hence the human being images the Trinity by a procession of a word[25] according to the intellect and a procession of love according to the will. By contrast with lower creatures, there is in us a *principium verbi*, a 'source of word', which implies that in our mind there is something that reflects the Father. To discover whether this is the mind itself, or something else, we go to the next article.

Article 7 explains that the image is present to a real but limited degree insofar as we have the relevant powers (i.e. intellect and will); it is present to a greater degree insofar as these powers are 'shaped' by appropriate habits; it is most present when we *actively* think and love. Thomas says:

> If the image of the Divine Trinity is to be recognized in the soul, we must chiefly look for it where the soul approaches as closely as possible to representing a specific likeness of the Divine Persons. Now the Divine Persons are distinct [from each other] on the basis of the procession of the Word from the Speaker, and [the procession] from the love connecting Both.[26] Now in our soul a word 'cannot exist without actual thinking', as Augustine says (*De Trin.* xiv, 7). Hence, first and foremost, the image of the Trinity is to be found in the mind on the ground of its acts, that is, insofar as from the knowledge which we possess, by thinking we form an internal word; and from this we burst forth into love.

We notice a reticence on Thomas' part. He does not say that if the human mind knew itself perfectly it would form a word that expresses itself perfectly, from which an impulse of love would arise that matches the mind's true worth, and by doing all this the mind would mirror the Trinity, in which by knowing himself perfectly the Father conceives a Perfect Image of himself, 'then' by loving himself-as-known breathes forth a coequal *Spiritus*. It is tempting to read Augustine's first analogy of the Trinity in this way. Edward Booth has argued that, even in his *Sentences Commentary*, Thomas gently corrected Augustine's exploration of the image, for Augustine expected too much: he wanted the created image of the Trinity, at least when brought to its perfection, to mirror the unity and equality of the Divine Persons in a fairly full way.[27] At the end of *De Trinitate* he admitted he had not done very well; Thomas takes seriously the impossibility of doing very well, and recognizes how far the image falls short of the Archetype. Thus in 1a 93 he is content to note that when we think of *any* good thing we have come to know (e.g. chocolate), we bring forth a concept; recognizing the goodness of what we know, we love it.

Thomas' reticence also marks the replies to the second and fourth objections. He points out that we are not always *actively* remembering, understanding and loving ourselves; he is cool towards the idea that a Trinity-mirroring activity is inescapably going on in the core of our mind. He reads Augustine as sharing this reticence, and suggests it was an awareness of the human mind's inability to know itself perfectly that led Augustine to propose his second psychological analogy, since there is less inequality between memory and understanding than between mind and (self-)knowledge. Hence at this point Thomas does make use of the memory–intellect–will triad, but adapted to his conviction that we have two powers at the spiritual level; ad 3 presents memory not as a third *faculty* but as our 'habitual retention of knowledge *and love*'.[28] We are not consciously thinking of every concept we have learnt. Nor are we consciously aware of all the desires and priorities we have! – we cannot tell by introspection whether we have grace,[29] and may surprise ourselves by what we find ourselves willing or unwilling to do!

Article 8 of Question 93 is a climax that clinches what Thomas has been arguing towards. The *sed contra* quotes *De Trinitate* XIV, xii, 15, which was given above, to support the claim that the 'trinity . . . of the mind is . . . the image of God . . . because it can . . . remember, understand, and love him by whom it was made'. We are most fully in the image of God insofar as we 'act on *God*' by knowing and loving the Most Holy Trinity:

> we look for an image of the Divine Trinity in the soul insofar as it represents the Divine Persons by some kind of specific likeness, as far as this is possible for a creature. Now the Divine Persons . . . are distinguished on the basis of the procession of the Word from the Speaker, and the Love from both. Now the Word of God is born of God through his knowledge of himself; and the Love proceeds from God according as he loves himself . . . Hence we recognize the divine image in the human being on the basis of a word conceived from the knowledge of God [*verbum conceptum de Dei notitia*], and of a love derived therefrom. Hence the image of God is found in the soul according as the soul is carried into God, or is naturally apt to be carried into God.

We are to become the image of God in the fullest sense by communion with God. The final article (93, 9) reaffirms this by saying that 'likeness' to God can refer to the image's *perfection*. We think of John 17.3 and 1 John 3.2 – eternal life is knowing God, and when we know him as he is, we shall be like him. The promise of Article 4 leads us to expect 8 and 9 to be about the Beatific Vision, yet Thomas is again reticent. *Verbum conceptum de Dei notitia* makes sense as applied to our present pilgrimage in which, from the graced knowledge of God we have, a *verbum* can be conceived: we can make acts of faith, we can in Wisdom judge what should be done or avoided *sub specie aeternitatis*. This hardly seems to fit the Beatific Vision. What affirmation or judgement can be adequate to the immediate knowledge of God's Essence?

Maybe Thomas is claiming that even in this life we really can resemble the Trinity, and is whetting our appetite to wonder what will happen when we pass from this degree of glory to the glory of heaven. We cannot conceive what this will be like but are given pointers (cf. 1 Cor. 2.9f.). Thomas intended to discuss our final bliss at the end of *Tertia Pars* but did not live to write a mature extended treatise on the Beatific Vision or the Resurrection.[30] Taking cues from what he has said we might tentatively propose the following:

1 In the Beatific Vision, the triune God gives himself to the glorified, strengthened mind; this presence of God as actively known replaces the 'habitual knowledge' of Faith.

2 Since we can never fully comprehend God, God's self-giving is 'met' by some limited 'grasp' of God; this non-conceptual, limited possession of the Trinity very approximately corresponds to the 'word conceived' (i.e. the concepts and judgements we now bring forth from memory).

3 But we will be able to draw out from the Beatific Vision 'words born therefrom', truths to be held in concepts, as we contemplate God's ways, able at last fully to appreciate their wisdom and beauty. We will be able to share these truths with other saints as we rejoice together in thanksgiving.

4 This will especially take place between death and the Final Judgement, while we receive new revelations and are able to respond with intercession as well as with new outbursts of love.[31] New revelations will cease at the Judgement, after which we will rest together in a participation in God's Eternity.

Love especially comes in as a response to the possession of God: we *delight* in the God who gives himself; by our will we *enjoy* the Ultimate Goal possessed (1a2ae 11, 3 and 4).

Thus Thomas is able to say, with Augustine, *to the Holy Trinity*, 'Lord, you have made us for yourself, and our hearts are restless till they rest in you.' The Father has planned us in his Word; the Father and his Word have loved us in the Spirit; Father, Son and Spirit want to give themselves to us. In this overflowing love the triune God has made us in his image; through the Son's and the Spirit's revelatory and salvific Missions, the image that we are is being brought to the perfection which is to have and to hold our triune Friend.

Notes

1 Karl Rahner, *The Trinity*, trans. Joseph Donceel (London: Burns & Oates, 1970), Part I, sections A and B.

2 *Ib.*, section E; Part III, section C. Also 'Some Implications of the Scholastic Concept of Uncreated Grace', *Theological Investigations* I (London: Darton, Longman & Todd, 1961), pp. 319–46.

3 Recent re-evaluations of Thomas' Trinitarian theology are spearheaded by Gilles Emery, OP, for example in *The Trinitarian Theology of Saint Thomas Aquinas* (Oxford: Oxford University Press, 2007).

4 'What Does Love Know? St. Thomas on the Trinity', *New Blackfriars* 82:964 (2001), pp. 260–72.

5 The title of this section alludes to *The Hitchhiker's Guide to the Galaxy*, in which it turns out that the answer to 'life, the universe, and everything' is 42. I see *Prima Pars* 43 as providing the answer.

6 For this phrase see, for example, 1a2ae 106, 1. (The parts of the *Summa Theologiae* will be referred to as 1a, 1a2ae etc., and followed by the number of the question, the article and, if appropriate, the reply to an objection.)

7 By the end of 1a 11 it has become so clear that God is 'wholly other' that it might seem we can neither know him nor speak of him, and so must call off our theological project and despair of the very possibility of a *reditus*. But Thomas argues that we *will* be made able to know God's very Essence, so we *can* hope to rest in him; and (in 1a 12, 11–13 and in 1a 13) that even in this life we can speak validly of God, and can do so not merely in metaphors.

8 The Latin word *processio* is less specific than the Greek *ekporeusis*, the Greek is reserved for the coming of the Spirit from the Father, whereas *processio* is used for: (i) the Son's generation by the Father; (ii) the Spirit's being breathed forth by the Father as Fount of the Divine Being; (iii) the Spirit's being breathed forth by the Son as one Principle with the Father and in dependence on the Father.

9 Thomas takes for granted that the Son is sent visibly and the Spirit invisibly; he sees a need to argue that the Son is sent invisibly (1a, 43, 5) and the Spirit visibly (1a 43, 7). Augustine and Thomas agree that God's friends receive the invisible missions *throughout* human history.

10 *Gratia gratum faciens* is often translated as 'sanctifying grace', which does not seem to capture very well the way this gift makes us 'pleasing to God', nor, for that matter, the *interpersonal* hints in 1a2ae 110, 1. It is basically the adoptive sonship that makes us 'sharers in the Divine Nature' (cf. 2 Peter 1.4). My paraphrase, 'the gift that makes us gracious, graceful and grateful', tries to capture: (i) the *moral beauty* God imparts; (ii) the fact of *being graced*; (iii) how, as a rule, the virtues that flow from God's grace render people 'beloved by God and man' (Sirach 45.1, referring to Moses); (iv) the meaning of *gratia* as 'thanks' that Aquinas includes in 1a2ae 110, 1.

11 There is debate about whether sanctifying grace is cause or effect of the divine indwelling. In 'Some Implications of the Scholastic Concept of Uncreated Grace', *Theological Investigations* I (London: Darton, Longman & Todd, 1961), pp. 319–46, Rahner agreed with Thomas that, insofar as they 'craft' us, the Divine Persons work with the single divine power. But in their inseparable yet *distinct* presences the Divine Persons give *themselves* to us to 'inform' us, roughly as the thing known 'structures' the knowing mind – with the caveat that *God* cannot be contained by a created mind. It would be interesting to investigate whether Rahner missed hints of his own position in Thomas; also whether Thomas' account of the divine indwelling makes more than Rahner does of the *reciprocity* between God and us.

12 Thomas returns to this in 2a2ae 23, 2 ad 1 and 24, 2.

13 2a2ae 45 explains that Charity brings about a 'connaturality' with God, so that the 'Wisdom from above' (James 3.17) is an instinctive fellow-feeling with our Divine Friend, a divine outlook that we share with the Spirit.

14 That is, what you *are* typically reveals itself in what you can *do*.

15 1a2ae 110, 3–4. The Gifts are mentioned explicitly in, for example, 3a 62, 2.

16 In traditional technical terminology, this could be seen as an 'appropriation'. Augustine develops this technique in *De Trinitate* VI, x, 11 –VII, 4, 6. Terms like 'almighty' and 'wise', which belong to all three Divine Persons, can be fittingly applied to *one* of them as reflecting his intra-Trinitarian 'personal role'. It became usual to appropriate to one Person both certain acts common to all Three, and various created realities that all Three cause.

17 *De Trinitate* VIII, I, 1.

18 For a full exploration, see John Edward Sullivan, OP, *The Image of God: The Doctrine of St. Augustine and Its Influence* (Dubuque, IA: The Priory Press, 1963).

19 Lewis Ayres, *Augustine and the Trinity* (Cambridge: Cambridge University Press, 2014), pp. 308–13.

20 *De Incarnatione* 3.

21 A point made in Edmund Hill, OP, *The Mystery of the Trinity* (London: Geoffrey Chapman, 1985), p. 126.

22 With my *imagination*, I recall learning about endoplasmic reticulum in a 1974 biology lecture; when I say, 'I remember what endoplasmic reticulum is', I mean that the concept is in my *intellect*. In 1a 93, 7 ad 3 Thomas rejects Lombard's understanding of *memoria, intellegentia* and *voluntas* as three natural powers of the soul.

23 In 1a 1, 9 Thomas defends metaphors; he does not have a distinct concept of 'model'. Edmund Hill sees Augustine as 'constructing' models (*Mystery of the Trinity*, pp. 125–6); I see him as *discerning* an image and using it as a model.

24 The Question focuses on 'image' because in Thomas' Latin, 'likeness' is ambiguous: it can mean something vaguer than 'image' or it can express a perfection of the image as it becomes more like its Exemplar.

25 For a detailed analysis of *verbum cordis*, see Bernard Lonergan, *Verbum: Word and Idea in Aquinas* (Notre Dame, IN: University of Notre Dame Press, 1967). Also John O'Callaghan, '*Verbum Mentis*: Philosophical or Theological Doctrine in Aquinas?', *Proceedings of the American Catholic Philosophical Association* 74 (2000), pp. 103–19.

26 The more natural translation of *Amoris connectentis utrumque* is: '[the procession] of the Love connecting Both'; that is, the procession of the Spirit, who is the Love connecting Father and Son. But 1a 37, 2 has denied that the Spirit is the Bond of Love by which Father and Son love each other; rather, he is Love Proceeding from the love by which they love each other. Of course, in 93, 7 Thomas may have had a lapse of precision, or, more likely, is expressing himself succinctly and assuming the reader will supply necessary qualifications. My translation imposes a strict consistency on Thomas.

27 Edward Booth, OP, 'Saint Thomas Aquinas's Critique of Saint Augustine's Conceptions of the Image of God in the Human Soul', in Johannes Brachtendorf (ed.), *Gott und sein Bild: Augustins 'De Trinitate' im Spiegel gegenwärtiger Forschung* (Paderborn: Ferdinand Schöningh, 2000), pp. 219–39.

28 Emphasis added.

29 1a2ae 112, 5.

30 *Compendium Theologiae* I, 104 (209)−106 (214) and 165 (327)−166 (330) cover the issues succinctly.

31 1a 43, 6 ad 3 associates missions (of the Word?) with these revelations.

9

Cranmer's *Gnadenstuhl:*
Continuity and Change in the Liturgy

GAVIN DUNBAR

Among the rare survivals of English medieval art is an altarpiece in painted and gilded alabaster, made in England for the flourishing export market in such things, in the early or middle of the fifteenth century. Purchased in Munich in the 1830s by Lord Swansea, it is now in the Victoria and Albert Museum in London. Four of its five panels depict the joys and glories of Mary – the Annunciation, the Adoration of the Magi, the Ascension and the Assumption. At the centre, however, is the image of the crucified Christ, much popularized by the Franciscans from the thirteenth century onwards. As in other crucifixes, the Son hangs crucified, naked except for his loincloth, his head bowed in death; and there are angels with chalices to catch the precious blood that pours from his sacred wounds. But the cross on which Christ hangs itself hangs from between the knees of the much larger figure of God the Father – bearded, robed, enthroned in majesty, his hands raised in blessing and flanked by angels blowing trumpets. In its current state, there is no representation of the Holy Spirit, though in other versions of this image he often appears, hovering over the Son or perched on the wood of the cross. Yet the dove's absence is not uncommon in such images, and even when it does appear, it is inconspicuous.

This type of image was dubbed the *Gnadenstuhl* (Throne of Mercy) by nineteenth-century German art historians, in an allusion to Hebrews 4.16: 'Let us therefore come boldly unto the throne of grace, that we may obtain mercy, and find grace to help in time of need.' But properly speaking it is an image of the Trinity, in which the Son is represented as the crucified one. It first appears late in the thirteenth century as an expression of 'a new theological emphasis on the outworkings of the eternal Trinity in the life and death of Jesus',[1] and is widespread from the fourteenth century through the Catholic Counter-Reformation. Celebrated examples are Masaccio's early fifteenth-century fresco in Santa Maria Novella, in which he made revolutionary use of

Brunelleschian perspective; and Dürer's early sixteenth-century Landauer Altarpiece, now in Vienna. But there are no traces of the influence of the Italian Renaissance on the Swansea Altarpiece, which is thoroughly Gothic. Later versions develop the theme of the Father's pity for his Son (perhaps under the influence of the Pietà or Virgin of Pity), but that is not the case here. As Sarah Coakley comments:

> the emphasis here . . . is not on an empathetic Father, but on a stern and merciful acceptance by him of the 'satisfaction' for sin effected in Christ's death. And all the drama of . . . the *Gnadenstuhl* resides in the relationship of the Father and the Son: the Spirit, we might say, is virtually redundant to the theme . . . Hence it is not surprising to find the Spirit actually missing from the *Gnadenstuhl* visual type on occasion.[2]

Is the Father accepting the sacrifice of his Son, or is he showing or even giving his Son to the faithful viewer, as one whose sacrifice has already been accepted? This showing or giving of his crucified Son has an obvious reference to its sacramental realization in the Mass, which was celebrated before this image. By the miracle of transubstantiation, the sacrifice of the crucified Son is made present on the altar under the appearances of bread and wine, that it may be offered as the sacrifice of the Mass.

Continuity and Change in the English Reformation

In this essay I wish to explore the implications of the disappearance of this *visual* image, the *Gnadenstuhl*, from English churches and altars in the middle of the sixteenth century, and its reappearance in *verbal* form, still in a eucharistic context, in Cranmer's *Order for the Administration of the Lord's Supper or Holy Communion* (1549, 1552 and its later revivals in 1559 and 1662).

An objection needs to be addressed before proceeding further. There was a time when Anglo-Catholics promoted a romantic and aesthetic vision of the English Reformation, as a *via media* between Geneva and Rome. Making ingenious use of the Ornaments Rubric and the furnishings of Elizabeth I's chapel, they painted the English Reformation as a kind of moderate catholic reform that (in original intention at least) was quite unlike the more 'extreme' continental reformation – and rather like the medievalizing ritualism that they themselves promoted.

Though this view has a lingering popular influence in Anglican mythology, and an undoubted effect on Anglican liturgy, it now commands little support among historians. The English Reformation was not without its distinctive quirks of order, polity and liturgy, quirks whose latent potential was to be taken up by the catholic revival of the nineteenth century; but in all essential points of doctrine, the English Church of the sixteenth century was altogether committed to the theological consensus of Protestant, and especially Reformed, orthodoxy, held in common by the reformed churches of the continent as well as the British isles. Anglicanism as a distinct strain of Christianity was not to emerge until the later seventeenth century.

This being so, one must also acknowledge a conservative aspect to the Protestant Reformation, including its English version. This is most evident in the reformers' retention of the Trinitarian and christological dogmas of catholic antiquity, an adherence reflected in the frequent use of the three ancient Creeds in Cranmer's liturgy: the Apostles' Creed, said twice daily; the Nicene Creed, at every celebration of the Lord's Supper; and the Athanasian Creed thirteen occasions through the year. This conservatism also appears in the fact that their distinctive doctrines are revisions of the three great pillars of the medieval doctrine of grace: justification, predestination and the sacraments. As Oliver O'Donovan has put it, in the doctrine of the sacraments, rather than rethinking it from the ground up, 'they defended as much of the developed scholastic doctrine of the sacraments as they could, and altered it only when they felt they had to.'[3] In the Church of England this general reformed conservatism was reinforced by the desire of the English reformers to maintain at least an apparent continuity with the recent past in things inessential – which largely accounts for the quirks of order, polity and liturgy, which the catholic revival of the nineteenth century was to run with.

In short, one does not have to adopt a mythological version of Anglican history to acknowledge that in the English Reformation there are striking elements of continuity with the late-medieval Church, as well as striking elements of change. The disappearance of the *Gnadenstuhl* in its visual form, and its reappearance in a verbal form, is another significant instance of this phenomenon.

Cranmer's *Gnadenstuhl*

Other reformed liturgies scrapped the Roman eucharistic prayer, the Gelasian canon, whose language of sacrifice and offering was deeply

associated with the objectionable late-medieval doctrines of transubstantiation and the sacrifices of masses, 'in the which', as Article XXXI
puts it, 'it was commonly said, that the Priest did offer Christ for the
quick and the dead, to have remission of pain or guilt'. Cranmer, however, took a different approach – retaining the language of sacrifice
and offering but recasting it in accord with the emerging reformed consensus of eucharistic doctrine, and the teaching of the Epistle to the
Hebrews. The sacrificial language no longer refers to the ritual action
centred on the elements but rather to Christ's once-for-all sacrifice for
sin that he offered on the cross, now commemorated – and not offered
again – in the Lord's Supper, *and* to the Church's continual sacrifice of
praise and thanksgiving for his sacrifice, which it offers in the Lord's
Supper.

Thus the very same elements that we find in the medieval image of
the *Gnadenstuhl* are present also in Cranmer's eucharistic prayer: the
crucified Son, the stern and merciful acceptance of his sacrifice by the
Father in satisfaction for sin – or rather, the Father's showing or giving
of the Son in all the benefits of his sacrificial death to those partak-
ing of the sacrament. Cranmer's eucharistic prayer corresponds to the
Gnadenstuhl even in the low visibility of the Spirit.[4] The contention of
this chapter is that the very *Gnadenstuhl* that disappeared from English
churches in the iconoclasm of the mid-sixteenth century in fact lived
on and flourished but now in verbal form in the Cranmerian *Order of
Administration of the Lord's Supper* – with, of course, this critical difference: that it has been extracted from the context of medieval eucharistic theology and practice and replaced within the context of reformed
eucharistic theology and practice. The Father gives the Son not so that
we may offer him anew in the mass but so that we may receive him in
all the virtue of his once-for-all and already accepted sacrifice for sin.

In Cranmer's rite, therefore, the verbal *Gnadenstuhl* comes first, with
an acknowledgement of the cross as the work of the Father and the
Son, of the Eucharist as its memorial, a prayer for faithful receivers of
the sacrament to partake in Christ's body and blood, and the institution narrative:

ALMIGHTY God oure heavenly father, whiche of thy tender mercye
dyddest geve thine onely sonne Jesus Christ, to suffre death upon
the crosse for our redempcion, who made there (by hys one oblacion of hymselfe once offered) a full, perfecte and sufficiente sacrifice,
oblacion and satisfaccion, for the synnes of the whole worlde, and
dyd institute, and in hys holye Gospell commaund us to continue,

a perpetuall memorye of that his precious death, untyll hys comynge agayne: Heare us O mercyefull father wee beeseche thee; and graunt that wee, receyving these thy creatures of bread and wyne, accordinge to thy sonne our Savioure Jesus Christ's holy institucion, in remembraunce of his death and passion, maye be partakers of his most blessed body and bloud: who, in the same night that he was betrayed, tooke bread, and when he had geven thanks, he brake it, and gave it to his Disciples, sayinge: Take, eate, this is my bodye which is geven for you. Doe this in remembraunce of me. Lykewyse after supper he tooke the cup, and when he had geven thankes, he gave it to them, sayinge: Drink ye all of this, for this is my bloud of the new Testament, whiche is shed for you and for many, for remission of synnes: do this as oft as ye shall drinke it in remembraunce of me.

After which, in prompt obedience to the Lord's command, the elements are immediately delivered to the communicants in this form:[5]

Take and eate this, in remembraunce that Christ dyed for thee, and feede on him in thy hearte by faythe, with thankesgeving.
Drinke this in remembraunce that Christ's bloude was shed for thee, and be thankefull.

They are received 'in remembrance' because Christ died already, and once for all. Nonetheless the recipients are to 'feed on him in thy heart by faith, with thanksgiving', because he is present now and in the future. This note of thankful faith informs the prayers that follow communion; and it is here, only *after* receiving the sacramental elements, that the rite provides for the offering of the Church's sacrifice, which is a self-offering in praise and thanksgiving for the benefits of Christ's all-sufficient satisfaction for sin:

O LORDE and heavenly father, we thy humble servaunts entierly desire thy fatherly goodnes, mercifully to accept this our Sacrifice of prayse and thanksgeving: most humbly beseching thee to graunt, that by the merites and death of thy sonne Jesus Christe, and through fayth in his bloud, we and al thy whole church may obtayne remission of oure synnes, and all other benefytes of his Passion. And here we offre and presente unto thee, O lord, our selfes, our soules, and bodies, to be a reasonable holy, and lively Sacrifice unto thee: humbly beseching thee that al we which be partakers of this holy

Communion, maye bee fulfylled with thy grace and heavenhy ben-
ediccion. And although we bee unworthy throughe oure manifolde
sinnes to offre unto thee any Sacrifice: yet we beseche thee to accept
this our bounden duetie and service, not weighing our merites, but
pardoning our offences, through Jesus Christ our Lord; by whom
and with whom, in the unitie of the holy ghost, all honour and glory
bee unto thee, O father almightie, world without ende. Amen.

Cranmer's liturgy is sometimes taken to task – or timidly defended – for
this narrow focus on the motif of sacrifice. Modern eucharistic rites by
contrast – especially in the Anglican Church of Canada and the Episcopal
Church of the USA – have sought to minimize such language and to
employ a much broader range of language and imagery from Scripture
and the Church's tradition. The result is that recognizable continuity with
the theology and liturgy of the classical Prayer Books has disappeared.
Moreover, among many clergy and in seminaries there is often resistance
to the use or even exploration in thought of the biblical and traditional
language of sin, satisfaction and sacrifice. Yet Cranmer's narrow focus
on satisfactory sacrifice is not without a compelling logic. There are no
doubt other ways of speaking of the saving act of God in Christ – as a victory over evil, for instance, a divine deliverance or an inspiring example
of human virtue. Yet victory over evil and divine deliverance is a matter
between God and the powers of evil; moral example is a matter between
Christ in his human nature and other men. Only sacrifice has to do with
the relation of man to God, and therefore it alone accounts for the communion and fellowship of sinful men with the Father, accomplished by
Christ, the God-man, who as man offered himself in death, and as God
offers a sacrifice of infinite value. There is of course a place in the liturgy
for other images of God's saving act; but in the Lord's Supper, the Holy
Communion, it is sacrifice that matters, because it is communion with
God that is sought, and it is his sacrifice, and his sacrifice alone, that
establishes and sustains us in communion with God. As Augustine said,
'the true sacrifice is done in every work which is designed to unite us to
God in a holy fellowship, every act, that is, which is directed to that final
good which makes possible our true felicity'.[6]
Cranmer follows Augustine in understanding that the sacrifice of
Christ is a sacrifice in head and members, and that through the sacrifice
of the head the members learn to offer themselves. Nonetheless, in common with other reformers he makes a much sharper distinction between
the propitiatory sacrifice of the head and the gratulatory sacrifice of the
members. For Cranmer, the *Gnadenstuhl* – the Father's free gift of the

crucified Son in all the virtue of his accomplished and accepted sacrifice, shown forth in the ministry of Word and sacrament, and received by means of faith alone – awakens an overwhelming gratitude to God, which is the dynamism and direction of the Christian life. This eucharistic self-offering, this return of the creature to the Creator, has no other basis and cause than the Son's own offering of himself for us to the Father, and in the Father's acceptance of that offering to our benefit. Where it is shown forth, in Word and sacrament, above all in the Lord's Supper, it moves the faithful receivers to 'offer ourselves, our souls and bodies, to be a reasonable, holy and living sacrifice unto thee'.

It is commonly said in North America that the new eucharistic prayers of the North American churches are more fully Trinitarian than Cranmer's narrow focus on Christ and the cross, because they rehearse the whole history of salvation from creation to eschaton. Yet if Cranmer's focus is narrow, it is also deep. What he retains from the *Gnadenstuhl* is the awareness of the cross as the point where the operations of the Trinity *ad extra*, God's work in the world, is integrated into the life of the theological or immanent Trinity, God in himself, the Father, the Son and the Holy Ghost. The entire motion of the liturgy is one of return to God out of utmost alienation, through the going forth of his Word and Spirit, in which the sacrifice of the cross is the decisive moment. This is why the relocation of the *Gloria in excelsis* from its pre-Reformation place just before the Collect of the day, to its 1552 place after the post-communion Prayer of Thanksgiving, is a masterstroke of liturgical craft. Not only is it psychologically appropriate, as the natural point for the release of joy, it also dramatizes the end that we have attained by the sacrifice of Christ, which we are moved to proclaim: 'Glory be to God on high, and on earth, peace, good will towards men.' Man attains his end in God, and the congregation may therefore be dismissed with the authoritative declaration of God's peace, which passeth all understanding, and which '[keeps] your hearts and minds in the knowledge and love of God, and of his Son, Jesus Christ our Lord'. It is all God, God's knowing and loving his own infinite goodness by his Word and Spirit, a knowing and loving of God in which the faithful are gathered, that we may rest in his peace also.

Mission and Liturgy

For Cranmer, the end of the liturgy, the action of God it celebrates, is not in the world but in God, in the world's finding its true end, the rest of the restless heart, in the knowledge and love of God and of his Son Jesus Christ. Mission, witness and service thus are not an alternatives to worship but arise out of it and return to it. Worship is the form of all our works of witness and service. The transformation of the world that we seek is found precisely in the world's discovering its true end in the glorification and enjoyment of God, through the sacrifice of his Son. Worship otherwise risks becoming a kind of pep rally or consciousness-raising exercise for some other agenda, however worthy. It is in the context of grateful self-offering that Cranmer situates the works God has prepared for his elect to walk in, the works of the Christian life (Eph. 2.10), and that is the frame within which any missional emphasis finds it proper place. This is why the minimization of sacrificial language in the newer rites of the North American churches is worrisome. One cannot but note the somewhat chilling dismissal of the last Cranmerian elements of Rite I in the 1979 American Prayer Book by the late Marion Hatchett: 'it is time to relegate the Eucharistic Prayer I to the appendix of historical documents.' Whatever else one might say about the English church's *Common Worship*, one of its strongest features is the willingness to incorporate in its eucharistic rites – and not just in the 'traditional language' version – elements of Cranmerian language and theology of sacrifice and offering in recognizable forms. As the Episcopal Church in the USA looks towards a new revision of the 1979 Prayer Book, there is an opportunity for a fresh and more sympathetic apprehension of the Cranmerian tradition.

Conclusion

The late medieval Church's devotional and liturgical image known as the *Gnadenstuhl* or Throne of Mercy brought together the mysteries of the Trinity, the Atonement and the Eucharist and, despite the iconoclasm of the Protestant reformers, the same mysteries are brought together in the Eucharistic Prayers of the Cranmerian Prayer Books, a striking instance of the conservative aspect of the Protestant Reformation and of the continuities between late-medieval and reformational Church. At the same time, this continuity highlights the changes involved in the reshaping of the Gelasian canon and its motif of sacrifice, to exclude late-medieval eucharistic doctrines, especially the propitiatory claims made for the 'sacrifices of Masses', in conformity with the emerging reformed consensus about the Eucharist, as a memorial of Christ's once-for-all sacrifice for sin, and the Church's own self-offering in praise and thanksgiving for his sacrifice. Cranmer's focus on the motif of sacrifice may be narrow but it accords with the end that is sought: communion with the triune God, and participation in the life of the Trinity. It is on the cross that the economic outworkings of the Trinity in the world are united with the immanent or theological Trinity, in the Father's giving of the Son and the Son's offering himself to the Father. As such, the motif of sacrifice articulated by Cranmer provides a frame within which the Church's own mission of witness and service in the world may be better understood within a Trinitarian context. It is deeply revealing of the continuity and change embodied with characteristic genius and economy in the language and structure of Cranmer's liturgical reform.

Notes

1 S. Coakley, *God, Sexuality, and the Self: An Essay 'On the Trinity'* (Cambridge: Cambridge University Press, 2013), p. 211.

2 Coakley, *ibid.*

3 O'Donovan, *On the Thirty Nine Articles: A Conversation with Tudor Christianity* (Exeter: Paternoster Press for Latimer House, 1986), pp. 1–23.

4 There was of course an explicit reference to the Spirit as well as the Word in the Epiclesis of the 1549 rite, which is altered in 1552. There are enough references to the Spirit's work in Cranmer's liturgy to know that he did not discount it. It is rather to be read as a late instance of a long tradition that goes back to the Gloria in Excelsis, the Te Deum Laudamus and the first version of the Nicene Creed, in which the Spirit receives only minimal attention.

5 Subsequently modified in the Elizabethan Prayer Book of 1559 and its successors.

6 *De Civitate Dei*, x, 6.

10

Hooker's Trinitarian Theology and the Everyday

GARY THORNE

Introduction

As a university chaplain in Canada, I observe that the majority of thoroughly secular students who arrive on campus each year have an intuition and experience of 'transcendence' that enriches the natural world and human communities. Unlike their previous generation who currently govern the university as administrators, staff and faculty, and who hold on to a rather sterile definition of secularity simply as the 'absence' of God, these young people seek to discover a deeper transcendence in the created order and human community than they perceive institutional religion to have on offer. They seek a world enchanted – or perhaps re-enchanted – with wonder and transcendence. This experience of transcendence is a large part of what motivates their uncompromising commitment to honouring and caring for the natural order. These students also differ from their previous generation in that many suffer from an anxiety of impotence both in regard to their personal well-being and in regard to their potential to influence large-scale and global significant change through collective political action. Their existential personal anxiety reflects a deep solidarity with the suffering of so many in the world.

In the sixteenth century, Richard Hooker's presentation of reality in terms of law described a natural order of transcendence and beauty that is simultaneously accompanied by a suffering that is beyond human resolution. Hooker proposes that the discovery of this enchanted world is through the revelation of the Trinitarian character of the natural order,[1] and that a healing solidarity with the suffering of the world is achieved in the Christian sacraments. This chapter will suggest why Hooker's emphasis on a thoroughgoing notion of participation that pervades all of reality resonates powerfully with many young people today.

It is regularly noted that the concept of participation is the theme that holds together the entirety of Richard Hooker's theology from Book I to Book VIII of his *Lawes of Ecclesiastical Polity* (hereafter *Lawes*).[2] One critical discussion of participation occurs in Book V as part of Hooker's commentary on the sacraments of baptism and the Eucharist as found in the 1559 Book of Common Prayer.[3] There Hooker makes clear that Trinitarian and christological theology, outlined in *Lawes* V.50–5, provides the key to an understanding of the sacraments.

Lawes V.56 has been called the theological heart of Book V[4] and thus of the entire *Lawes*. It is the hinge that sums up the consideration of Trinitarian and christological theology in *Lawes* V.51–5 and introduces the discussion of the sacraments proper.

Hooker begins this bridge chapter, *Lawes* V.56, by summing up the notion of how Christ is in us (the argument of *Lawes* V.51–5) in terms of participation:

> Wee have hitherto spoken of the person and of the presence of Christ. Participation is that mutuall inward hold which Christ hath of us and wee of him, in such sort that ech possesseth other by waie of special interest propertie and inherent copulation.

Hooker then briefly reviews the overall argument of the *Lawes* in terms of participation. He recollects his teaching from Book I that law is to be discovered in the nature of God the Trinity: 'The being of God is a kinde of lawe to his own working: for that perfection which God is, giveth perfection to that he doth.'[5] This first eternal law, which governs God in himself (*in se*), is like unto the second eternal law that governs all created reality (*ad extra*). All law reflects the following principles:

> *Everie original cause imparteth it selfe unto those things which come of it,* and *Whatsoever taketh beinge from anie other the same is after a sorte in that which giveth it beinge.*[6]

These universal principles of knowing and being[7] necessarily determine and limit our ability to say anything of the mysteries of the Trinity and the Incarnation but they also make clear that our knowing and being is dependent throughout on a notion of participation that runs through all reality, both created and uncreated. In this chapter Hooker outlines his intent to describe the various types and degrees of participation within the Trinity itself, between the two natures of Christ in the Incarnation, and between the created order and God the Trinity both as Creator and as Saviour.

All created things participate in God the Trinity through the natural law:

> All thinges are therefore partakers of God, they are his offspring, his influence is in them, and the personal wisdom of God is for that verie cause said to . . . reach unto everie thinge which is . . . Whatsoever God doth worke, the hands of all three persons are joyntlie and eqaullie in it according to the order of that connexion whereby they ech depende upon other . . . The father as goodness, the Sonne as wisdom, the holie Ghost as power doe all concurre in everie particular outwardlie issuing from that one onlie glorious deitie which they all are . . . So that all thinges which God hath made are in that respect the offspring of God, they are in him as effects in theire highest cause, he likewise actuallie is in them, thassistance and influence of his deitie is theire life.

The final desire of man is God, and since 'desire tendeth unto union with it that it desireth', union with God, return unto our highest cause, is our happiness.

> If then we be blessed it is by force of participation and conjunction with him [i.e. God] . . . Then we are happie therefore when fully we injoy God . . . although we be men, yet by being unto God united we live as it were the life of God.[8]

But by the sin of pride man's reason is corrupted so that the knowledge of good and evil is confused, and this return of the effect unto the cause is desired but unattainable. In the Incarnation, Christ makes the ascent possible again because he 'is in us as a moving and working cause'.[9] Humankind's return to God, and participation in God the Trinity, is restored by supernatural grace in the divine law:

> These were in God as in theire Savior and not as in theire creator onlie. It was the purpose of his *savinge* goodness, his *savinge* wisdom and his *savinge* power which inclineth it selfe towards them. Life as in all other guiftes and benefites growth originallie from the father and commeth not to us but by the Sonne, nor by the Sonne to anie of us in particular but through the Spirit . . . which three St Peter comprehendeth in one, the *participation of divine nature* . . .[10]

Thus in broadest terms outlined in *Lawes* V.56, all creatures participate in God through following the laws of their nature. The law of man's nature is that he desires the good but in fact he cannot will the good and his return to God is frustrated.[11] Christ has come to be the new law, the divine law that makes it possible for man to obtain, by degrees, that highest good which he seeks, and thus to live the life of God.

> Finally since God has *deified* our nature, though not by turning it into himself, yet by making it his own inseparable habitation, we cannot now conceive how God should without man either exercise divine power or receive the glory of divine praise. For man is in both an associate of Deity.[12]

In subsequent chapters Hooker will proceed to describe the sacraments as the instrumental means by which we participate in that divine law. Baptism provides 'that saving grace of imputation . . . [and] that infused divine virtue of the holie Ghost which giveth to the powers of the soule theire first disposition towards newness of life',[13] and participation in the Eucharist increases, by degrees, one's growth in 'holiness and virtue'.[14] That's the overall argument, too briefly considered.

But since our theme is that of knowing and loving the triune God, let's return to the beginning of Hooker's commentary on the sacraments in the Book of Common Prayer, where he argues that the Prayer Book doctrine of the sacraments depends directly on the doctrine of the Trinity and Incarnation.

In *Lawes* V.50, Hooker describes sacraments as 'powerfull instruments of God to eternall life' and the means whereby humans are made partakers of God in Christ. In his own much quoted words:

> For as our natural life consisteth in the union of the bodie with the soule; so our life supernaturall in the union of the soule with God. And for as much as there is no union of God with man without the meane between both which is both, it seemeth requisite that wee first consider how God is in Christ, then how Christ is in us, and how the sacraments soe serve to make us partakers with Christ. In other thinges wee may be more briefe, but the waight of these requireth largeness.[15]

Generally speaking this scheme is unexceptional. Hooker will rehearse several times how the first Council of Nicaea insisted that the Son was not in the Father simply by an undefined 'participation' but that the Son shared the same uncreated divine essence as the Father. Subsequent Councils up to Chalcedon describe how the Eternal Word, the Son of

God, assumed human nature so that, though an unconfused yet indivisible union of the divine and human natures defined by *communicatio idiomatum*, this human nature became deified human nature in the Son. In baptism and the Eucharist we participate in Christ's deified humanity and thus we become partakers 'with Christ' of the divine life of the Trinity.

Although this scheme is commonplace, Hooker's selection of sources and authorities in *Lawes* V.50–6 is what interests us. In Hooker's 852 patristic references throughout the *Lawes*, the Latin Fathers – Augustine, Tertullian, Cyprian and Jerome – dominate. Yet in *Lawes* V.50–6, Theodoret of Cyrrhus, Cyril of Alexandria and John of Damascus are prominent and in these chapters there are only six medieval and no classical or contemporary references.[16] That Hooker privileges these three Greek authors is unquestionable from any plain reading of this section of the text. It is natural to ask why Hooker determines these three particular Greek authors to be authoritative in establishing the Trinitarian and christological theology that best explains the nature of the sacraments in the Book of Common Prayer.

Some bits of the answer to this question are well established, even if often overlooked by scholars. For example, Hooker is entirely in step with sixteenth-century magisterial reformers in their humanist cry of *ad fontes*. The general response of the magisterial reformers to the scholastic arguments over the localized presence of Christ in the Eucharist was to turn to an earlier Greek Patristic Christology as the key to understanding the nature of the presence of Christ in the Eucharist. The early reformers had discovered that in the pre-scholastic Greek patristic tradition, eucharistic theology was directly and intimately connected with Trinitarian and christological doctrine. Melanchthon wrote to Matthäus Alber in 1526:

> The Greek doctrine of the Lord's Supper holds that the real presence of the Eucharistic Christ is analogous to the mode of being of the historical Christ. The Greeks understood the presence of the Body of Christ as an anamnesis of the Incarnation, and the Eucharist itself as an anamnesis of the whole Christ-event. Thus, the doctrine of the Eucharist recapitulates the doctrine of the person of Christ.[17]

Second, that Hooker should highlight Theodoret of Cyrrus in this doctrinal introduction to the sacraments is also to be expected.

Theodoret had been introduced to the English context by Peter Martyr when he arrived in 1547 with a fresh copy of Theodoret's

Eranistes, or *Three Dialogues*. It is likely that Cranmer borrowed Peter Martyr's copy of Theodoret in composing his 1550 *Defence of the True and Catholic Doctrine of the Sacrament of the Body and Blood of Christ*.[18] In his response to *The Defence*, Stephen Gardiner engaged both Peter Martyr and Thomas Cranmer over their interpretation of Theodoret's theology and thereafter Theodoret's *Three Dialogues* became a central text in the continuing eucharistic controversies in England in the sixteenth century. As Marvin Anderson rightly suggests: 'The Christological observations in this ancient Greek treatise became integral to the Tudor reformation at a critical juncture.'[19] What remains to be explained, however, are Hooker's references to John of Damascus, and particularly his extended use of Cyril of Alexandria.[20]

The main argument of this chapter is that in these central chapters of the *Lawes*, Hooker specifically leans on the theology of Cyril of Alexandria as a determining influence on his interpretation of the sacraments in the Prayer Book tradition. Although I think Hooker could not be more direct in pointing to Cyril's theology, commentators on Hooker have not acknowledged sufficiently this dependence. But first a very brief excursus to Hooker's use of the *De Fide Orthodoxa* of John of Damascus, which will help set the context for Cyril's contribution.

John of Damascus and *Perichoresis*

In *Lawes* V.51, Hooker begins his argument of how God is in Christ by reminding us that the statement, 'The Lord our God is but one God' refers to the 'indivisible unitie' of God. Here Hooker brings to mind his discussion in Book I.2.2: 'God is one, or rather verie Oneness, and mere unitie, having nothing but it selfe in itself, and not consisting (as all things do besides God) of many things.' Nonetheless, says Hooker, we adore that 'indivisible unitie' as Father, Son and Holy Ghost: the father being of none, the consubstantial Word which is the Son is of the Father, and the coessential Holy Ghost proceeding from both. The Persons of the Trinity share one substance but in each there is also 'that propertie which causeth the same person, reallie and trulie to differ from the other two'. Each person of the Trinity has its own 'subsistence' (because of the uniqueness of origin) and thus when God became man it was not the Father nor the Holy Spirit but only the Son or the Word that was made flesh. In Christ divine nature assumed human nature so that God might be in Christ reconciling the world to himself. Christ took to himself our flesh to offer it to God on our behalf: he took

manhood to suffer for the sins of the world, to humble himself unto
death, and to make intercession for sinners with 'a true, a natural, and
a sensible touch of mercie.'

In this introductory chapter to his Trinitarian and christological doctrine, Hooker turns to John of Damascus[21] to support his summary of
how God is in Christ in the Incarnation.

In *De Fide Orthodoxa*, as the Damascene moves to consider the
revealed *theologia* and *oeconomia* (Trinity and Incarnation) he quotes
the dictum of Gregory the Theologian that Hooker would acknowledge
to be the principle that guides all of christological doctrine, and which
will encourage him to turn to Cyril:

> [Christ] in His entirety assumed me in my entirety and was wholly united
> to the whole, so that He might bestow the grace of salvation upon the
> whole. For that which has not been assumed cannot be healed.[22]

Although Hooker's several summaries of the oecumenical councils in
these chapters always conclude with Chalcedon in 451, and he asserts
that all errors in Christology can be reduced to one of the four principal heresies refuted in the 'fower most ancient general Councels',[23]
in turning to John of Damascus Hooker acknowledges that there was
continued debate after Chalcedon about just how this individual person
Jesus Christ could be both of, and in, the two natures of divinity and
humanity. John of Damascus's *De Fide Orthodoxa* is a recapitulation
and resolution of three centuries of debate among various groups of
Neo-Chalcedonians, Nestorians and Monophysites over the definitions
of the notions of *ousia*, *physis*, *hypostasis* and *prosopon*. Thus Hooker's
first quotation acknowledges this history in presenting John's definition:

> The hypostasis has that which is common (τὸ κοινὸν) along with
> that with is individuating (ἰδιάζοντος), [i.e. substance plus accidents
> or characteristic properties.] Ousia does not subsist in itself but is to
> be perceived/contemplated (θεωρεῖται) in individuals (ὑποστάσεσι).[24]

In Hooker's second quote from John of Damascus in this section the
Damascene quotes Dionysios the Areopagite (Hooker's chief source in
his general philosophy of Law, or *lex divinitatis*):[25]

> The Father and the Holy Ghost have no communion (κεκοινώνηκεν)
> with the incarnation of the word (τῇ σαρκώσει τοῦ λόγου) otherwise
> than by approbation and assent (their good pleasure and will).[26]

But most interesting is Hooker's third passage from John of Damascus, where he points to John's notion of *perichoresis*. The Damascene had gathered up and reconciled various strands of christological thinking after Chalcedon in his embellishment of the notion of *perichoresis* that had roots back to Gregory the Theologian. In the section of *De Fide Orthodoxa* to which Hooker refers,[27] John promotes the term *perichoresis* as adequate both to Trinitarian and christological doctrine in describing a type of mutual indwelling or immanence that protects the identity and difference of the Persons of the Trinity on one hand, and of the divine and human natures of Christ on the other.[28] In Hooker's consideration of the *communicatio idiomatum* he cautions that the union must not be seen as 'any mutuall *participation* whereby the properties of the one are infused into the other'[29] but rather the notion of *perichoresis* serves to protect the asymmetry of the union, allowing the divine nature to take the initiative and essentially to remain unaffected by that which it indwells or pervades; or as Hooker says, the 'union doth ad perfection to the weaker, to the nobler no alteration at all.'[30]

> Such then is the manner of this exchange by which each nature (φύσεως) communicates its own properties to the other through the identity of their person (τῆς ὑποστάσεως) and their mutual immanence (τὴν εἰς ἀλληλα αὐτῶν περιχώρησιν).[31]

Thus Hooker learns from John of Damascus that the notion of *perichoresis*, or mutual indwelling is adequate to how God is in Christ (*theologia*) and how Christ is in us (*oeconomia*).

We also note that in this section of John's *De Fide Orthodoxa*,[32] which Hooker has before him, John quotes Cyril more than any other author. More significantly, John alludes to Cyril's controversy with Theodoret over theopaschitism, and we shall now see that this controversy becomes an important theme in Hooker's understanding of how Christ has assumed the totality of humanity for its salvation.

Cyril of Alexandria and Theopaschitism

At the beginning of *Lawes* V.52, Hooker cautions that in respect to the Incarnation:

> It is not in mans habilitie either to expresse perfectlie or conceive the maner how this was brought to passe . . . Howbeit because this

divine mysterie is more true than plaine, divers having framed the same to theire owne conceipts and phancies are found in their expositions thereof more plaine than true.[33]

After Hooker presents one of his several summaries of the four ecumenical councils, most of *Lawes* V.52 is given to a close examination of the error of Nestorius, introduced by a quote from Cyril's letter to Eulogius, a priest in Constantinople (*c*.433–5). The passage states that Nestorius errs in denying the union of natures in Christ. Hooker focuses positively on Cyril's role in identifying the Nestorian heresy condemned at Ephesus in 431, and then goes out of his way to insist that Cyril did not hold the position that 'even as in the bodie and the soule, so in Christ God and man make but one nature'.[34] Hooker clearly knows that the most recurring image in Cyril of the union of godhead and humanity in Christ is precisely that of the manner of the union of the soul and body in man. It is this image in particular that Cyril uses to support his strong claim that in the Incarnation the Eternal Word suffers, and that the Word's engagement in human sorrows is the supreme redemptive principle. I think that this aspect of Cyril's thinking is embraced by Hooker and critical to his argument, and that is why Hooker insists that Cyril uses this image appropriately. The inappropriate use of the image of body and soul to suggest that there is one nature in Christ is the error of Eutyches, who was condemned at Chalcedon. In keeping with Hooker's appropriation of Cyril's teaching that the suffering of the Word brings within the Godhead the fragile and suffering flesh for the purpose of redemption and return of the creative order to its First Cause, Hooker concludes his discussion with reference to a passage from Theodoret's third *Dialogue*: 'The divine nature must be confessed inseparable from the flesh even on the cross and in the tomb.'[35] This is a surprising passage for Hooker to quote because it appears in Theodoret's third Dialogue in the *Eranistes*, written a year or two after the death of Cyril, in which under the guise of his literary heretic Theodoret ridicules Cyril's paradoxical turn of phrase that the Son suffered impassively. Nonetheless, because of Theodoret's continuing influence on English eucharistic theology since Peter Martyr introduced the *Eranistes* to Cranmer,[36] Hooker must show substantial agreement between Theodoret and Cyril, and this expression is the closest Theodoret would come to Cyril's extreme language of the suffering God. I suggest that for Hooker's overall argument of how God is in Christ, how Christ is in us and how we are partakers of Christ in the sacraments, Hooker seeks to embrace a Cyrillian Christology that allows the fullness of God's presence in the world by bringing suffering within the life of the Trinity while at the same time denying suffering in the inner life of the Trinity.[37] This paradoxical language is an instance where 'this divine mysterie is more true than plaine.'

As Hooker says in *Lawes* V.52:

> in Christ there is no personal subsistence but one, and that from everlasting. By taking only the nature of man he still continueth one person . . . Whereupon it followeth against Nestorius, that no person was born of the virgin but the Sonne of God, no person but the Sonne of God baptized, the Sonne of God condemned, the Sonne of God and no other person crucified . . .

Hooker concludes his discussion of the *communicatio idiomatum* in *Lawes* V.53 by pointing to the fifth-century christological debate between Cyril and Theodoret over divine impassivity:

> Theodoret disputeth with great earnestnes that God cannot be said to suffer. But he thereby meaneth Christes divine nature against Apollinarius which held even deitie it selfe passible. Cyrill on the other side against Nestorius as much contendeth, that whosoever will denie verie God to have suffered death doth forsake the faith. Which notwithstandinge to hold were heresie, if the name of God in this assertion did not importe as it doth the person of Christ, who being verily God suffereth death, but in the flesh, and not in that substance for which the name of God is given him.[38]

Hooker is referring to Cyril's third letter to Nestorius in AD 430, to which were attached twelve anathemas. The twelfth anathema pushed the limits of Trinitarian doctrine:

> If anyone does not confess that the Word of God suffered in the flesh, was crucified in the flesh, and tasted death in the flesh, becoming the first-born from the dead, although as God he is life and life-giving, let him be anathema.

Theodoret – representative of the Antiochene tradition – was convinced that this language violated the impassible God of Nicaea and that Cyril allowed the human pathos of Jesus to touch the godhead. Indeed, the entire argument of the three dialogues of Theodoret's *Eranistes* (*c.*447–8), so influential in the development of eucharistic doctrine in England in the second half of the sixteenth century, was to reject Cyril's notion of 'impassible suffering of the Son' as nonsensical. In Frances Young's phrase, Theodoret accused Cyril of destroying 'the Godness of God'.[39]

Hooker knows all this, and he knows that Cyril refused to recant. Cyril was primarily a biblical exegete and in passages like John 1.14, Hebrews 2.14–17 and Philippians 2 (all cited by Hooker in this section), Cyril read how the Son participated fully in human limitation. The biblical text spoke of a Christ who both suffered and was God. For Cyril, the Antiochene position represented by Theodoret meant that the great gulf separating God and the world had not been bridged at all. In respect to the 'divine mysterie', Theodoret's position is 'more plaine than true'.

The paradox of impassible suffering points to the soteriological purpose of the Incarnation, inviting our participation in the eternal life of triune love. The Son's suffering does not merely demonstrate God's solidarity with us. By being incarnate the Eternal Son took on a state in which he could in some real sense experience suffering and death.[40] That which is not assumed is not healed. Or, as Cyril says, our deification and enjoyment of the life of God requires that 'he took what was ours to be his very own so that we might have all that was his'.[41] Hooker tells us (*Lawes* V.54): 'The union therefore of the flesh with deitie is to that flesh a guift of principall grace and favor. For by virtue of this grace man is reallie made God.'[42]

Hooker concludes *Lawes* V.53 by championing both Theodoret and Cyril, allowing Hooker to embrace Theodoret as an authority yet at the same time to affirm a Cyrillian emphasis on how Christ is in us.

Conclusion

In these chapters (*Lawes* V.50–6), Richard Hooker shows 'How God is in Christ, how Christ is in us', and in subsequent chapters he will consider how the sacraments make us partakers with Christ. We have seen that the structure of Hooker's commentary on the sacraments in the Book of Common Prayer is in keeping with the general tendency of the magisterial reformers who avoid the scholastic question of how Christ is localized in the eucharistic elements, and rather embrace the Greek Patristic tradition in which the Eucharist is an anamnesis of the whole Christ-event: the doctrine of the Eucharist recapitulates the doctrine of the person of Christ.[43] Thus the doctrine of the sacraments is essentially Trinitarian and christological doctrine.

Theodoret, Cyril and John of Damascus all consider the meaning of the Eucharist itself in these passages we have been considering. In the second Dialogue of *Eranistes*, Theodoret writes that as the flesh assumed by the Son of God remains flesh while deified, so likewise the bread and wine of the Eucharist retain their creaturely natures after the consecration. This is the critical theme of the magisterial reformers in response to the doctrine of Transubstantiation of the Church of Rome, and is emphasized likewise by Hooker.

But significantly, Hooker also highlights Cyril's language of the Eucharist, referring several times to Cyril's third letter to Nestorius in which his use of the expression 'impassible suffering' is followed by a description of how communicants are sanctified by 'becoming participants in the holy flesh and the precious blood of Christ'. Communicants receive 'the personal, truly vitalizing (lifegiving) very-flesh of God the Word himself'.[44] In his commentary on John's Gospel, Cyril emphasizes that Christ comes to dwell in us more and more fully as we partake of the eucharistic flesh and blood. Thus as Christ is more fully in us, we participate more fully in the divine nature. When Hooker speaks powerfully of 'our participation also in the fruit grace and efficacie of his bodie and blood, whereupon there ensueth a kind of transubstantiation in us, a true change both of soule and bodie . . .', he cites Cyril's commentary on John: 'Since the redeeming flesh, joined to the word of God, which is by nature life, has become life-giving, when we eat it, then have we life in us, being joined to that Flesh which has been made life.'[45]

At the beginning of this chapter we noted that Hooker promises that through the 'meane between both which is both' we are made partakers of the divine nature (1 Peter 1.4). Hooker tells us that in the Incarnation God has deified our nature,[46] that man is an associate of God both in his deified humanity and in his divinity, and that by virtue of the unity of flesh with divinity man is 'reallie made God'.[47] Lately several scholars have pointed to the theme of 'deification' in Cyril, and we suggest that Hooker's robust understanding of deification can reasonably be traced to his reading of Cyril of Alexandria. Norman Russell says that 'Cyril brings the doctrine of deification . . . to full maturity'.[48] But as a recent study of divinization in Cyril suggests, Cyril faced the challenge of untangling the complicated notion of participation in order to speak of deification without collapsing the primary distinction between the uncreated and the created. Cyril struggles to maintain the asymmetrical character of the union of the natures in Christ. We have identified that it is precisely here that Hooker depends on the mature notion of *perichoresis* in John of Damascus to protect his Trinitarian and christological orthodoxy.

Hooker also discovers in Cyril another side of the fifth-century christological debates that informs and deepens the efficacy of the Prayer

Book liturgy. Cyril represents a tradition that emphasized God's intimate presence in and to creation. For Hooker, Theodoret was too narrow in his relentless efforts to avoid the potential 'confusion' of God
and creature and thus (representative of the Antiochene position) too
much emphasized God's *otherness* in regard to creation. Cyril, on the
other hand, represents a tradition that stretches language to paradox
and is willing to rest in the poetry and paradoxes found in Scripture,
embracing the fullness of God's presence in His creation. Thus in Cyril's
hermeneutic we find the possibility of the re-enchantment of nature.
The Word has taken all of our human flesh and human experiences,
including our limitations and our suffering, to be His own. In the gift
of the Holy Spirit, and in the personal, substantial eucharistic presence
of Christ we become partakers of the divine nature. Cyril's theology is
consistent with Hooker's all-embracing *lex divinitatis* that he inherits
from Dionysius and is summed up in *Lawes* V.56 in terms of exitus/
reditus, cause and effect, creation and redemption. As for Dionysius, so
for Richard Hooker, the whole of the created order is theophany: both
divine transcendence and divine immanence simultaneously.

Equally for Hooker, in the sacramental principles drawn from the
Scriptures, interpreted by the Greek Patristic tradition, and expressed
in the Prayer Book liturgy, the whole of the created order can be
described as sacramental in character. The natural order does not lose
its autonomy, beauty or integrity but the divinity is made present to
the individual believer precisely through the integrity of the natural
order. The conversion, *metanoia*, and transfiguration occur within the
believer himself by participation in Christ.

As theophany and sacrament the goodness and integrity of the natural order is fully acknowledged, yet it is not exhaustive of its meaning:
the natural points to a transcendence and immanence that ultimately,
in return, gives the deeper meaning and reverence to nature itself that
many young people of our generation are seeking. On the one hand, the
thoroughly secular students who arrive at my small liberal arts university each year typically are convinced that an objectifying and reduction-
ist view of nature has contributed to its exploitation and destruction. On
the other hand, these students reject the God of institutional Christianity
that represents an unresolved separation or duality between the divine
and the world. Thus many of these students remain restless for a way of
'thinking' that makes sense of their apprehension of transcendence and
immanence in the natural world and human community.

They seek to know the world as theophany: to acknowledge the presence of the divine throughout a natural order that is 'drenched with

divinity'. They also seek to know the world as sacrament: our return to what makes us truly human is through the natural order that is deified, and not in overcoming or destroying the natural order.

The Anglican sacraments, as interpreted by Hooker in the light of the Greek Fathers, encourage a particular world view: a way of seeing and interpreting the whole of experience as theophany and sacrament, making us partakers of the divine within the created order and leading us to know our happiness by living the life of God the Holy Trinity. As Thomas Traherne, next generation to Hooker, would express it:

From dust I rise
And out of nothing now awake;
These brighter regions which salute mine eyes
A gift from God I take:
The earth, the seas, the light, the day, the skies,
The sun and stars are mine; if these I prize.

Long time before
I in my mother's womb was born,
A God preparing did this glorious store,
This world for me adorn,
Into this Eden so divine and fair,
So wide and bright, I come, his son and heir,

A stranger here
Strange things doth meet, strange glories see,
Strange treasures lodg'd in this fair world appear,
Strange all and new to me:
But that they mine should be who nothing was,
That strangest is of all; yet brought to pass.[49]

Notes

1 As C. S. Lewis points out, Hooker's universe is 'drenched with Deity'. C. S. Lewis, *English Literature in the Sixteenth Century, Excluding Drama* (Oxford: Clarendon Press, 1954), p. 462.

2 John Booty calls the concept of participation 'the philosophical-theological key to Hooker's theology in Book V' (*The Folger Library Edition of the Works of Richard Hooker* [hereafter FLE], vol. VI, pt 1, p. 197), but the consideration of participation provides integrity to the whole of the *Lawes*.

3 *Lawes* V is an *apologia* and commentary on the entire Book of Common Prayer and *Lawes* V.50 begins the commentary on the sacraments.

4 John Booty, FLE, *ibid.*

5 *Lawes* 1.2.2; FLE 1:59.5.

6 *Lawes* V.56.1; FLE 2:235.1–3.

7 In concluding these to be the very principles of knowing and being, Hooker looked to the sixth-century Dionysius, who in turn was explicating in Christian terms the thinking of his near-contemporary Proclus: 'Every effect remains in its cause, proceeds from it, and reverts upon it' (*The Elements of Theology*, Proposition 35).

8 *Lawes* I.11.2; FLE 1.

9 *Lawes* V.56.10; FLE 2:242.8.

10 *Lawes* V.56.6–7; FLE 2:238.6–18.

11 The divine good, says Aristotle, is 'a life too high for man' (*Nicomachean Ethics*, X.7), though, at the same time, it is the only end of human longing and man's only final happiness.

12 *Lawes* V.54.5; FLE 2:224.14–18.

13 *Lawes* V.60.2; FLE 2:255.9–13.

14 *Lawes* V.67.1; FLE 2:330.

15 *Lawes* V.50.3; FLE 2:208.22–209.2.

16 Cf. A. S. McGrade, 'Classical, Patristic and Medieval Sources', in Torrance Kirby (ed.), *A Companion to Richard Hooker* (Leiden: Brill, 2008), pp. 51–87 (p. 67).

17 H. Ashley Hall, *Philip Melanchthon and the Cappadocians: A Reception of Greek Patristic Sources in the Sixteenth Century* (Göttingen: Vandenhoeck & Ruprecht, 2014), p. 192.

18 Marvin Anderson, *Peter Martyr, A Reformer in Exile (1542–1562): A Chronology of Biblical Writings in England and Europe* (Nieuwkoop: De Graaf, 1975), pp. 90–1.

19 Marvin Anderson, 'Rhetoric and Reality: Peter Martyr and the English Reformation', *Sixteenth Century Journal* 19:3 (1988), pp. 451–69 (p. 462).

20 Hooker would have been familiar with Thomas Cranmer's use of Cyril's Commentary on John in his *Writings and Disputations Relative to the Sacrament of the Lord's Supper*. Cf. *ibid.* (Parker Society: Cambridge, 1844), pp. 165–72. But Hooker reads Cyril more broadly and significantly considers Cyril's dispute with Theodoret over divine impassibility, thus introducing aspects of Cyril's theology not referenced by Cranmer.

21 *De Fide Orthodoxa* III.3–11. Note that quotations are taken from Frederic H. Chase (trans.), *St. John of Damascus: Writings* (Washington, DC: Catholic University of America Press, 1958).

22 *De Fide Orthodoxa* III.6.

23 '. . . the Council of Nice to define against Arians, against Apollinarians the Council of Constantinople, the Council of Ephesus against Nestorians, against Eutichians the Calcedon Councell', *Lawes* V.54.10; FLE 2.227.3–5.

24 *Lawes* V.51.1; FLE 2.209.note m; *De Fide Orthodoxa* III.6.

25 This same sentence is repeated at *De Fide Orthodoxa* III.11 as a conclusion to John's consideration of Cyril's expression, 'the One Incarnate Nature of the Word of God'. Since Hooker also directly discusses the orthodoxy of this

Cyrillian expression, Hooker points the reader to both places where this passage appears in the text of *De Fide Orthodoxa*, Bk III.

26 *Lawes* V.51.2; FLE 2.210.8–9. Note that FLE 5.717 cites *De Fide Orthodoxa* III.11 as Hooker's source, which is a close variation, but the actual quote is from III.6, several paras after Hooker's first quotation in this section.

27 *De Fide Orthodoxa* III.5, 6.

28 'One must know . . . that although we say that the natures of the Lord (τοῦ κυρίου φύσεις) are mutually immanent (περιχωρεῖν ἐν ἀλλήλαις), we know that the immanence (περιχώρησις) comes from the divine nature (τῆς θείας φύσεως). For this last pervades all things and indwells (περιχωρεῖ) as it wishes, but nothing pervades it. And it communicates its own splendours to the flesh while remaining impassible (ἀπαθὴς) and having no part in the affections of the flesh.'

29 *Lawes* V.53.3; FLE 2.219.3.

30 *Lawes* V.54.4; FLE 2.223.7.

31 *De Fide Orthodoxa* III.7.

32 *De Fide Orthodoxa* III.3–11.

33 *Lawes* V.52.1; FLE 2.211.29–32.

34 *Lawes* V.52.4; FLE 2.215.25ff.

35 *Lawes* V.52.4; FLE 2.216.4.

36 Theodoret's discussion of the Eucharist is in the second Dialogue of the *Eranistes*, also quoted by Hooker in this section.

37 See the insightful consideration of this theme in John McGuckin, *Saint Cyril of Alexandria and the Christological Controversy* (Crestwood, NY: St Vladimir's Seminary Press, 2004), pp. 198–207. Cf. John O'Keefe, 'Impassible Suffering? Divine Passion and Fifth-Century Christology', *Theological Studies* 58:1 (1997), pp. 39–60 (p. 43).

38 *Lawes* V.53.4; FLE 2.220.8–17.

39 Frances M. Young, *From Nicaea to Chalcedon: A Guide to the Literature and its Background*, 2nd edn (Philadelphia, PA: Fortress Press, 2010), p. 333. Cf. O'Keefe, 'Impassible Suffering?', pp. 39–60.

40 Young, *op. cit.*, p. 337.

41 St Cyril of Alexandria, *On the Unity of Christ*, trans. John McGuckin (Crestwood, NY: St Vladimir's Seminary Press, 1995), p. 59.

42 *Lawes* V.54.3; FLE 2.222.21.

43 Hall, op. cit., p. 192.

44 Third Letter of Cyril to Nestorius, p. 270.

45 *Lawes* V.67.11; FLE 2.339.6–8, quoting Cyril, *In Evangelium Joannis*, 4.14. In keeping with the reformers, Cyril nowhere explains how the elements are transformed, or the manner in which the consecrated bread and wine may be understood as Christ's body and blood.

46 *Lawes* V.54.5; FLE 2:224.14–18. 'Finally since God has *deified* our nature, though not by turning it into himself, yet by making it his own inseparable habitation, we cannot now conceive how God should without man either exercise divine power or receive the glory of divine praise. For man is in both an associate of Deity.'

47 *Lawes* V.54.3; FLE 2:222.21.

48 Norman Russell, 'The Concept of Deification in the Early Greek Fathers' (unpublished doctoral thesis, Oxford University, 1988), p. 436, cited by Daniel Keating, 'Divinization in Cyril: The Appropriation of Divine Life', in Thomas G. Weinandy and Daniel A. Keating (eds), *The Theology of S Cyril of Alexandria* (Edinburgh: T. & T. Clark, 2003), p. 149.

49 From 'The Salutation', in Lord David Cecil (ed.), *The Oxford Book of Christian Verse* (Oxford: Clarendon Press, 1940), p. 272.

11

The Gothic Revival, Pre-Raphaelitism and Trinitarian Art in Britain

AYLA LEPINE

In his multi-volume publication *The Stones of Venice*, the Victorian artist and critic John Ruskin wrote:

> . . . imperfection is in some sort essential to all that we know of life. It is the sign of life in a mortal body, that is to say, of a state of progress and change. Nothing that lives is, or can be, rigidly perfect; part of it is decaying, part nascent . . . All admit irregularity as they imply change; and to banish imperfection is to destroy expression, to check exertion, to paralyse vitality.[1]

This chapter explores the source of life and creation itself, the Trinity, through Victorian and early twentieth-century British art that searched for spiritual understanding in visual terms for this sense of changeful vitality. The artworks that engaged with the vitality of the triune God did not do so by attempting to mirror God's own profound perfection but by attempting to represent something bespoke and personal as a response to the ultimate, changeless, perfect vitality of God. The artworks considered here are explorations of the Trinitarian impulse to love, give, share, relate and to differ in tension with unity. Art in this context is a reification of theological possibility, at once made concrete through material means and also created as a deliberate and ongoing task of destabilization; the artworks discussed here pose questions about the Trinity as well as attending to Trinitarian theology's assertions in new ways. Stained glass by Edward Burne-Jones or an early twentieth-century rood screen by Temple Moore remind us of what we consistently need to know: 'The Trinity makes creatures distinct in order to unite them: they differ in order to love.'[2] The visual arts present a challenge in this regard in numerous ways. In one sense, art creates an apparently easy route towards simplicity of perception of the complexities of the Trinity by establishing symbolic and iconographical language.

This apparent ease is an aspect of intersecting priorities in theology and the arts, which must be acknowledged and then, if possible, kept in check unless there is a claim to be made that art in the service of religion cannot do more than illustrate. Sarah Coakley's work on the Trinity and the arts is sensitive to this, as she presents a veritable catalogue of Trinitarian artwork across more than a thousand years, several media and over thirty examples. This survey is an 'introductory reflection' that stimulates further consideration of how the Trinity operates within the visual arts, spurring new theological dialogue.[3] Janet Martin Soskice and Sarah Coakley both affirm that art does not – and indeed cannot – 'describe what it is like chez God', but instead it advances a prospect of imaginative and creative visualization of Trinitarian possibility in terms that go beyond classic tropes of 'threeness', literalist or banal representations of family relations and so on.[4] As Coakley affirms:

> art does not simply illustrate doctrine as a kind of anodyne teaching aid for something already settled theologically elsewhere. No, theological art at its best can enable – in a way that on this supposition *only* the arts can – doctrine's creative new expression, animus, and efficacy.[5]

Moreover, the use of art as a horizon of engagement with Trinitarian theology can constitute a productive disturbance and reshaping of points of access to belief and theological debate that Coakley sees as a feminist impulse, and asks questions of interpretation and production that align with feminist art historical methods across decades of research and analysis.[6]

There are several classic types of Western and Eastern depictions of the Trinity:

- three figures, in the spirit of Genesis 18 and the three strangers who visited Abraham;
- the *Gnadenstuhl* or Throne of Grace;
- a three-headed body; a three-leafed clover;
- Christ at his baptism with the Spirit descending like a dove and the Father overhead;
- the three-pronged shield inscribed with text stating 'is' and 'is not' to relate the Father, Son and Holy Spirit to one another as three Persons and one God.

In another sense, the visual arts and architecture – differentiated from though sharing much in common with music, dance and even poetry – cannot, it would seem, pin down the dynamic energy of the Trinity in that the medium can never be the message. Oil paint affixed to a treated board or canvas is necessarily a medium bound in stasis not in movement, from the moment it is completed. However, even without entering into the vast theological and aesthetic zone of Orthodox icons and their capacity to be prayerful windows on to the lives of the saints in the realm of human sensorial experience, the potential for visual art – painting, stained glass, sculpture and indeed architectural form – to elucidate something of the Trinity's energies in a profound and insightful manner is rarely explored and too often overlooked. Art as theology, not merely as illustrative or adjacent to theological concepts and debates, can create a fruitful nexus through which visual culture may connect humanity with the divine.

Art, Trinity and *Imago Dei*

As Eugene F. Rogers observes, 'In the Trinity, God is always on the move, and God's movement is love. The Trinity enacts perfect love already in itself, and gives it to rational creatures without cost or cause – an act unnecessary but characteristic.'[7] The nature of that move – love – is attended to in a provocative phrasing by Rowan Williams too: the Trinity's 'whole life is a "being-for", a movement of gift';[8] joyfully relational and bound together in being propelled by participation in and through love among persons. Rogers, when interpreting Aquinas' position on the Trinity, writes:

> In love, the Father regards the truth with joy, generating the Son; in love, the Father wills the good with joy, breathing the Spirit. Love completes itself in three persons, no more, no fewer, and all God's moves come from gratuitous love.[9]

He hooks this claim to his understanding that for Aquinas, there are 'two occasions of joy' that invite the flow of love that characterizes the on-the-move Trinity: 'understanding truth and willing good'.[10] The production of art itself and the spiritual conditions in which creativity thrives is a reflection of that 'movement of gift' and the human capacity for 'gratuitous' making is both a sign of love for God and a sign of our own shared identity as the *imago Dei*.[11]

Recent postulations on the *imago Dei* and theological aesthetics help to forge a path towards understanding what is at stake in the artworks produced by Moore, Burne-Jones and others in modern Britain. As Gerhard Ebeling has observed, as an image points to more than its own reality – and this is particularly true of theological imagery – the image is threefold: that which is represented; the creator; and the viewer.[12] Interacting with Ebeling's ideas, Claudia Welz writes:

> Thus, the God-relationship takes place through God's image in that the image conveys an awareness both of God and of the human being. The relations between the signified, the creator and the viewer of the image interpenetrate each other insofar as God is at the same time the content and the origin of the image and insofar as the image shows something about God and man alike, and insofar as the image can be viewed by God and other human beings.

For Welz, then, 'Being God's image is the human way of being related to God, and this relation includes personality and linguisticality (*sic*).'[13] Welz rides out the threshold of being and becoming, and of the distinction between image, icon and idol, with care in her discussion of the inherent human essence of what it is – and is not – to be made in the image of God. While she does not extend her discussion to art-making in a sustained way, she does offer a pertinent reminder in relation to the present task of considering a cluster of British artworks that invoke Trinitarian themes in surprising and against-the-grain as well as more conventional ways. Welz asks:

> . . . is the *imago Dei* a pure icon? If it were, it would be an idol, because it would lose that which is essential for it: the reference to the invisible God. If the *imago Dei* were nothing more than self-referential, then it would serve the human being's apotheosis.

Avoiding this trap, then, Welz turns to relationality and difference in the midst of intimacy in order to parse the delicate textures of human–divine image-inhabiting:

> If we wish to preserve the idea of the dissimilarity between God and man, we must preserve the relationality implied in the *imago Dei*. The idea of dissimilarity is, in turn, derivative of the idea of similarity.[14]

It is nearness and distance as well as similarity and dissimilarity – not only between God and humanity in God's artistry and our own artistic capacities but also between the Divine Persons of the Trinity – that is engaged when Trinitarian visual theology takes place. These images are by their very nature unsettling, representing the trifold unrepresentable I AM in ways that necessarily open out new theological questions about who God is not only in the moment of the image's making but also in all subsequent moments of perceiving and interpreting. There is a tantalizing energy, therefore, in the rhetorical question Grace Jantzen has asked in her work towards a new and urgent theology of beauty: 'what if beauty and truth were to mutually destabilize and enrich one another?'[15] In every instance of Trinitarian art, I suggest, this productive destabilization is no less than unavoidable, and this is both exciting and positive for research in visual culture and in theology.

To make art at all is to participate in a sacramental manifestation of Trinitarian reflection. So claimed numerous modern artists in Britain, including David Jones and Eric Gill, both of whom interwove art, craft, worship and liturgy and both of whom were seeking critical and innovative perspectives on the artists in religious contexts who had gone immediately before them in Britain's creative history. In the works of art addressed here, produced in the final decades of the long nineteenth century, notions of surface and depth as well as distance and intimate nearness are put into play by artists who explore Trinitarian mystery with a variety of views. 'Humans image God best when they vary most in their ways', suggests Rogers. Encounter with God as Three-in-One through grace and by analogy not only encourages art but also demands it – a love beyond words requires other forms of thought and communication, aware that none would ever be sufficient. And indeed, this is a crucial point. Neither in the artistic traditions of baptismal imagery and the *Gnadenstuhl*, nor in the artworks assembled here that touch on prayer, the passion and frail yet persistent hope, can the Trinity be depicted in a truly stable, truly articulate way. Like theological enquiry, the question must be asked, teased out and explored, even if the answer remains with God. It is in this zone of the mind and of the soul that Rogers can suppose, with language helpful for the investigation of Trinitarian British modern art, that: 'The Trinity is not just the farthest out in theological speculation: it is also the deepest in.'[16]

Gothic Revival Trinities

The first pair of artworks expressive of Trinitarian theology are the most apparently conventional of the five works discussed here. The first is the rood imagery chosen by Temple Moore for Pusey House's chapel, together with another Trinitarian image in the context of university sacred space. While the rood is painted wood, the Trinity image by Edward Burne-Jones in Jesus College Chapel in Cambridge is in stained glass, part of a complex programme of windows that align images of the four Evangelists between two sibyls with a trio of narratives from their respective Gospels.

In October 1914 the chapel of Pusey House in Oxford was consecrated; it represented an assertion of Catholicity within the heart of the Church and yet as it was not a college chapel its cultural significance was to be on the blurred edge of the University's relationships between religion and education.[17] The rood's western façade, facing into the nave from above the high altar, offers a typically medievalist image of Christ on the cross between the Virgin Mary and St John the Evangelist. Beneath, three angels hold a banner stating 'Deus scientiarum Dominus' – the Lord is the God of knowledge. This passage from 1 Samuel 2, the Song of Hannah and its immediate context is a reminder of God's power in relation to the need for humility. The eastern façade of the rood contains a less conventional array of symbols that connect the salvific scandal of the Crucifixion to the reality of the Trinity.

There are four roundels: the topmost is a hand with its index finger pointing downwards, a symbol of the Father's will. The bottom is the dove of the Holy Spirit facing outwards; at the north and south ends of the cross, surrounded by crockets and florets, are mirror images of the crucified Son on the reverse of the wooden polychromed sculpture. On the south side, four ears of wheat are arranged with a circular dynamism around a central host; on the north, a chalice is suspended between two bunches of grapes. All of these symbols are highly legible; their arrangement is innovative and stylistically striking. Moreover, in the centre of the cross another roundel, containing the IHS monogram, re-inscribes Christ yet again. There is a threeness beyond threeness at work here in relation to the Trinity and Christ's crucial passion role within it: on the eastern façade of the cross the image of Christ in the Eucharist and in his holy name form a horizontal triad; they intersect with the verticality of Christ's corpus on the reverse, and together these four images form a trinity of their own between the Eucharist, the name of Jesus and the body of the crucified God, suspended between the Father's will and the Spirit's immanent witness at the lower and upper edges of the cross. The eastern façade's symbolic language assists in offering theological heft to the western nave-facing surface of bodies. The opacity of the object creates a theological lucidity regarding Trinitarian identity and the work of atonement in the round.

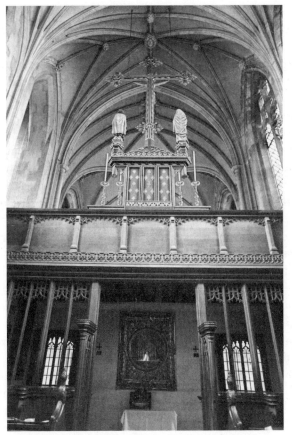

Temple Moore, Pusey House Chapel rood, 1914, Oxford.

From Oxford to Cambridge and from Moore's work to that of a medievalist Victorian predecessor, the Trinitarian visual theology of Edward Burne-Jones in the stained-glass scheme for Jesus College Chapel considers the relational distinctiveness of Father, Son and Holy Spirit in a different way. Jesus College benefits from one of the most extensive stained-glass schemes undertaken by Morris & Company. Burne-Jones' glass designs were always highly alive to the translucency and fragility of the medium, so different from the necessary opacity of painting. As Caroline Arscott explains in relation to a late scheme in Birmingham: 'part-picture, part-assemblage, [Burne-Jones' panels] combine the weightiness of silica and lead with acute awareness for the viewer of weightless, channelled light and transmitted colour . . . They activate questions about ornament, embodiment, literal presence, illusion and spirit.'[18]

Produced in the late 1870s, the glass programme in the chapel at Jesus includes images of the nine orders of angels and the *imago Dei* in ten lights, allegorical Christian virtues standing above their opposites, Old Testament prophets and, in the north transept, the four Evangelists in the act of writing with sibyls at either side.[19] In these four windows the long upper panels are matched with three smaller panels beneath, each of which depicts a narrative episode or a theological element of the Evangelist's Gospel. In the Johannine window, an image of the Trinity appears on the right of the lower trio. Here, the Father and the Son occupy a double-seat, holding an orb, with an image of the Spirit as a dove hovering between them. The bird is not stylized as motionless but is evidently in a delicate state of dynamic movement; the Father and the Son exert a tenderness in their emotive faces and countenances, and the universe-orb they hold is reminiscent of another moment, connected to Christ's pre-existence as *logos* in the making of the world. Burne-Jones had considered the orb-world as a visual trope before, in his *Days of Creation* series, and the inclusion of this abstract form in the Jesus Chapel window indicates a Trinitarian paradox of representation as much as a Creation one. Burne-Jones' interactions with the Bible were myriad, and as Caroline Arscott observes, his unconventionality was a door to impactful theological experimentation:

> His own religious beliefs were somewhat unorthodox, aligned neither with the Methodism of his wife's background nor with the Church of Rome, nor with the high church fashion of the Church of England. A conviction of the importance of the divine remained with him through his life, though. The terrors and joys of experience that are conveyed in his work and the fascinating mystery that colours his scenarios have a spiritual aspect that is fundamental to his outlook.[20]

The envisaging of Genesis' creative ultimacy as spherical is hardly new, but the relationship between the Father, Son, Spirit and sphere offers a theological insight in visual terms. The world's creation as a whole cannot be contained in an image and thus the orb becomes a sign of inability to represent the act or its outcomes fully. Similarly, the trope of two males, one older, one younger, sharing a seat and in the presence of a bird points to the inability to represent God as well as the act of doing so. As Coakley writes: 'There is the importance, too, of the avoidance of crassly literal male anthropomorphisms, or an overdominance of the Father–Son relations to the exclusion of the Spirit.'[21] Arguably, Burne-Jones' image is both a part of this classic masculine divine trope as well as a complication of it in the feminized masculine sensibility of his Christ figure as well as the composition overall. Burne-Jones' strategy is both compelling and understandable as he was an artist who spent much of his career transgressing conventions in representing masculine and feminine figures by producing provocatively androgynous imagery. The artist's androgynous depictions can be seen in numerous panels of the Jesus College Chapel glass scheme, and Burne-Jones' Christ in the Trinity window is part of this androgynous aesthetic.

Trinitarian Returns and Embodiments

The co-founder of the Pre-Raphaelite Brotherhood, John Everett Millais, exhibited *The Return of the Dove to the Ark* at the Royal Academy in 1851, the same year as Charles Allston Collins' *Convent Thoughts*. Both were owned by Thomas Combe in Oxford, and together with William Holman Hunt's monumental image of a Christian family sheltering a fleeing monk from a crowd of angry druids, these three religious paintings formed a triptych in the Combe household before being given to the Ashmolean in 1893.[22]

The painting, for which Millais also designed the verdant frame, with its olive foliage a contrast for the dry wisps of straw that line the bottom of the picture, depicts Noah's young daughters comforting the dove who has returned with a sign of the receding waters – a small sprig of olive – in its mouth. The theme, in addition to Millais' unique approach to representing the Noachic narrative in Genesis, is surely that of the surprising gratitude with which one may respond to new life. The girl on the left holds the bird and scrutinizes the little leaves of green, fresh olive. Her sister reacts differently, holding onto the other girl's arm for tender balance as she presses her lips and nose gently into the dove's feathers, as a kind of Thomas pressing his fingers into Christ's wounds, needing material sensual contact in order to believe that a decimating tragedy could be transformed by God's love. Without resorting to the banality of threeness, it is notable to point out the trio of heads – the two girls with the dove between; the cluster of emerald green leaves; the trio of hands creating a kind of unstable delicate horizontal plinth above which that action of tender hopeful scrutiny of God's nature and God's will takes place in the holy darkness, no longer oppressive but a place from which freedom might begin again with a 'bow in the clouds', a reminder to God to preserve creation despite humanity's perpetual limitations.

John Everett Millais, The Return of the Dove to the Ark, *1851, Ashmolean, Oxford.*

In Coakley's discussion of art and the Trinity she is particularly drawn to and convinced by a sketch of the Trinity by William Blake, which he produced *c.* 1793. The Spirit's wingspan exceeds the grieving Father and the outstretched arms of the lamented Son, their faceless heads and ambiguously gendered bodies overlapping and entwined. The trio of circles at the centre of the image, distinct yet energetically connected, reflects the triad of the medieval shield depiction of the Trinity but loosens it in sketched repeated lines that register intensity and a kind of spontaneity. For Coakley: 'here is the circle of divine desire perfectly enacted, under the aegis of the Spirit's own longing for love.'[23] Can this divine desire and its intimate intensity in this small rough sketch be offered in a different way by images produced by Moore, Burne-Jones or Millais? They can, and the way this takes place is through the concentration on the vulnerable strength of touch and the expression of a private, deep-rooted tenderness.

Focusing on the Trinity through the arresting image of two girls attending to a frail bird in the dark hollow of a straw-lined ark at the centre of a five-artwork discussion allows us to reimagine art's Trinitarian capacity in a way that admits new thinking regarding gender and God. There are no straightforward paths in this territory, and this is a positive statement regarding the intersections of theology and the arts rather than a claim for discouragement. Indeed, as Coakley notes:

> there can be little doubt . . . of this prevailing paradox in classic Christianity: the persistent orthodox refrain that God, qua God, is beyond gender; and the equally persistent appearance of gendered visual representations of that God, often in forms which vividly display cultural assumptions about 'normative' gender roles.[24]

Victorian Visions of the Trinity and Incarnation

Victorian art frequently forged new ways of expressing gendered experience through art that comingled past and present with religious ideas. *Convent Thoughts* is a painting that heralded, together with Charles Allston Collins' Pre-Raphaelite circle's work in the mid-nineteenth century, a new way of seeing and a new way of making.

It was painted under John Everett Millais' supervision in Oxford, and the flowers are based on the garden of its first owner, Thomas Combe, in the Clarendon Press quadrangle.[25] Resisting the artistic traditions of previous generations, the Pre-Raphaelites were determined to fill their canvases with details of historic and modern life in which a blade of grass was as powerfully articulate as a sparkle of vitality in an open eye. Fingernails could be as important as chalices in conveying meaning and offering new ways of considering narrative and emotion. Completed in 1851, *Convent Thoughts* was also collaborative: the frame, featuring pronounced lilies and the biblical inscription *Sicut Lilium*, was designed by Millais. Its scriptural reference connects the sensuality of the Song of Songs with the prayerful attitude of the painting's isolated and monumental female figure, whose attention to natural beauty leads to a contemplation of devotion itself in relation to Trinitarian belief and Trinitarian mutual love.

Charles Allston Collins, Convent Thoughts, 1851, Ashmolean, Oxford.

Convent Thoughts was painted as a semi-companion, or at least a fruitful pairing, for Millais' *The Return of the Dove to the Ark*, and both had frames designed by Millais that drew on natural themes and symbolism, connecting the meanings in the paintings to the borders that surrounded them. Moreover, when exhibited at the Royal Academy in 1851, *Convent Thoughts* was accompanied by a quotation from Shakespeare's *A Midsummer Night's Dream*: 'Thrice blessed they, that master so their blood / To undergo such a maiden pilgrimage.' The reference is to be applied to the young nun and it can also be a hinge between the nun's prayer and the Trinitarian blessing bestowed on those who follow God as proclaimed at baptism and in other sacramental rites: 'in the name of the Father, and of the Son, and of the Holy Spirit'. The nun's trifold blessing – and indeed by implication the Christian Victorian viewer's own trifold blessing – is inscribed into the artist's layering of cultural meaning from vantage points including the Old Testament and Shakespeare around the central theme of the Passion of Christ and its Resurrection promise. The Clarendon Press quadrangle is re-envisaged as a holy Eden.

The painting depicts a nun in an enclosed garden bursting with colour and diverse life. In one hand she holds a passion flower, contemplating Christ's own passion; in the other she holds open an illuminated small medieval-style book (it is unclear whether, though certainly medievalist, this image may reference a contemporary Victorian nun or may be an imagined scene from a medieval convent). Her fingers mark two pages, made partially visible at an angle and meticulously painted by Collins to show just enough of these scenes – painting within a painting – to create theological meaning. The nun holds this book, which is likely a Book of Hours, open between an image of the Blessed Virgin Mary praying and reading in what appears to be an Annunciation, and also displays an image of the crucifixion with Christ between the Virgin and St John, with another roundel of Christ's head in the marginalia that surrounds the central image.

Convent Thoughts, detail showing book pages.

The red-edged pages the nun grasps between these two open surfaces of the book are a representation of the passage of time, of duration in prayerful and contemplative reading, and in the duration of Christ's own life from conception to crucifixion. In *Convent Thoughts* the advancement of Pre-Raphaelite painting technique that Allston Collins chose to deploy speaks to another element of Trinitarian dynamism. As in much of the Pre-Raphaelite and Gothic Revival artwork generated in this period, there is meticulous attention to detail. Blades of grass and delicate cuticles are given as much painterly attention and crispness as facial expressions and the passion flower the nun contemplates. The technique itself is a sign of Trinitarian attentiveness to life, love and mutual regard, with differentiation itself as an engine of generative desire, as every single element within the artwork is equally prioritized in a paint-world in which each created entity counts, is valued, has life and gives life.

In a cope designed by the architect Ninian Comper and produced by the Anglican Society of the Sisters of Bethany, the presence of the Spirit and the contemplation of the passion are interwoven with a twist.

Ninian Comper and the Society of the Sisters of Bethany, Pentecost Cope Hood, c.1900, V&A, London.

This too, like the other four examples explored in this chapter, have a stasis rather than a swirling movement or intimation of abstraction in their depictions. However, there is a difference in the Comper/Sisters of Bethany cope hood, in its liturgical context. Cope hoods are, like all vestments, not intended for static use. They enfold and emblazon the body of the wearer, stimulating theological thought and prayer in the worshipper as well as she or he who presents the cope's imagery to the people and speaks and acts alongside and through its sacred visual vitality. The presentation of a revivalist, Neo-Opus Anglicanum image of Pentecost with the Virgin in the centre surrounded by Apostles receiving the gift of the Spirit and the related gift of profoundly empathetic communication with one another and with the nascent Church, enflames the body and ignites the liturgy in its signal of the presence of God's Spirit in a particular way. For Coakley, the goal of engaging with Trinitarian art is to 'find in these art forms a means and goad towards the *purgation* of (often unconscious) idolatry; and then to *redirect* our minds, hearts, and imaginations towards a new participation in the Trinitarian God'.[26] That is precisely what this Comper/Sisters of Bethany sacred artwork does, and it is the tension, too, that the nun in Allston Collins' *Convent Thoughts* explicates, her own embodied faith devotionally set between the passion flower and the painted image of the crucifixion, apophatically caught up in prayer, her face pressed close to the petals and her delicate fingers grasping the freshly cut stem, as her left hand holds open the page of the book at which she stops, offering this to the viewer as a set of interlaced visions of God's dynamic presence in human life, spirituality and creativity, both now and in echoes of history.

Near and Far: Trinitarian Visual Culture

Many of the theological insights into the triune God that these artworks provide operate within a tension between the distant and the close at hand. More than this, they are relational mediators between intimacy with God and the necessary impairment of comprehension of the mystery of the Godhead. There is a depth of acceptance of mystery that characterizes much of the art engaged with Trinitarian themes – however unexpected or surprising that engagement might be – in this fruitful period for artistic production and theological debate. Throughout this study, there has been an attentiveness to artists' efforts to see distantly outwards towards the changeless vitality of God through the means provided by the intimate salvation of the Incarnation itself, cherishing it and deploying its gifts in order to suggest new ways in which Trinitarian life poured out for us all might be envisaged. This chapter began with a Victorian writer exploring finitude and the changeful, imperfect nature of humanity. The last word is given to another Victorian writer. Elizabeth Barrett Browning's publication *Aurora Leigh* offers a meditation on the oscillation between near and far that characterizes how the artists considered here have in different ways explored Trinitarian life:

> But poets should
> Exert a double vision; should have eyes
> To see near things as comprehensively
> As if afar they took their point of sight,
> And distant things as intimately deep
> As if they touched them.
> Let us strive for this.[27]

Notes

1 John Ruskin, *The Stones of Venice*, 1853.

2 Eugene F. Rogers, 'Trinity', in Philip McCosker and Denys Turner (eds), *The Cambridge Companion to the Summa Theologiae* (Cambridge: Cambridge University Press, 2016), p. 121.

3 Sarah Coakley, *God, Sexuality and the Self: An Essay 'On the Trinity'* (Cambridge: Cambridge University Press, 2013), p. 198.

4 Coakley, *God, Sexuality and the Self*, p. 197. Coakley acknowledges that the evocative phrase 'chez God' was coined by the theologian Janet Martin Soskice.

5 Coakley, *God, Sexuality and the Self*, p. 191.

6 Though Coakley does not reference these scholars, her questions regarding patronage, systems of production and patterns of interpretation align with feminist art historians including Linda Nochlin, Tamar Garb and Mignon Nixon, to name but a few.

7 Rogers, 'Trinity', p. 117.

8 Rowan Williams, 'The Body's Grace', in Eugene F. Rogers Jr (ed.), *Theology and Sexuality: Classic and Contemporary Readings* (Oxford: Blackwell, 2002), p. 317.

9 Rogers, 'Trinity', p. 118.

10 Rogers, 'Trinity', p. 118.

11 For more on the relationship between making, creativity and human spiritual impulse, see John Ingold, *Being Alive: Essays on Movement, Knowledge and Description* (London: Routledge, 2011).

12 Gerhard Ebeling, *Prolegomena: Erster Teil: Der Glaube an Gott den Schöpfer der Welt*, vol. 1 of *Dogmatik des christlichen Glaubens*, 2nd edn (Tübingen: Mohr Siebeck, 1982), p. 377.

13 Claudia Welz, 'Imago Dei', *Studia Theologica – Nordic Journal of Theology* 65:1 (2011), pp. 74–91 (p. 82).

14 Welz, 'Imago Dei', p. 86.

15 Grace M. Jantzen, 'Beauty for Ashes: Notes on the Displacement of Beauty', *Literature and Theology* 16:4 (2002), p. 429.

16 Rogers, 'Trinity', p. 119.

17 See Ayla Lepine, 'Modern Gothic and the House of God', *Visual Resources* 32:1–2 (2016), pp. 76–101.

18 Caroline Arscott, *William Morris and Edward Burne-Jones: Interlacings* (New Haven, CT and London: Yale University Press, 2008), p. 206.

19 See Duncan Robinson and Stephen Wildman, *Morris and Company in Cambridge* (Cambridge: Cambridge University Press, 1980).

20 Caroline Arscott, 'Edward Burne-Jones', in Elizabeth Prettejohn (ed.), *The Cambridge Companion to the Pre-Raphaelites* (Cambridge: Cambridge University Press, 2012), p. 224.

21 Coakley, *God, Sexuality and the Self*, p. 261.

22 Tim Barringer, Jason Rosenfeld and Alison Smith (eds), *Pre-Raphaelites: Victorian Avant-Garde* (London: Tate Publishing, 2012), p. 122.

23 Coakley, *God, Sexuality and the Self*, p. 256.

24 Coakley, *God, Sexuality and the Self*, p. 248.

25 Barringer, Rosenfeld and Smith (eds), *Pre-Raphaelites*, p. 121.

26 Coakley, *God, Sexuality and the Self*, p. 260.

27 Elizabeth Barrett Browning, *Aurora Leigh*, 1853–6 (London: Women's Press, 1978), pp. 200–1.

PART FOUR

The Trinity in Prayer, in Life and in the Church

Sermon

Transformed by Encounter

JONATHAN GOODALL

Eucharist, Friday 1 July
Lectionary: Psalm 84.8–end; 1 Peter 3.8–15; Luke 5.1–11

'They abandoned everything, and followed him.' (Luke 5.11)

We're told at the end of the Gospel reading: 'Immediately they brought their boats in to land. Then they abandoned everything, and followed him.'

As I remarked yesterday, as Luke presents the calling of Simon, James and John, the process was longer than it appears in the other Gospels. The moment of Jesus' challenge to the disciples – 'Put out into the deep' – was the culmination of many events in which they had witnessed Jesus healing Simon's mother-in-law, his teaching of the crowds, healing the sick and casting out demons, all leading to the life-changing encounter on the lake.

Through it all they observed and pondered. And then in the boat they found themselves confronted with the discovery of the profound personal distance that separated them from the Lord, which paradoxically seems to have drawn them to him also. Captivated by the Lord's insight and love towards them, a true journey of conversion and new life opened up before them.

Their futures were transformed by the encounter, and the revelation that in Jesus' hands, in his company, ordinary fishermen would become fishers of human hearts; that is, people capable – in Jesus' company – of leading men and women to God. It was a promise addressed to Simon Peter even as he confessed his manifest inadequacy, demonstrating that he could only lose his fear, and accomplish what would otherwise be quite impossible, through staying close to the Lord.

The story ends with a note that, in its brevity, sums up the meaning of a lifetime: the three fishermen 'pulled their boats to land, left everything, and followed Jesus'. They said 'yes' to Jesus and followed him, but it was a clear-cut choice that also involved a 'no'. They gave up their livelihoods, and abandoned their families and homes (cf. Luke 18.29). In this way, the evangelist shows how the first disciples followed Jesus, trusting him, relying on his word. Their decisions make sense because they are under no constraint. An irresistible choice has opened up before them, and they act as those who freely agree, to quote St Benedict's later advice, 'to prefer nothing to the love of Christ'; and to 'be with him' (Mark 3.14) in the certainty that 'his love is better than the life they have' (Ps. 63.4). It is a path of response, confirmed by desire and conviction, that has been experienced by many throughout history. But it is the work of God, and a clear reminder that human beings are *not* the authors of their own vocations. They respond; the initiative and invitation are God's.

This insight took on a particular meaning in 2013, when this reading coincided with an extraordinary moment in history, the act that has defined Pope Benedict's ministry as pope: his resignation. Poignantly in retrospect, commenting on this Gospel passage during the Sunday Angelus the day before the world knew of his decision to resign, he spoke these words:

> Human weakness should never be afraid if God calls. It is necessary to have confidence in his strength, which acts in our poverty; we must rely more and more on the power of his mercy, which transforms and renews us.
>
> Dear brothers and sisters, may this Word of God revive in us, and in our Christian communities, courage, confidence and enthusiasm in proclaiming and witnessing to the gospel. Do not let failures and difficulties lead you to discouragement: it is *our* task to cast our nets in faith. The *Lord* will do the rest. We trust, too, in the intercession of the Virgin Mary. Well aware of her own smallness, she also answered the Lord's call with total confidence: 'Here I am.' With her help, let us renew our willingness to follow Jesus, our Master and Lord.

12

Father Sergii Bulgakov on the Doctrine of the Trinity

ANDREW LOUTH

Bulgakov's theology was always controversial; his teaching on the Trinity even more so. Put rather bluntly, it is difficult to get a grasp of his doctrine of the Trinity, as you can pick up book after book by Bulgakov and find nothing obvious on the question. His first philosophical-theological work, *Unfading Light*, has nothing very obvious on the Trinity, save where he is discussing others (Palamas, for instance). Neither his lesser trilogy – *The Burning Bush, The Friend of the Bridegroom, Jacob's Ladder* – nor his greater trilogy – *The Lamb of God, The Comforter, The Bride of the Lamb* – have much that is explicit about Trinitarian doctrine. One sometimes is tempted to think that Bulgakov is deliberately avoiding broaching the subject directly. Critics of Bulgakov have a ready explanation for this: the doctrine of the Trinity, along with much else in traditional Christian doctrine, has been swallowed up in his speculation about Sophia, the Wisdom of God. Vladimir Lossky, in his critique of Bulgakov, issued in defence of the *ukaz* of Metropolitan Sergii and published as *Spor o Sofii*[1] (published, as his son Fr Nicholas Lossky made clear only a few years ago, at the insistence of his colleagues in the Confrérie de St-Photius, and somewhat against his own will),[2] drew attention to the way sophiology distorted fundamentals of Christian theology. As Ivana Noble has recently put it: Lossky 'criticized sophiology for becoming a kind of Christianized version of pantheism, and for blurring a clear Trinitarian teaching'.[3] Brandon Gallaher, in an article on Bulgakov's debt to, and criticism of, Solov'ev quotes a passage from *Spor o Sofii* in which Lossky sums up his gravamen against Bulgakov: 'The Christianity (*sic*) of Fr S. Bulgakov dissolves into a cosmic panchristism, swallowing up both the Holy Spirit and the Church, thereby annulling human personhood in a sophianic-natural process of deification, accomplished through the Incarnation.'[4] Recent articles, not least by Brandon Gallaher, have shown how much common ground there was between Bulgakov and even his most severe critics (such as Lossky), and the piece by Lossky's son just referred to suggests that, had Lossky lived, he might have essayed a presentation of Bulgakov's theology, shorn of the dangers posed by his speculations about Sophia.

Much of the case against Bulgakov is undeniable, though it is often, it has to be said, a matter of guilt by association. Bulgakov's mentors – Solov'ev and Florensky – were deeply in hock to nineteenth-century German Idealism, especially the strand represented by Fichte and Schelling, and for all his attempts to distance himself from, at least, elements of their thinking, Bulgakov himself never shook off habits of thought and expression that he owed to them and the intellectual tradition on which they drew. This seems to me particularly true of what he has to say about the Trinity, where ideas of the Absolute expressing itself in the non-absolute of human history and thereby echoing in some way a Trinity implicit in the Absolute's fashioning of, and encounter with, the Other seem to haunt the way Bulgakov sketches out what the Trinity means for him. This is markedly true of the principal treatise he wrote on the Trinity, *Chapters on the Trinity* – a long and difficult essay, which starts with an engagement with Fichtean idealism and remains, it seems to me, in that thought-world, even as he goes on to discuss, in detail and in depth, the doctrine of the Trinity that he finds in the Fathers. One could argue that, in this treatise, one can see *both* the Bulgakov, continually criticized by such as Lossky and Florovsky, as exemplifying the 'Babylonian captivity of the Church', *and* the Bulgakov whom some are beginning to claim as a fundamentally patristic theologian. Quite how they relate I am not sure: *Chapters* is a difficult and complex work, both in the prose of the text and the multitude of footnotes. However, even in the most impenetrable passages, where the indebtedness to German idealism is clearly manifest, there are strands of thought that seem to me to point away from his philosophical heritage to what seems to me the heart of Bulgakov's theology as it developed. Let me quote a passage from this work:

> Thus [concluding a piece of complex analysis], religion in general begins here where the human *I* encounters the divine *I* as *Thou*; or, conversely, God, the divine *I*, turns towards the human as *us*. It is a *dialogue* of the human with God in prayer, or of God with the human in revelation. That is why praying is the indispensable sign of religion – where there is no prayer, there is no religion either (although maybe contemplative or mystical immersion). A great but faceless *it* extinguishes *I*, but for that reason extinguishes religion, which always and invariably presupposes

the bright light of self-awareness, long before release from the boundaries of createdness, long before deification. When a human being standing 'before God in grace' lives the divine life, he nevertheless preserves his personal consciousness, without which there is no place for love.[5]

What strikes me about that is the way it is *prayer* that is the 'indispensable sign' of religion, and prayer understood in a kind of Buberian *I–Thou* way. There seems to me to be a hint here of the way the Trinity is going to find a place in Bulgakov's theology. For that place is by no means obvious: right through to the end of his life, his theology is expressed in terms that owe everything to what I find the turgid tradition of – I am tempted to say – deliberate obscurity introduced into philosophical discourse by Kant and his *epigoni*. *Chapters* is a relatively early work, completed during Bulgakov's time in Prague (1922–3), though it is likely that its origins date back to his time in Crimea (1918–20), as its theology overlaps with that seen in his *Tragedy of Philosophy*, which belongs to those years.[6]

I am, eventually, going to come back to analysis of some of Bulgakov's texts, but before that I want to reflect more generally on the way Bulgakov wrote his theology. The two monuments to his mature work as a Christian theology are the two trilogies I mentioned early: the little trilogy belonging to the mid-1920s, his early days in Paris, and the great trilogy, *On Godmanhood*, that occupied the last decade of his life and was left, as I understand it, in an incomplete state. The first trilogy evokes a triptych of icons: the group, often depicted in a single icon, known as the *Deisis*, or 'Intercession'. At the centre is Christ the Pantocrator, sitting holding the book of the Gospels; on his right (his proper right, as art historians put it) is the Mother of God, interceding with her Son for humankind; on Christ's left is St John the Forerunner, or Baptist, not pointing to Christ, as is common in Western art (notably in the Isenheim altarpiece by Grünewald), but like the Mother of God opposite him beseeching Christ in prayer. Above the three of them, usually above Christ's shoulders, and therefore above and between the three, are often depicted angels. Bulgakov's trilogy concerns the Mother of God, John the Forerunner, and the angels; it is as if he were writing his treatises to expound what it means to stand in prayer before this icon. And standing before this icon is something he would have been very familiar with: the *Deisis* icon, often expanded sideways, with other saints, is almost invariably found as the first layer, or rank, of icons above the iconostasis. The priest begins his preparation to celebrate by standing beneath these icons. The experience of celebrating the Divine Liturgy was clearly very important for Bulgakov, possibly because he came to it somewhat late in life: he was nearly 50 when he was ordained in 1918 – deacon at Pentecost, Trinity Sunday for the Russians, and priest the next day, the Day of the Holy Spirit. In this little trilogy, there are frequent references to liturgical texts and the liturgical action: the association of the angels with the liturgy is obvious; his constructive account of Orthodox veneration of the Mother of God is drawn almost entirely from liturgical texts; in *The Friend of the Bridegroom*, Bulgakov makes much of the fact that St John the Forerunner is the first to be commemorated, after the Mother of God, in the anaphora after the epiclesis. In the preface to *Jacob's Ladder*, Bulgakov talks about another experience that seems to me to link up to the liturgy. For he speaks of his own experience of his guardian angel, in particular the near-death experience he had, shortly after his arrival in Paris, as a result of a heart attack. Those with him had already made a start on the prayers for the departed, when he began to come to. Reflecting on his experience, he spoke of the guardian angel that called him back from the joy that awaited him after death, saying 'that we had gone too far ahead and it was necessary to return . . . to life'.[7]

More immediately relevant is Fr Alexander Schmemann's recollection of Fr Sergii celebrating the Divine Liturgy. Let me remind you, before I read it, that Fr Alexander had very little time for Bulgakov as a theologian, regarding his theological work as a 'ponderous philosophical edifice':

My third memory of Fr Sergii, the third image, is . . . of Fr Sergii before the altar, celebrating the liturgy . . . He was not accomplishing a well-established rite, traditional in all its details. He delved down to the very depths, and one had the impression that the liturgy was being celebrated for the first time, that it had fallen down from heaven and been set up on the earth at the dawn of time. The Bread and the Chalice on the altar, the flame of the candles, the smoke of the incense, the hands raised to the heavens: all this was not simply an 'office'. There was accomplished here something involving the whole created world, something of the pre-eternal, the cosmic – the 'terrible and the glorious' [*strashnoe i slavnoe*], in the sense these liturgical words have in Slavonic. It seemed to me that it is not by chance that the writings of Fr Sergii are very often laden – so it seems – with liturgical Slavisms, that they themselves so often resonate with liturgical praise. It is not just a matter of style. For the theology of Fr Sergii, at its most profound, is precisely and above all liturgical.[8]

It is not just a matter of 'liturgical Slavisms', mostly lost in translation, but the way his theology is continually illustrated, or rather carried forward, by reference to liturgical details. It is not without reason that Fr Boris Bobrinskoy remarks of Bulgakov – alluding I think to a kind of priestly proverb – that 'the whole of his theological vision he had drawn from the bottom of the eucharistic chalice.'[9]

We misread Bulgakov if we forget that Fr Sergii celebrated the Divine Liturgy almost daily; that we are reading not just a theologian but a celebrant. This, it seems to me, explains the structure of his great trilogy, *On Godmanhood*, for it needs explanation. It does not take a broadly credal form, as has generally been the case with accounts of theology, from Origen's *De Principiis*, through the catecheses of the fourth century and St John Damascene's *Exact Exposition of the Orthodox Faith*, to textbooks still in use today. Its structure is quite original, though also, in a deeper way, profoundly traditional. For Bulgakov, picking up an idea from the greatest early theologian, St Irenaeus, sees revelation not as God's communicating various theological truths but rather as God's engaging with his creation through his 'two hands', the Son and the Spirit. As we stand before God in prayer and grasp something of the revelation of God (think back to the passage I quoted earlier from his *Chapters on the Trinity*), we encounter the Son and the Spirit: it is that encounter with God through his two hands that constitutes revelation, our coming to know God, and more deeply our being transfigured by those hands that created us into the divine, our deification. The first volume of the trilogy is on the Son, *The Lamb of God*; the second on the Spirit, *The Comforter*. And the Father? There is an appendix, or epilogue, to *The Comforter*, entitled 'The Father', for we know nothing about the Father, save through the Son and Spirit. We do not know God the Father apart from the Son and the Spirit, but only through the Son and the Spirit. And the deepening of that knowledge is found in our experience within the Church, as we move towards the eschaton: the subject of the final volume of the trilogy, *The Bride of the Lamb*, a work of Orthodox theology unusual in the attention paid to the last book of the Bible, the Apocalypse (on which, towards the end of his life, Bulgakov wrote a commentary, a French translation of which has been recently published).[10]

I could go on and show how the doctrine of the Trinity emerges within the great trilogy, but that would take far more space than this chapter allows. There is, however, a shortcut, for Bulgakov provides a concise summary of this approach in the most unlikely of places: the book published in English in 1937, *The Wisdom of God*. There he has two chapters on the Trinity: 'The Divine Sophia in the Holy Trinity' and 'The Divine Sophia and the Persons of the Trinity'. He begins, rather bizarrely to my mind, by appealing to a 'Latin Creed of the fifth century', the *Quicunque vult*, or the so-called Athanasian Creed. Here 'the dogma is most clearly expressed', we are told.[11] I am old enough to remember the days when, in the Church of England, this text (not properly a creed), ordered to be sung at Matins on feast days in most months of the year, was actually sung in many churches on Trinity Sunday. So far as clarity is concerned, there was a joke about a choirman singing one of the verses: 'The Father incomprehensible, the Son incomprehensible: and the Holy Ghost incomprehensible', and commenting under his breath, 'and the whole thing incomprehensible'! Enthusiasm for the creed, in a slightly modified form, seems widespread in Orthodoxy: Fr Sophrony was, I seem to remember, quite fond of it,[12] and you can find it, in Greek, in the *Horologion*.[13] Quite how the Athanasian Creed made its way to the East I have no idea; Kelly has nothing to say about it in his otherwise admirable short study, *The Athanasian Creed*.[14] More interesting, perhaps, is a footnote in which Bulgakov quotes the way the doctrine of the consubstantiality of the Trinity is expressed in the Athanasian Creed – *unum Deum in Trinitate, Trinitatem in unitate veneremur. Neque confundentes personas, neque substantiam separantes* – and adds to that some 'ejaculations' of the priest in the Orthodox liturgy, expressing the same doctrine: 'Glory to the Holy, Consubstantial, Life-giving, and Undivided Trinity, now and for ever . . .' (which occurs at the beginning of the Vigil Service), 'For Thine is the Kingdom, the power, and the glory, of the Father, and of the Son, and of the Holy Spirit . . .' (the conclusion, or *ekphonesis*, sung by the priest at the end of the Lord's Prayer).[15] It is thus with appeal to liturgical worship that Bulgakov begins his treatment of the Trinity.

The first of these chapters develops the notion of Wisdom in connection with Glory: both of these, though relatively undeveloped, expressing something of the meaning of the one substance, or οὐσία, of God, a notion, Bulgakov comments, developed in a purely abstract way in the Fathers. It is to the notions of wisdom and glory that we need to look to find a more fully developed sense of what is meant by consubstantiality (this is something we also find in Solov'ev). We can do little more than note this here: he speaks, for example, of 'two aspects of the Godhead in its revelation: Wisdom, the first, concerns its content; Glory, the second, its manifestation' and continues:

Nevertheless, these two distinct aspects can in no way be separated from each other or replaced by one another, as two principles within the Godhead ... for the one personal God possesses but one Godhead, which is expressed at once in Wisdom and Glory.[16]

Let us move on to his treatment of the persons in the second chapter noted above. It is the Father who is revealed in the two hypostases of the Son and the Spirit:

He is, so to speak, the divine Subject, the subject which manifests itself in the predicate. He constitutes the divine Depth and Mystery. He represents, as it were, that speechless Silence which is pre-supposed by the Word. He is intelligence contemplating himself (νόησις τῆς νοήσεως) – even 'before' the articulation of his thought. He is the Primal Will, the principle of all volition, the Fullness participated by all being. He comprises the Unity of all, and is prior to all distinction. He is the source of Beauty which must exist before beauty can come to be. He is Love, although this love is withheld within Himself and as yet unmanifested. He is the Father, the source of being and of love, that love which cannot but diffuse itself.[17]

This is a fascinating passage, pregnant with allusions to the philosophical tradition, ancient, medieval and more recent, both thoroughly traditional and less so, even heretical (more than a whiff of the Gnosticism Myrrha Lot-Borodine sensed about Bulgakov).[18]

A constant of Bulgakov's theology, and especially his Trinitarian theology, is a warning against abstractness; something that, for him, sophiology dispels. So here we find Bulgakov's insistence that 'we must eliminate any *abstract* interpretation of the words of the Word'. Such an abstract interpretation would have these words to be 'but powerless, lifeless symbols'. In truth:

the words of the Word in themselves possess reason and life. They are, as it were, certain intelligible essences, which can best be described as, like the Platonic *ideas*, ideal and real at the same time, and endowed with the power of life.[19]

This links to his defence of the *imiaslavtsi*, the venerators of the Name. But one might think, too, of Bulgakov's own experience of standing beneath the dome in Hagia Sophia in January 1923, of the sense of being:

neither in heaven or on earth . . . [but being] in Hagia Sophia –
between the two: this is the *metaxu* of Plato's philosophical intuition . . . the last silent testimony to future ages of the Greek genius: a
revelation in stone . . . Plato's realm of ideas in stone rising above the
chaos of non-being and subduing it through persuasion: the actual
pleroma, all as a single whole, pan-unity.[20]

One might also recall the reflections of the modern Romanian philosopher, Andrei Pleşu, for whom 'concepts are the corpses of angels. While
those who, in the exercise of thought, see nothing beyond concepts
practise – not necessarily in bad faith – a pathetic form of necrophilia.'[21]
And then there is St Maximos' doctrine of the words, the λόγοι, of
creation.

Let us glance too at the way Bulgakov speaks of 'the conception of the
self-revelation of the Godhead in the double figure of Wisdom-Glory,
which corresponds to the dyad of the Word and of the Spirit'.[22] This is
one of the aspects of Bulgakov's thought that seems most intransigently
bound up with a kind of Gnostic idealism, found, especially, perhaps in
his reflection on sexual difference in creaturely Sophia, mirrored in the
relationship between Christ and his Mother, one of the driving themes
of his reflection on the human and the Church.

I suggest that we see these aspects of Bulgakov's doctrine of the
Trinity as not just wisps and hints of the murky thought that emerges in
nineteenth-century German Idealism, with its inspiration, as Berdyaev
insisted, in the visionary philosophy of such as Jakob Boehme, but
also growing out of Fr Sergii's reflection on what is meant by praying
to God the Father, through the Son and in the Spirit: a notion of the
Trinity that contains both monad and dyad, as one is made aware,
throughout, for example, the anaphora of St John Chrysostom, the
one usually used in the Divine Liturgy of the Orthodox Church, which
addresses God the Father but recalls at least three times that we are
addressing him together 'with your only-begotten Son and your Holy
Spirit'. Or, more concisely, when we read Bulgakov we should remember that we are not just reading a philosopher-theologian, learned in
the language and ways of thought of nineteenth-century idealism, sitting in his study, but rather a priest, Fr Sergii, reflecting on and interpreting what he is doing when he stands before the altar, celebrating
the Divine Liturgy.

Notes

1 *Spor o Sofii, Stat'i raznykh let* [Dispute about Sophia, Articles from various years] (Moscow: Izdatel'stvo Svyato-Vladimirskogo Bratstva, 1996; *Spor o Sofia* first published in 1936).

2 Vladimir Lossky, ed. Nicholas Lossky, *Seven Days on the Roads of France, June 1940*, trans. Michael Donley (Yonkers, NY: St Vladimir's Seminary Press, 2012), pp. 117–18 (first published in French – Paris: Éditions du Cerf, 1998).

3 Ivana Noble, 'Three Orthodox Visions of Ecumenism: Berdyaev, Bulgakov, Lossky', *Communio Viatorum* 57:2 (2015), pp. 133–40, at p. 135.

4 Brandon Gallaher, 'Antinomism, Trinity and the Challenge of Solov'evëan Pantheism in the Theology of Sergij Bulgakov', *Studies in Eastern European Thought* 64:3–4 (2012), pp. 205–25, at p. 206, quoting Lossky, *Spor o Sofii* (original version: *Spor o Sofii: 'Dokladnaja zapiska' prot. S. Bulgakova i smysl ukaza Moskovskoy Patriarkhii*, Paris: Brotherhood of St Photius), p. 61 (in the edition cited in n. 1, pp. 56–7; more precisely it is the 'Christology' of Bulgakov Lossky is talking about, not just Bulgakov's 'Christianity').

5 *Glavy o Troichnosti* [Chapters on the Trinity], in *Trudy o Troichnosti* [Works on the Trinity], ed. Anna Reznichenko (Moscow: O.G.I., 2001), pp. 54–180 (reprint of original 1928 [chapters 1—9 and excursus] and 1930 [chapters 10—13] editions), at p. 67.

6 I owe these precisions, as well as a scan of the text of *Chapters on the Trinity*, to Brandon Gallaher.

7 *Jacob's Ladder: On Angels*, trans. Thomas Allen Smith (Grand Rapids, MI: Eerdmans, 2010), p. 19.

8 Alexandre Schmemann, 'Trois Images', *Le Messager Orthodoxe* 57 (1972), pp. 13–14 (my translation from the French, with reference to the Russian original).

9 B. Bobrinskoy, *La compassion du Père* (Paris: Éditions du Cerf, 2000), p. 160, cf. p. 173; *Le mystère de la Trinité* (Paris: Éditions du Cerf, 1986; 1996 imprint), p. 149 (presumably a reminiscence, as no reference is given).

10 Serge Boulgakov, *L'Apocalypse de Jean* (Paris: Parole et Silence, 2014).

11 S. Bulgakov, *The Wisdom of God* (London: Williams & Norgate, 1937), p. 43.

12 See Archimandrite Sophrony, *La Félicité de connaître la voie*, trans. Hieromonk Symeon (Geneva: Labor et Fides, 1988), p. 15.

13 *Orologion to Mega* (2nd, rev. edn, Athens: Astir, 1984), pp. 487–8. The text in the *Orologion* and that quoted by Fr Sophrony omit the *Filioque* (or rather: *et Filio*), which omission damages the rhythmic prose of the Latin original.

14 J. N. D. Kelly, *The Athanasian Creed* (London: A. & C. Black, 1964).

15 S. Bulgakov, *Wisdom*, p. 44, n. 1.

16 Bulgakov, *Wisdom*, p. 54.

17 Bulgakov, *Wisdom*, pp. 65–6 (translation slightly modified).

18 See the remark quoted by Marianne Mahn-Lot in her memoir of her mother, 'Ma mère, Myrrha Lot-Borodine (1882–1954 (sic)): Esquisse d'itinéraire spirituel',

Revue des sciences philosophiques et théologiques (2004), pp. 745–54, at p. 748; referred to in my *Modern Orthodox Thinkers: From the Philokalia to the Present* (London: SPCK, 2015), p. 100 and n. 22.

19 Bulgakov, *Wisdom*, pp. 69–70.

20 James Pain and Nicolas Zernov (eds), *A Bulgakov Anthology: Sergius Bulgakov 1871–1944* (London: SPCK, 1976), p. 14.

21 Andrei Pleşu, *On Angels: Exposition for a Post-Modern World*, trans. Alistair Ian Blyth (Whitby, Ontario: Cross Meridian, 2012), p. 180.

22 Bulgakov, *Wisdom*, p. 80.

13

Hans Urs von Balthasar:
The Trinity and Prayer

LUCY GARDNER

Introduction

Hans Urs von Balthasar is explicit about the link that he perceives between Christian prayer and the doctrine of the Trinity, acknowledging his own repeated return to it in his short book on prayer when, for example, he writes: 'Once again, we see that the very possibility of Christian contemplation is founded entirely on the doctrine of the Trinity.'[1] In the first section of this chapter, I focus on Balthasar's understanding of prayer as I sketch something of the ways in which he sees the practice and possibility of Christian prayer as grounded in the doctrine of the Trinity.

For all that Christian prayer depends on the Trinity, however, and our understanding of Christian prayer therefore depends on our understanding of the doctrine of the Trinity, Balthasar's theology also suggests that the doctrine of the Trinity itself grows out of Christian prayer and reflection on it. In the second section, therefore, I turn to consider Balthasar's understanding of the doctrine of the Trinity as I outline something of the character of his presentations of this doctrine, which proceed via reflection on particular moments of prayer.

The frequent expositions of the Trinity encountered in Balthasar's theology, in which we read of his perception and understanding of the eternal, seemingly dramatic relationships between Father, Son and Holy Spirit in disturbingly sensory and even sensual language, are as strikingly idiosyncratic as that theology's overall approach, structure and style, provoking no little comment among critics and admirers alike, particularly on its relationship to the life, work and prayer of Adrienne von Speyr. In my third section, I consider Balthasar's understanding of theology as I suggest and explore some of the ways in which these idiosyncrasies are connected precisely to his understanding of the relationships between Christian prayer and theology, and between contemplation and the doctrine of the Trinity in particular. In conclusion, I outline two questions which I think consideration of these interconnections between Christian prayer and the doctrine of the Trinity in Balthasar's theology pose for the Church today.

Understanding Prayer from Prayer in the Trinity

For Balthasar, prayer might appear to begin as our stammering attempts to address God, but the more we pray, the more we realize that this stammering must in fact be understood as our attempt to articulate a response to the God who has already addressed us,[2] not least in the very act of creating us. Moreover, from praying and considering the Lord's Prayer, we grow to understand that a fundamental aspect of Christian prayer is learning to repeat words already spoken to God, by God, learning to make our own words that are given and taught us by the Son of God, who is himself God's Word, spoken from and in all eternity and therefore never merely in the past tense.[3] Prayer, then, is a conversation, in which God speaks first, in which we need to watch and listen for and to that Word, and in which ultimately we speak God's words back to God, participating in the eternal conversation between the Son–Word and the Father, which precedes, outlasts and encompasses us.

Conversations with Christ recorded in the Gospels, therefore, can offer important examples of the responses and prayers we might make; but they are also a means through which that same Word continues to address us in our particularity today. To pray, for Balthasar, is to become a hearer of God's Word;[4] but in a sometimes bemusing exchange of the senses, it is also to contemplate that Word, to learn to 'look to the LORD our God' (Ps. 123.2).[5] In this, the Blessed Virgin is the most perfect example. Reflection on the Annunciation, Mary's obedient response to God's address upon her life and the fulfilment of her unique vocation in relation to her unique Son, enables Balthasar to introduce the Holy Spirit who acts and speaks to reveal the Father in the Son, to Mary, in Scripture and in the Church, and so in every age and to each individual believer.[6]

Turning from this thoroughly Trinitarian account of prayer and the necessity of contemplation as the structure of our obedient attention to God's Word, Balthasar moves to consider the very possibility of contemplation, reflecting on the roles of and interchanges between the Persons of the Trinity:

the Father provides the original blessing of creation for fulfilment in the beatific vision by means of his plan for creation, which is nothing other than his own creating and blessing 'vision' for it and simultaneous 'contemplation' of it;[7]

the eternal Son, begotten of the Father, provides the eternal image brought forth in and enjoyed by the Father's loving gaze, in whom the Father predestines and chooses humanity; in his return to the Father, the Son intervenes as our sponsor, and in him we are justified and ultimately glorified by the Father, coming to share in his eternal, responding, thankful contemplation of the Father;[8]

and the Holy Spirit, coactive with the Father in bringing forth the Son, in some sense completing the divine life, likewise coactive with the Son in revealing the Father by preparing human history and individual human hearts to hear, see and receive the Word, enables us to respond obediently and faithfully within the Son's own faithful obedience, implanting God's life in our souls and us in God's life, and making us likewise coactive with him.[9]

Balthasar then turns from considering the necessity and possibility of contemplation as rooted in the eternal divine conversation and contemplation within God, to attend to the object of Christian contemplation. Here he is at pains to disrupt the antitheses of subjective and objective, active and passive, which might be suggested in speaking of God as the object of our contemplation, and achieves this by another swift move to the Trinity in an exposition of the triune life and the possibility for our inclusion in it. He writes:

We would never come to a knowledge of the triune life in Jesus Christ, not even on the basis of the 'objective' elevation we have received in the 'state of grace' (assuming that such a 'state' could exist in pure objectivity), unless we had also been participants, from all eternity, in the subjective relationship of the incarnate Son with his heavenly Father in the Holy Spirit.[10]

The very purpose of the Incarnation is to open up God's triune life to us, for us to share in it; this is made possible by the Son's intentional inclusion of us in his love of the Father from even before our creation. Here, Christian prayer is again construed as contemplation but explicitly contemplation of Jesus Christ, the Word made Flesh, and in or via him the triune life he shares with the Father in the Spirit.

Taking up one of his favourite Johannine motifs, Balthasar echoes 1 John 1.1–3[11] and explains that in contemplating and responding to Christ's revelation, and through participation in the sacraments, we too can 'see, hear and touch', sense and experience, both subjectively and objectively (we might also add both actively and passively), the Word of life. This, theologically speaking, he adds, mediates to us a true and objective knowledge of God's triune life.[12] Prayer and faith together constitute a spiritual seeing, hearing and touching that take the form of always seeking, and finding, as we cease merely to contemplate the Son and are drawn into his 'station' of facing the Father, his contemplation and even worship of the Father, in the Spirit, and in complete openness, experiencing 'with our very being, and hence also with our minds and senses, what it means to say that God is love'.[13]

Understanding the Trinity from Prayer in the Trinity

It comes as no surprise in the book on prayer, therefore, that towards the end of the chapter on the triune life, Balthasar writes that: 'The New Covenant's Trinitarian revelation is not only inseparably interwoven with the Son's Incarnation; it is also inseparable from the obedient response of the praying believer.'[14] For him, Christian prayer is only to be understood in conjunction with consideration of revelation of the Trinity; at the same time, that doctrine itself only comes to light through the involvement of Christian prayer in revelation. We do not come to understand God as Trinity simply by reflecting on biblical and ecclesial witness and narrative; we understand God as Trinity because we have met and experienced God as Trinity, particularly in prayer.

Since he sees prayer as grounded in the prayer of the Son, Balthasar's expositions of the Trinity often turn to Christ's prayer as intimate disclosure of the relationships between Father, Son and Holy Spirit, drawing on particular prayers for the logic and the content of his accounts. In and from the Lord's Prayer, for example, he reads the Son's adoration of the Father and obedience to his will, his whole being and existence to hallow and glorify the Father's name in both heaven and earth; his desire to feed only from and on the life he shares with the Father; his thanksgiving for that life translated into a commitment to the forgiveness of sins and deliverance from evil; and his testimony to the fact that these originate in and from the Father.

More infamous, perhaps, are his readings of the radical, unimaginable difference and distance between the Father and the Son from the 'cry of dereliction' in *Mysterium Paschale*[15] and the *Theo-drama*. Rather than reading this witness to and assertion of the Son's experience of God-forsakenness as a theological embarrassment to be explained away, as an invitation to an Arian interpretation of Christ, or as an excuse for an un-Chalcedonian decoupling of the two natures, Balthasar embraces this moment as central to the coordinated revelation of: (i) the Son's true identity and faithfulness to his mission; (ii) the relationships between the Father and the Son; and (iii) also indirectly between them and the Spirit, within which that identity and mission exist. At the Crucifixion, read adamantly, even at the moment of dereliction, as the Johannine hour in which the Son is glorified in glorifying the Father, we see and hear more of God than we could otherwise understand or imagine, in ways that disrupt our usual binary understandings of identity and distinction, active and passive, subject and object, here and there, first and second, same and different.

The Son does not and cannot lie or misunderstand; his God-forsakenness must be real, but for Balthasar, this very abandonment itself evidences rather than challenges or undoes the Persons' love for each other. The incarnate Son's abandonment and even death are made possible by and in the very form of his generation from the Father who, in the *Urkenosis* (a term borrowed from Bulgakov) of (eternally) begetting the Son, in a sense (eternally) lets go of divine being, or at least renunciates any sense of being God alone or merely for himself; this Balthasar reads as itself something like a divine godlessness, 'which cannot be in any way confused with the godlessness found within this world, although it is also, transcendentally, the ground of the possibility of this worldly godlessness'.[16]

The cry of the Son from the cross, his prayer already echoed in the Psalmist's, does not open up a new distance in God but reveals the infinite distance the real and eternal distinction between the Father and the Son can as it were 'contain' without breaking. Here the identity and work of the Spirit is critical, if less visible; he springs from the Father and Son's love for each other, and is also in a sense that love which holds them together beyond all difference and any distance. This moment is, moreover, also a revelation of the Son's eternal conformity or obedience to the character of the Father's eternal self-bestowal. Even in his dereliction, at the moment in which he experiences true God-forsakenness, the Son remains committed to the Father and the Father's will, still faithfully turning to him, addressing him, trusting him, giving his all to and for him, thus revealing his true identity and mission, and also making truly Christian prayer possible for others in and from any situation. The 'ending' of the incarnate Son's life, his death, is conducted (enacted, performed) in complete consonance with the living of that incarnate life and with his eternal existence.

The Son's eternal worship and contemplation of the Father in the Spirit, indeed their mutual adoration and joyful contemplation of each other, forms the ground for human prayer, and is revealed to us in the incarnate Son's life lived as a prayer, an offering, a sacrifice and a thanksgiving, which is ultimately the true Christian prayer. But again and again it is Mary's prayer that offers the most perfect example of human participation in that one true prayer. In this she presents a prototype of the Church but also a series of cameos, an enacted icon, through which the identity and mission of the Spirit in relation to those of the Son can be particularly clearly discovered. Here we see even more clearly how the Trinitarian revelation 'is inseparable from the obedient response of the praying believer'[17] and ultimately that of the Church.

At the Annunciation, Mary is addressed by the angel, who in their conversation reveals to her the Father's will for her life and for the world, which will unfold in her acceptance of the Son into her body and life but therefore also her acceptance of her future with and in the Son. He also discloses to her the role of the Holy Spirit, who will overshadow her and bring this about. Mary meets the angel's announcements with obedient prayerfulness, even in her wondering questions, and consents to the Father's will, allowing the Spirit to prepare her to receive the Son. This reflection leads Balthasar to make the striking claim that Christian obedience is the medium in which the Trinity is revealed,[18] but it is also an example of his persistent refusal to separate economy and immanence in his accounts of the Trinity, showing that how the three Persons interact with each other in their shared action in and towards the world is always contained within and only ever a kind of extension of how they coinhere eternally, present to, with and in each other, fulfilling each other in and as Love.

This co-infusion of economic and immanent is perhaps most tangible in Balthasar's brief exposition of the transfiguration, which follows his meditation on Mary's fiat at the end of his chapter on the triune life in the book on prayer. While Jesus is praying, the disciples see his face transformed; the glory of the Lord streams forth from him as he speaks with Moses and Elijah, who represent the law and the prophets, and proclaims to them, in a 'horizontal' plane, 'the Trinitarian form of God's entire revelation of salvation'. But this conversation is, 'at the same time', also 'the exposition of the most "sublime" vertical dialogue, since the Father's word resounds over the Word-made-flesh and the Spirit's *shekinah* completes the whole theophany'.[19] Prayerful contemplation of the Son in prayer yields to a transforming vision and audience of the fullness of the glory of the triune God, both for the three pillars of the Church, Peter, James and John, present on Mount Tabor, and also for the institutional Church herself.

Understanding Theology from Prayer in the Trinity

At the very end of the chapter on the triune life in the book on prayer, Balthasar announces that: 'The contemplative, Trinitarian mystery which the Church has gazed upon and which it cherishes in its heart, is not to be belittled by much talking; it brings forth its genuine fruit in those who follow Christ into suffering.'[20] The doctrine of the Trinity is not given us as a mystery for interminable discussion and disagreement, nor is it a section of theology to be dealt with in one place, be that beginning or end, or middle, and otherwise left alone. It marks the structure, the conduct and the content of Christian theology through and through. Here I offer brief comments on just three interlocking aspects of this in Balthasar's own work.

Aspect 1

If Balthasar is explicit about the link which he perceives between Christian prayer and the doctrine of the Trinity, he is equally convinced of Adrienne von Speyr's accompanying perception of the same link (if sometimes from a different perspective), explaining in the Foreword to his collection of some of her thought on prayer in *The World of Prayer* – published four years earlier than his own book on prayer – that the fundamental idea of the book, from which it continually draws and to which it repeatedly returns, is that 'prayer is ultimately rooted in God himself and in his triune exchange of life',[21] and that he has therefore placed the section on 'Prayer in the Trinity' at the beginning, as the first 'source' of Christian prayer, although it might just as fittingly have been placed at the end as a summary or conclusion to which the rest has worked.[22] The proximity of these two understandings, the conviction of a shared, even a twin vocation, and Balthasar's several explicit references to Speyr's thought in his own theology, and especially at those points where he is setting out a 'vision' of the Trinity, provoke further thought on the relationships between prayer and theology, and the doctrine of the Trinity in particular.

For Balthasar, Christian prayer, the Church's Spirit-empowered participation in Christ's prayer to the Father, and contemplation in particular, appears to provide not only a resource for Christian theological reflection but in a sense also both its horizon and its content. This intuition, however, can never be left as a mere unfocused abstraction, nor could it be obeyed by an attempt to deduce a summary, definitive account of the Trinity from accounts of prayer that could then be subjected to a subsequent rigorous theological investigation. Throughout his work, Balthasar draws on the particular lives and writings of many saints, side by side. Famously there are points where he seems personally and acutely captivated by the vision he believes Speyr has opened to him, particularly, for example, in his accounts of the Trinity in volume 4 of the *Theo-drama*. Many have noted that this is far from unproblematic, particularly if we read his references to her insights as appeals to Speyr's experience as to an unimpeachable authority.

But Balthasar's method appears to intend something rather different; as he reflects on the witness of many saints, theologians and mystics alike, he seems to move not so much in straight lines as in circles, seeking to capture and sketch something of their many and various partial visions of the whole, drawing them together into another, theological, literary – expansive but nevertheless still partial – vision of that same whole, offered as an invitation to see what they have seen, and thus to see and hear what the Church holds, hears and sees, in her very heart. The test of this theology will not be so much whether we believe their testimony or the authenticity of their experience, nor even whether we trust Balthasar's faithfulness to their own understandings. On its own terms, the test of this theology will be in whether it enables others to see, hear, learn, understand something more of the triune God and our salvation in Christ to which it seeks to point. This is not to make truth relative, nor even to subordinate truth to justice or beauty; but it is to require truth and beauty and goodness to be coordinated to each other. Theology cannot merely describe the process of our transformation, it must contribute to it.

Aspect 2

As I have already hinted, throughout his many discussions and presentations of the triune life, Balthasar is apt to employ a rich and at times bemusing vocabulary of the senses. At first meeting this can appear as rhetorical flourish, or perhaps even as metaphorical and almost grammatical attempts to capture in language that which transcends and exceeds it. On further reflection, however, this can be better understood as linked quite specifically to the Johannine motif mentioned above – 'what we have heard, what we have seen with our eyes, what we have looked at and touched with our hands, concerning the word of life . . . we declare to you' (1 John 1.1–3). In the context of the first letter of John, this can surely be read precisely as reassurance of a sure, unimpeachable, unassailable, evidential, perhaps even experiential, basis for the proclamation to follow: we know what we are talking about; we have experienced it for ourselves with our own eyes and ears and hands, each sense confirming the other. From Balthasar's pen, however, it seems to become inextricably linked with echoes of Psalm 34.8, 'O taste and see, how gracious the Lord is', in a deliberate synaesthesia in which the senses do not only confirm and complement one another but cross each other, such that we can see the Word or perhaps hear a vision, and in which light can appear as a type of darkness.

This confusion of the senses can usefully point to our physical and spiritual blindness and deafness, even when we do actually hear and see, both physically and spiritually. It also echoes language of the Incarnation, in which the Word of God has become flesh and thus available to us in new ways, such that it can be heard and touched, held and seen in ways we do not usually associate with the spoken or written Word; and such that we can make sense of the Word proclaiming love and good news even when it is silent (or silenced). It is also linked to reflection on the nature of the sacraments, in which that same Word-made-flesh becomes available to us in further new ways, such that it can be truly eaten and drunk, touched and adored, felt and shared, carried and received. This language thus helps to present the unbreakable bonds between Word and sacrament, both in the person of Christ and in the life of the Church, and it contributes to Balthasar's account of the ways we and our senses are transformed by being caught up into Christian contemplation.

The relationship between physical and spiritual senses is not, then, to be understood in merely metaphorical terms; there are real, analogical links between them, akin to the real links between the senses in our ordinary embodied lives. More than this, however, this human synaesthesia seems analogically grounded in something similar within the triune life itself, in which the Persons' presence to each other is as much their contemplation of each other as their conversation with each other; in which being and doing amount to the same thing in God, just as do thinking and knowing, and ultimately contemplation and action; and in which the Son not only hears and beholds the Father but in a sense even feeds on him.[23] In this, then, it seems that Balthasar co-opts a rich, dense and at times bemusingly sensual language of the senses both to capture for us something of our similitude to God and at the same time to mark something of his ever greater dissimilitude, locating that very law of analogy not simply in God's relationship to the world but grounding it in the eternal triune life itself, made available for us in the Incarnation and the sacraments, in which the Son who feeds from the Father becomes himself our food. With this language Balthasar also disrupts and discredits modernity's oppositions, not on account of their poverty, nor by simply offering an alternative opposition but through a rediscovery of the riches of the Church's own tradition and the fruitfulness of contemplating the Trinity.

Aspect 3

The centrality of contemplation for Balthasar's vision of the Christian life and therefore for his understanding of theology and his deployment of language of the senses can also explain for us something of the structure of his theology, and the impressive and at times bewildering structure of his triptych in particular. This begins not with a fundamental or foundational theology, nor with bald exposition of the doctrine of revelation, but with his theological aesthetic, *The Glory of the Lord*, in which he considers precisely our perception of beauty and in particular the glory, lordship and holiness of God. The aesthetic itself begins with an exposition of how we are 'to see the form',[24] and in particular the form of the Word of God, and here Mary reappears as a critical exemplar of beholding and resting with, remaining in, God. But the second, central panel, the *Theo-drama*, does not leave the senses or beauty, glory, lordship and holiness behind; rather it focuses on teaching us how to 'read' and indeed come to participate in divine action. In both expositions, we begin as apparent observers, maybe even seekers but find that the tables are turned: we are in fact beheld and sought.

Only after these two expositions does Balthasar turn to the considerations with which others might begin, in his *Theo-logic*, seeking to draw out and draw together the overall shape and structure of the Truth that has been observed, witnessed, contemplated and heard in the other two panels. Organized in three volumes considering in turn the truth of world, the truth of God and the Spirit of truth, with the Word as the Truth at their centre, the fundamental theme of this third panel is the transformative power of truth, particularly in the form of participation in Love, beholding the beloved, and receiving our own belovedness.

Conclusion: Reflecting on Theology, Prayer and the Trinity in the Church Today

Whether or not one warms to Balthasar's audacious vision of the Trinity, the tone of his writing or the key moves of his theology, his insistence on the links between prayer, Trinity and theology, and his own attempts to be faithful to this perception, suggest important, perhaps even urgent, questions about the place of prayer and theology in the Church today.

Balthasar presents the God who is Trinity as the ultimate ground of Christian prayer: its proper object, the beautiful and holy One on whom we gaze; its true subject, the good, righteous, powerful One who enables that rapt contemplation; and ultimately its particular content, its very truth and logic, its point and our end. This Trinity is in the same way the ultimate ground, the proper object, the true subject and particular content, point and end of Christian theology. There is in his scheme no ultimate division between these, just as there is ultimately no division between contemplation and action: obedient, grateful contemplation is not merely a particular type of action alongside others, it is the true form of faithful response and action. Mary does not simply stay seated frozen for ever in the moment of the Annunciation; her contemplation, her dwelling in God's gaze, persists throughout all the action of fulfilling her vocation.

My first question that arises from this exploration of Balthasar's perception of the links between the Trinity and prayer concerns individual Christian vocations: How does the Church today understand the relationships between vocations to contemplation and vocations to particular forms of activity? Are these truly alternative paths, offered to different people, mapping different walks of life? Or to what extent might we need to rediscover the sense of a vocation shared by all Christians, to contemplate the triune God through Jesus Christ, and to do so by following him and sharing in his mission?

My second question concerns the place of theology in the Church: How do we understand the relationships between vocations to prayer and vocations to theology, and their place in a Church that can seem at times consumed with the idols of effective leadership and efficient management? Balthasar's own attempt to be faithful to his vocation to prayer and theology, and to his sense of a shared vocation with Speyr, led to his painful departure from the Jesuits and also to the formation of a new community in which they could work and pray, and of a publishing house to present the fruits of their twin labours. In a world where universities seem ever more enamoured of theology as one of the humanities, understood in terms of correlation, cultural studies and comparative religion, how can the churches foster individual vocations to confident, praying Christian theology, and nurture and support communities and institutions, such as Pusey House, dedicated to a communal, eucharistic life in which those vocations may flourish and from which thoroughly ecclesial theological voices might be heard?

Surely the Church needs to value theology not as an alternative to prayer, nor simply as providing the useful, necessary basis and intellectual tools for faithful proclamation, wise decisions, just actions and obedient, loving service, but as itself a proper part of our Spirit-led contemplation of God in Jesus Christ, of our proclamation of the Word of his good news, and of our cooperation in his mission to the world. And the Church needs faithful, praying theologians, prepared, like Balthasar, to wrestle with the task of exposing and presenting anew the transforming vision of the triune God she carries in her heart.

Notes

1 Hans Urs von Balthasar, *Prayer*, trans. Graham Harrison (San Francisco: Ignatius Press, 1986), p. 77.

2 Balthasar, *Prayer*, p. 14.

3 *Ibid.*

4 Balthasar, *Prayer*, p. 20.

5 See Balthasar, *Prayer*, p. 24.

6 See Balthasar, *Prayer*, pp. 27–9.

7 See Balthasar, *Prayer*, pp. 38–51.

8 See Balthasar, *Prayer*, pp. 51–67.

9 See Balthasar, *Prayer*, pp. 67–82.

10 Balthasar, *Prayer*, p. 178.

11 '. . . what we have heard, what we have seen with our eyes, what we have looked at and touched with our hands, concerning the word of life . . . we declare to you . . . so that you also may have fellowship with us; and truly our fellowship is with the Father and with his Son Jesus Christ.'

12 Balthasar, *Prayer*, pp. 178–9.

13 Balthasar, *Prayer*, p. 178.

14 Balthasar, *Prayer*, p. 194.

15 Hans Urs von Balthasar, *Mysterium Paschale: The Mystery of Easter*, trans. Aidan Nichols (Edinburgh: T. & T. Clark, 1990).

16 Hans Urs von Balthasar, *Theo-drama: Theological Dramatic Theory: Volume Four: The Action*, trans. Graham Harrison (San Francisco: Ignatius Press, 1994), pp. 323–4.

17 Balthasar, *Prayer*, p. 194.

18 Balthasar, *Prayer*, pp. 194–5.

19 Balthasar, *Prayer*, p. 195.

20 Balthasar, *Prayer*, p. 197.

21 Adrienne von Speyr, *The World of Prayer*, trans. Graham Harrison (San Francisco: Ignatius Press, 1985), p. 9.

22 See Speyr, *World of Prayer*, p. 10.

23 Balthasar, *Prayer*, p. 184.

24 'Seeing the Form' is given as the title of the English translation of the first volume. Hans Urs von Balthasar, ed. Joseph Fessio SJ and John Riches; trans. Graham Harrison, *The Glory of the Lord: A Theological Aesthetics: Volume One: Seeing the Form* (Edinburgh: T. & T. Clark, 1982); from *Herrlichkeit: Eine theologische Ästhetik: Band Eins: Schau der Gestalt* (Einsiedeln: Johannes Verlag, 1961; 2nd edn 1967). The German, *Schau der Gestalt*, might perhaps be better rendered as 'the look of the form', which would also capture something of the way Balthasar moves between considering our beholding of the form – of beauty, Christ, God – and our being beheld in the divine gaze.

14

Participation in God: An Experiment in Trinitarian Philosophy

LYDIA SCHUMACHER

The Western doctrine of the Trinity, initially credited to Augustine and later codified by Thomas Aquinas, has come under criticism in recent years on a number of grounds. In his well-known treatise on *The Trinity*, for instance, Karl Rahner famously bemoans the fact that the Trinity is introduced only after the one God in Aquinas' *Summa Theologiae*. In practice, Rahner contends, the distinction between *deus unus* and *deus trinus* renders the doctrine of the Trinity something of a theological afterthought: a non-essential of Christian faith. To make matters worse, Rahner points out, Aquinas articulated his account of the Trinity nowhere near his discussion of the Incarnation, thus depriving Christians of an understanding of what it means to imitate or participate in the life of Christ who is, after all, the Image of the Trinity.[1] As if these allegations were not serious enough, theologians in Rahner's wake have added to them, among others, the charge that Aquinas' way of describing the Trinity promotes both individualism and authoritarian rule by a single power.

Following Rahner, there has been a revival of Trinitarian theology and a surge of new work to recast the doctrine of the Trinity in ways that evade the aforementioned problems.[2] In this connection, however, many have turned away from the Western doctrine of the Trinity, and Aquinas' in particular, to what they see as more Greek, 'social Trinitarian' models.[3] While it is not my purpose to assess these models in the present context, I do intend to give a reading of Aquinas' doctrine of the Trinity, which underlines its ability to evade the aforementioned objections.

On this basis, I will offer a constructive account of the way this doctrine may serve as a model for human participation in the life of the triune God. In developing this account, I will seek to establish the Christian doctrine of the Trinity as the ultimate foundation for enabling us to live the human lives – and be the human beings – we were designed by God to be. Since the whole purpose of much philosophy up to the time of Aquinas was to facilitate flourishing in ordinary life, and to help individuals overcome common hindrances to doing so, my discussion will provisionally support the conclusion that a philosophy that fully delineates the nature and conditions of human existence must be a 'Trinitarian philosophy'.[4] As a preliminary to this discussion, I will outline Aquinas' doctrine of the Trinity.

Aquinas on the One-in-Three God

From the start of Aquinas' treatise on the nature of God, it is clear that his uttermost concern in this context is to establish God's simplicity.[5] The doctrine of divine simplicity, upheld in some form by all three Abrahamic religions, asserts God's total otherness in the face of all known objects. While such ordinary objects are composed of parts, finite, temporal and therefore subject to development, God is not divided, limited or tensed in any way. He always completely is what he is, which is to be one being that is, that knows, wills and does all things good, and is perfect in that sense.

Following his account of the single, simple God, Aquinas turns in the way Rahner protests to a distinct discussion of God's triune nature, treating the two processions, three persons and four relations that subsist in the Trinity. On his account, the first principle of the two processions – that is, of generation and spiration – and therefore of the Trinity itself is God the Father. He alone is unbegotten: not produced by another. By contrast, the second person of the Son proceeds from the Father by way of knowledge or intellect. This is because his relationship to the Father is like that of one known by a knower.[6]

When the Father knows the Son, Aquinas suggests, he generates a thought of himself; that is, his image or a word of self-expression.[7] As God is the highest object of knowledge, his supreme knowledge as God consists simply in the knowledge of himself. Since the Father's knowledge of the Son is reflexive, it can be likened to self-knowledge. Thus, the Son can be said to know and make known the Father in the very experience of being known by him.

On the grounds that a good withheld is not truly good, Aquinas argues that a good incapable of communicating itself along these lines could not be considered the highest good. Because the communication of goodness is an expression of love, Aquinas identifies love as the ultimate attribute of the Trinity in which the Father and the Son communicate God's goodness to one another.[8] This brings us to the role in the Godhead of the Holy Spirit, who proceeds from the Father and the Son not by way of intellect but by way of the will – or love and desire – for that which is known, namely the Son by the Father and the Father, in turn, by the Son.[9]

In Aquinas' account, the Father's knowing of the Son and the Son's knowing of the Father ultimately reflect their mutual desire to know one another; that is, God's desire, consisting in the Holy Spirit, to know himself and make himself known as the highest good. Since the Spirit is indicative of the Father's will to make himself known in the Son, and the Son's will to know and make known the Father, he is generally described as the 'Love' or the 'Gift' exchanged between the Father and Son.[10] Thus, the Spirit is said to be spirated or breathed out by the Father and the Son (*filioque*), as the bond that clinches their unity.[11] Because this spiration enacts the knowledge shared by the knower and the known, the Spirit constitutes the very life or indeed the Spirit of the Trinity, which consists in honouring or loving God as the highest good or object of adoration, which he is known to be.

As the discussion above suggests, an appeal to the processions of the Son and Spirit from the Father generates an account of one God who does not merely exist as God but also knows and names or communicates himself as God, wants to act and indeed acts like God. Since a God incapable of knowing and being who he is along these lines could scarcely be regarded as divine, it follows that the doctrine of the Trinity constitutes the condition of possibility for affirming that the one God is worthy of the name 'God'. This is the upshot of Aquinas' affirmation that God *is* his act of understanding, such that whatever is understood by God is the very living or life of God, namely that God always completely is what he is, which is to be, know, say, desire and do all that is good, or consistent with love, because of a perfect correspondence within him between who he is, what he knows, what he communicates, what he wants and what he does.[12]

On this showing, it seems clear that Aquinas' work is not plagued by a sharp division in accounts of the one and the triune God, and a tendency to demote the doctrine of the Trinity. When his treatises on these topics are interpreted as above, the doctrine of the Trinity instead emerges as the means to delineating how the one God can be described as the supreme, self-communicating good monotheists believe him to be. That is not to undermine the validity of monotheisms that reject the teaching that God is triune. Rather, it is to offer a rationale for belief in the one

God that affirms this belief in the strongest possible terms. Since there is no certain knowledge of the unknowable God, let alone as triune, at least for us, apart from his self-revelation, however, this rationale only becomes fully available to us at the Incarnation of God's Son.

Thus, it remains to explain how the 'known unknown' made himself known as such to humanity by assuming human personhood at the Incarnation. On a broadly Thomist conception of this event, Christ relayed the knowledge of the triune God by continuing the work he eternally accomplishes within the Godhead.[13] That is to say, he operated in the awareness of God as the highest good and with a view to accomplishing God's good purposes. Since he carried on his divine work in the context of a human life, he brought his direct knowledge of God to bear in an indirect manner, namely by assessing how to go about ordinary activities and confront distinctly human situations in light of the knowledge of God as the highest good.

By these means he expressed his Spirit – life, mind, personality and so on – of love for the Father; that is, his desire to please the Father. At the same time, he revealed the triune nature of God in a manner with which human beings can identify. Furthermore, he demonstrated that all human beings were designed to image the Trinity as he did; that is, to express their individual spirits – lives, minds or personalities – given through the creative work of the Son with a view to subjecting every single circumstance to the knowledge of God's supreme goodness. On this showing, consequently, Aquinas' account of the Trinity and the Incarnation are naturally linked, even though they are located at the beginning and end of his *Summa*, for the purposes of rhetorical force.[14] The separation between them, and the Trinity and Christian life, that Rahner detected is not actually in evidence. Instead, the discussion of Christ as the image of the Trinity naturally gives rise to the question as to what it means for human beings to imitate Christ by participating in the life of the triune God.

Participation in God

On the basis of the account of the Trinity outlined above, human participation in the divine life can be said to entail efforts gradually to achieve the unity of being, knowledge, word, will and action that characterizes the divine. The point of participation, in other words, is to come to a place of personal maturity. While such fullness of being is a given for God, who always completely is what he is, it is a challenge for us to achieve as human beings, for at least two main reasons. One concerns our finitude – the fact that we are limited by space, time, embodiment and diverse levels and types of ability. While these features of our existence are by no means denigrating, they do necessitate that we strive – over time and often with considerable effort – to become what we are but cannot be from the outset of our existence or possibly even at any point in time.

This effort to 'become ourselves' is considerably complicated by a second factor, namely sin, which hinders even our best efforts along these lines. At a preliminary level, sin springs from pride; that is, the inaccurate self-image and inordinate self-love that result from a refusal to know and love God as the source of our purpose and value as finite beings. Such pride may manifest in the extreme forms of hubris and false humility that respectively nurse in us the desire to be something more or less and thus altogether other than we actually are. Indeed, both pride and false humility entail a refusal to confront our finitude – and the supremacy of God – either by denying it, in hubris, or devaluing ourselves on account of it, in false humility.

When acted on, this refusal leads to false forms of self-expression or self-actualization, or both. In fact there are as many ways to sin in terms of pride as there are permutations of self-knowledge, self-love or self-acceptance, self-expression or self-communication and self-actualization. For instance, there can be self-knowledge without self-love, in which case one knows one's vocation but does not love oneself enough to fulfil it, whether because of low self-worth or laziness, which hinders one's ability to self-communicate and realize personal potential. Conversely, there can be self-love without self-knowledge, wherein one bypasses reflection on one's rightful vocation but works for certain causes anyway, thus doing so in ways for which one is unsuited, or out of a disproportionate sense of authority and entitlement.

Of course, there are cases in which both self-knowledge and self-love are lacking. In these, one wonders ceaselessly what one should be doing with one's life, while wandering aimlessly through it. Depending on one's characteristic vices, consequently, one may be given to self-expression without self-actualization (that is, to talk without action); or to self-actualization without self-knowledge and/or self-love, which one is incapable of expressing appropriately. In the latter case, one tends to work for the well-being of others but does so without a sense of purpose or vocation, let alone an ability to articulate that vocation in ways that would help oneself – and others – understand where one's energies should be directed.

This deficiency renders one susceptible to being ever distracted from and torn between various purposes, or to define oneself in terms of what one does to fulfil the needs of others, which can ironically result in becoming excessively dependent on those served. In this regard one's desire to do good can ultimately alienate one not only from oneself but also from others. Without self-knowledge and self-love, moreover, these good works cannot build on and reinforce a sense of vocation and the pleasure one derives from fulfilling it, which may lead to a loss of energy to engage in self-actualization in the long term, or under difficult or new circumstances.

As the above suggests, there are many excesses and deficiencies in self-knowledge, self-acceptance, self-expression and self-actualization that can result from pride. Put differently, there are many ways of failing through pride to participate in the life of God. While pride distorts our sense of self on an initial level, it further skews our whole perspective on and capacity to appreciate other realities, not to mention other persons. It causes us to attribute too much – or too little – significance to temporal objects and circumstances. Thus, it prevents us from evaluating our experiences in the light of the knowledge of God as highest good, which enables us to see all things – including ourselves – in terms of the actual value they possess and to reckon with them accordingly.

Although such a 'divine perspective' on reality, supremely modelled and made possible by Christ, does not afford the direct knowledge of God, which Christ himself enjoyed, it arguably provides a sort of indirect knowledge of the maker, which comes by discerning the difference belief in him makes to the way we think and live in ordinary ways. It offers us a means of participating in the life of God that we can possess while still in the time-bound process of working to achieve the state of maturity that the divine being enjoys eternally. To this end, correcting pride by cultivating an appropriate degree of self-knowledge and self-love represents a key first step. In this regard, we must start by abandoning any desire to be something other than God made us to be and will to be exactly that.

That is to say, we must accept ourselves in all our finitude and feebleness and come to see our limitations precisely as the locus of a personal vocation imparted by God, whose loving bestowal of individual human life calls for a return of the gift. By relinquishing resentment concerning the constraints of our existence, we satisfy the precondition for identifying and ultimately utilizing our abilities; that is, for seeing ourselves through the eyes of our maker and for expressing ourselves and living accordingly. Through such acts of self-expression and self-actualization, conversely, we reinforce and strengthen our self-understanding and self-love, which in turn generate more sophisticated acts of self-expression and self-actualization.

As we come by these means to a place of heightened continuity between who we are, who we know ourselves to be, who we want to be, how we relate to others or express ourselves, and how we act, I have hinted that we increasingly imitate or participate in the fullness of being that characterizes the triune God in an utterly simple and supreme manner that nevertheless remains foreign to us. Thus, it is through the ordinary operations of the human intellect, will, language and life that we are formed after the image of God in Christ, and come to reflect that image with increasing clarity and consistency.

Although it is only possible by these means to know God indirectly, by perceiving the difference belief in him makes to our way of evaluating ourselves and our world, it is by achieving the highest possible level of personal maturity with respect to self-awareness, self-acceptance, self-expression and self-actualization at any stage, that we become predisposed to see the divine being who is mature in the fullest and truest sense of the term. After all, the condition of possibility of gazing on a being who always completely is what he is, is to reach a state of complete self-awareness, self-acceptance and self-realization that is made possible by, and reflects the condition of Christ.

That is not to suggest that we cannot participate fully in the life of the Trinity while we are still in the process of cultivating maturity in any of these respects. Provided we strive for and achieve the level of personal maturity that is possible for us at any given point in time, we can be described as full participants in the life of the Trinity, even while still on the way to achieving the highest possible level of maturity that is objectively attainable by ourselves. Still, it remains impossible to attain maturity along these lines in the way that is proper to God. On account of the fundamental difference between the Creator and his creatures that is clinched by divine simplicity, human beings cannot share in the divine life in the way God is fit to participate in what is by definition *his* life. As mentioned, rather, we do so in ways that accord with our finite and created natures.

This difference between God and us has direct implications for our understanding of the function community life performs in the process of personal development. More specifically, it provides grounds for refuting the common objection that Thomist Trinitarian theology promotes excessive individualism by emphasizing the ultimate unity rather than plurality of the three persons. Though the very fact that this unity is enacted by the community of the three persons suggests that human individuality should likewise be nurtured in a communal context, the Creator–creature distinction already clues us in to the fact that the way human individuality is consummated in community will necessarily differ qualitatively from the way this happens in God, which I will clarify through a brief excursus on the nature of personhood in God versus human beings.

On Aquinas' understanding, the Father, Son and Spirit are unlimited, albeit distinct, as persons, precisely on account of the unbounded nature of God. Since their distinctive 'personalities', as it were, predispose them to enter into relations, the three persons are accordingly unlimited, albeit distinct, in terms of their capacity to relate to one another. Because of this unlimitedness-in-difference, there is nothing about the Father that is not made known to the Son in the Spirit and vice versa. So construed, the three persons of the Trinity are 'personal' and correspondingly 'relational' in the fullest possible sense. Aquinas goes so far as to indicate that persons are or are a function of their relations, which render God the one genuinely and supremely personal being.[15]

By contrast, human persons are limited in their personalities and thus in their ability to relate to others. While this means that it is impossible for human beings to experience complete fulfilment in any given relationship, or in relationships overall, it also means that human beings are not and cannot rightly be defined by their relations. Though many social Trinitarians have argued to the contrary in their enthusiasm to combat an unhealthy sense of autonomy from human community, they seem not to have noticed that their position logically entails human confinement to circumstances of personal upbringing, social status, gender stereotypes and instances of authoritarian or oppressive control that are all too common in human societies, not least within the Church. In trying to counteract individualism, in other words, they seem to pose a significant theoretical threat to the most vulnerable individuals.

The present account steers a middle course between the individualism that rejects community, and the communitarianism that potentially harmfully reduces individuals to a function of their social circumstances, by affirming that while we are like God in that our individuality can only flourish within community, we are unlike him in the sense that we are not ultimately defined by our relations with others.[16] In other words, human personalities remain prior to relationships, as predispositions for engaging in them, even though they can be called out in the context of interpersonal relationships.[17] Although the community poses a context in which to use our gifts, as well as a responsibility to use those gifts to the benefit of others, its purpose by this account is ultimately to facilitate the development of individuals, and to enable them to transcend gender stereotypes, disadvantage and forms of oppression to this end.

In this connection, the present account implies that a community should serve its members equally, since the persons of the Trinity are ultimately equal. As in the Trinity, this equality does not necessarily entail uniformity but may require different forms of service, to accommodate different human natures and needs and thereby contribute to the realization of different human potentialities. In that sense, this account evades the objection that Western theology promotes authoritarian rule by a single power, once again, by laying emphasis on the oneness of the three persons in God. To the contrary, this account calls for communities to be overhauled if they fail to promote equality, since it is in doing so that they fail in their purpose, which is to promote the thriving of individuals, who are in turn gifted to foster in different and equally necessary ways the functioning of the community itself.

Although the limitations of space prevent me from delineating in greater detail the possible responses to the principal objections concerning the Western doctrine of the Trinity, the arguments that have been developed thus far should suffice to show that a broadly Thomist understanding of the Trinity and human participation in the life of the triune God does not fall prey to the problems that have often been associated with it and that have motivated the development of alternative theologies.

An Experiment in Trinitarian Philosophy

Yet the doctrine as I have described it accomplishes a great deal more than merely evading recent and common objections. Since human and indeed all beings turn out on this showing to be patterned after and to participate in the life of the triune God, an appeal to the doctrine of the Trinity arguably makes it possible to delineate the nature and conditions of their existence in the most specific of terms. In sum, it provides the paradigmatic model and foundation for living our ordinary lives to the full – and thus for preparing us to meet God. This was the whole purpose of philosophy in many sectors of the pre-modern world, namely to facilitate the realization of human potential, and through the work of human individuals, to promote the well-being of human society. Put differently, the goal of philosophy originally and presumably in Aquinas was to teach human beings to live well and thus prepare them for death. When philosophy is defined along these lines, and the doctrine of the Trinity is recognized as the ultimate resource for achieving philosophy's ends, it therefore follows that a fully delineated philosophical account of the nature and conditions of human existence will ultimately require the development of what I would call a Trinitarian philosophy.

That is not to say that the affirmation of the triune God is the sole means for accomplishing the objectives of philosophy. After all, there are many observable cases in which human potential is realized and human society supported without reference to belief in the Christian God. Nevertheless, there are reasons why a Trinitarian foundation for philosophy is significant and even crucial to fulfilling the purposes of philosophy over the long term. Most notably, it stands to reason that human beings are more likely actually to *be* what they are as images of the Trinity – rather than some deficient or defunct version of themselves – if they are able to explain the nature and conditions of their being; that is, if they have recourse to the sort of explanation that Trinitarian philosophy would endeavour to provide.

By way of illustrating this point, I would mention the three criteria for authentic virtue that Aquinas follows Aristotle in deploying in the development of his famous virtue ethic, which is the tool he employs to teach readers how to further their own thriving and that of others.[18] In this regard, Aquinas firstly posits the necessity of knowing that virtuous acts are virtuous when performing those acts. Apart from this knowledge, he avers, virtuous act might be a matter of mere 'moral luck'. To guarantee such knowledge, the second criterion stipulates that virtuous acts must be performed precisely because they are virtuous and out of no other primary motivation. Where a virtuous act is committed with any other goal than the achievement of virtuous ends, that act potentially springs from pride. As a result, it is not intentionally virtuous and cannot therefore generate consistently virtuous behaviour.

In order to ensure this consistency, the last criterion holds that genuine virtue must proceed from a habit of virtue. Put differently, it must flow from a fundamental impulse to engage in the virtuous activity. Without such a conscious and consistent habit of virtue, Aquinas concludes that there is no way to explain, defend, motivate and instruct others in what is virtuous. On a grand as well as an individual scale, consequently, a habit of virtue is essential to ensuring that acts that appear virtuous are non-accidental and intentional, and that they can therefore be repeated on a consistent basis, regardless of circumstances. Since circumstances are contingent and subject to considerable variation, only such a habit can predispose moral agents to discern how to act virtuously on short notice or under new, unfamiliar or difficult conditions.

On the basis of Aristotle's three criteria, I submit that Aquinas' doctrine of the Trinity provides necessary grounds for explaining what we are or ought to be doing when we are living our ordinary human lives, for living them accordingly and for striving to do so with the consistency that characterizes the life of God himself. When it comes to doing this, arguably, other theological doctrines – to do with creation, sin, redemption, ecclesiology, eschatology and so on – perform a variety of essential functions. Taken together with the key doctrines of Trinity and Incarnation, whereby the Trinity is revealed to humankind, these doctrines fully outline the contours and conditions for the possibility of our participation in the Trinity. As such, therefore, Trinitarian philosophy represents something of a method in systematic theology, whereby doctrines are defined in terms of the way they enable human flourishing – which in turn represents the locus of the Christian life.

In this connection, the approach to systematic theology that a Trinitarian philosophy proffers overcomes a common tendency in the discipline to bifurcate spiritual and ordinary life – to construe the Christian life as something separate or altogether other from the simple effort to be oneself and pursue one's abilities and interests in the world in order to make some kind of difference in it. On this account, rather, participation represents nothing but the rationale behind or formality under which human beings engage in their ordinary lives, namely from a standpoint of faith in God as the highest good. By the same token, Trinitarian philosophy creates a natural point of connection between the Christian believer and all those who seek to grapple with the purpose and conditions of natural life, without ceding territory to those who might challenge the legitimacy of faith.[19] By establishing human and all life as a matter of joining in the God-glorifying life of the Trinity, in fact, it renders theology not only relevant but even crucial to unlocking the meaning of life in this world.

Notes

1 Karl Rahner, *The Trinity*, trans. Joseph Donceel (London: Burns & Oates, 1970), pp. 16–17.

2 See, for example, Leonardo Boff, *Trinity and Society* (Eugene, OR: Wipf & Stock, reprint, 2005); Sarah Coakley, *God, Sexuality and the Self: An Essay 'On*

the Trinity' (Cambridge: Cambridge University Press, 2014); Paul S. Fiddes, *Participating in God: A Pastoral Doctrine of the Trinity* (London: Darton, Longman & Todd, 2000); Colin Gunton, *The Promise of Trinitarian Theology* (London: Continuum, 2003); Jürgen Moltmann, *Trinity and the Kingdom of God* (London: SCM Press, 2000); Samuel M. Powell, *Participating in God: Creation and Trinity* (Minneapolis, MN: Fortress Press, 2003); Miroslav Volf, *After Our Likeness: The Church as the Image of the Trinity* (Grand Rapids, MI: Eerdmans, 1998); John Zizioulas, *Being as Communion* (London: Darton, Longman & Todd, 2004).

3 Kathryn Tanner, 'Social Trinitarianism and Its Critics', in Robert J. Wozniak and Giulio Maspero (eds), *Rethinking Trinitarian Theology* (London: T. & T. Clark, 2012); especially pp. 382–6.

4 Pierre Hadot, *Philosophy as a Way of Life: Spiritual Exercises from Socrates to Foucault* (Oxford: Blackwell, 1995).

5 *ST* (*Summa Theologiae*) Ia.3. See David Burrell's defence of divine simplicity in *Aquinas: God and Action* (Chicago: University of Chicago Press, reprint 2008).

6 *ST* Ia.33.

7 *ST* Ia.27.2; *ST* Ia.34–5: on the Son as Word and Image.

8 *ST* Ia.37.

9 *ST* Ia.36.

10 *ST* Ia.37–8.

11 *ST* Ia.27.3–4.

12 *ST* Ia.18.4.

13 *ST* IIIa.10.

14 Mark D. Jordan, *Rewritten Theology: Aquinas After His Readers* (Oxford: Wiley Blackwell, 2005).

15 *ST* Ia.40.

16 See David Fergusson's work to chart a course between communitarianism and individualism in *Community, Liberalism and Christian Ethics* (Cambridge: Cambridge University Press, 2005).

17 See Harriet A. Harris' superb article on this score, which responds to a number of accounts in which personhood is defined in terms of relations: 'Should We Say that Personhood is Relational?' *Scottish Journal of Theology* 51:2 (1998), pp. 214–34.

18 Aristotle, *Nichomachean Ethics* II.2, 1105a28–1105b1: 'the acts that are in accordance with the excellences [virtues] themselves have a certain character . . . the agent must also be in a certain condition when he does them. In the first place, he must have knowledge [of what he is doing]; secondly, he must choose the acts, and choose them for their own sakes [rather than any other motive]; and thirdly, his action must proceed from a firm and unchangeable character.

19 Furthermore, our 'being human' serves as a testimony to the power of Christian faith in the triune God: a sort of proof for its rationality if you will. Indeed, the Christian faith in the triune God proves rational on this showing by providing the ultimate resource for ensuring that we become what we were made to be; that is, rational animals who function in ways that support personal flourishing and that of a wider community.

15

The Trinity and the Moral Life
In memoriam John Webster

OLIVER O'DONOVAN

Dogmatics and Ethics are often distinguished for pedagogical purposes, though among theologians there is rather little engagement with why they should be distinguished. But both John Webster and I have given our minds to this question from time to time, and in his last-published work, *God without Measure*, there is a great deal about it. He possessed a remarkable skill in making distinctions, that gift unusual in our age but much cultivated in scholastic disputation and prized above every other by Martin Luther. Modest and circumspect, the master-distinguisher did not scatter oppositions promiscuously across the page, merely to dazzle or bewilder. He did not brandish them violently, slashing a path through country where a delicate balance and complementarity ought to reign. Each distinction, however remote, was brought before the bar of the founding distinctions between God and man, holiness and sin; each had to bear witness to the gracious act of God, who reaches out across the gulf of these distinctions to embrace sinful man in partnership. John Webster made his distinctions like a surgeon teasing apart the tissues of a living body, as respectful of organic unity as of difference, knowing that when the operation is over the tissues must bind together again. In that scrupulous and patient discrimination he was a standing example to his generation, serving the harmony with which theology must fulfil itself in calling on God, a task unified in its object though differentiated in its offices.

In his last work he posed the relation of dogmatics and ethics by way of the scholastic phrase, *agere sequitur esse* ('action follows being'). On the one hand, dogmatic reason had to have its 'prospective' moment in which it looked to 'temporal enactment', open to being 'enlarged' by moral theological reflection. On the other hand, practical-moral theology, orientated towards deliberation, had its 'retrospective' moment, drawing on an understanding of what is said about God and God's works.[1] In an earlier essay, while warning of the 'disorder' of thinking of dogmatics and morals 'as discrete disciplines, each with its own domain and procedures', he goes on to suggest that they are 'coinherent reflective activities directed to some particular aspect of a common object – the mystery of God and the work of God'.[2] In the later essay the two enterprises come together on a field he calls 'moral theology', the 'first principles of human moral history', which dogmatics must reach and Christian practical reason must be able to draw on reflectively. A material priority, he thinks, is to be assigned to dogmatics, 'because the movement of Christian teaching is from God to created things'; yet since theology is 'a mixed knowledge, acquired not only speculatively but also practically', dogmatics must expect 'enrichment, illumination or expansion from the considerations of morals and ascetics'.[1]

The invitation to take up the topic left vacant by John Webster's early summons to leave the world leads me to address a neglected aspect of a thesis of my own. Moral reason needs to be understood, I have argued, as having a threefold reference: to the agent self; to the world that comprises an order of values; and to the horizon of emerging time before which we deliberate on action. The impasse into which modern moral reason has run, frequently diagnosed by philosophers in the last generation, springs from a tendency to be monothematic, and so unable to reconcile these points of reference, a horizon of constituted obligation, a horizon of future possibility and an imperative of action, each apparently absolute. This leaves modern man with the intolerable alternative of stagnation, on the one hand, and unrooted spasmodic exertion on the other, with no imagination of how we may be *ourselves* when we act, taking new steps in faithful reflection of the good we have seen and loved. I have developed my plea for a better and fuller account of moral reason in terms of the Pauline triad of faith, love and hope, but have deliberately made no connection between these two triads and the Holy Trinity. I expect the reason for that omission will be obvious. The Trinity is a dogmatician's theme, if ever there was one. An understanding of the triune God has to prove itself on terms proper to what we may know of the divine life; an analysis of moral reason has to prove itself on terms proper to human life. The seduction of the number three should not tempt us to confuse these tasks, and represent our moral reason as a direct image of the godhead, which would be the theological equivalent of what the political theorists have called 'living metaphysically'; that is, converting contingent practical decisions into ultimate statements of reality. A bishop, exhorting his church to a frank and charitable approach to their disagreements, was reported to have said: 'We do not have to be afraid of disagreements;

the godhead has disagreements among its members', a train of thought, one might judge, equally disastrous to dogmatic theology and to moral reason. Making God in our own image, we recall, is idolatry; divinizing worldly differences is an evasion of their challenges.

Yet if ethics cannot take a lead in discourse about the Trinity, it can listen and respond. In John Webster's view moral theology is 'distributed across the corpus of dogmatics', and 'there is a moral-theological derivate of all theological doctrines', beginning with 'the one principal Christian doctrine of God the Holy Trinity'.[2] Ethics, remaining within its own sphere of competence, can trace such correspondences as may appear between the form of human action and what it has been told of the being and acts of God. It will remain for dogmatics to decide whether such a correspondence can enrich, illumine or expand the knowledge of God. So let me begin with a broad thesis: it takes a Trinitarian God to elicit purposeful human action. Our task is to see whether that thesis could find theological support, in search of which we may turn to a *locus classicus* in the New Testament for the interplay of the triune godhead with the formation of the life of faith. I have in mind the Farewell Discourses of St John's Gospel, the whole of which is germane to the theme, though we shall concentrate mainly on chapter 14.

The agency of the disciples is right at the fore of the discussion in the opening words: 'Let not your hearts be troubled' – hearts, of course, not in the modern romantic sense as pure receptors of emotional stimulus but as always in the New Testament, representing the seat of practical reason. Confusion and instability threaten the disciples' capacity to live and act but the condition of a stable agency is fully realized: 'you believe in God.' But as anyone who has read the Gospel to this point knows, faith in God means faith in his presence in Jesus, so that the scope of the faith is immediately extended: 'you believe also in me' (John 14.1). The first of what I take to be three sections of the chapter explores the relation between Jesus and the Father as the way of approach to God, and the truth and life of God's being (John 14.6). When Philip demands, 'Show us the Father, and it will suffice us!' (John 14.8), he has not yet fully grasped this relation. He is the aspiring φιλόθεος (friend and lover of God, familiar to the ancient world), whose hope to see the Father is formed as a hope to be taken somewhere else than where the Father is visible in Jesus, which is to say, the world they have known with him, in the history they have lived with him. The relation of Jesus and the Father is then developed (John 14.10) in terms of Jesus' 'words' and 'works'. The disciples have received teaching, teaching about how to live before God, and they have seen 'works', a life of effective activity in the power and presence of God. And in these words and works they encounter the Father too.

And thus the thought returns to where it began, the disciples' faith (John 14.11). They are to believe in the mutual indwelling of Father and Son, and they are to believe in it because of the active life displayed before their eyes. From this point a new horizon opens up: *the disciples who believe, are themselves to be active*. The new theme is stated in the bold promise of verse 12: 'One who believes in me will do the works I do, and greater works, because I go to the Father', and the ground on which this is to happen is the focus of the remainder of the chapter. The condition for their works to be 'greater', of course, is paradoxically that they are to be *the same* works; they will do Jesus' works, works morally and evangelically consistent with what he has done, a faithful representation of them and an active participation in his active life. Yet since the time of Jesus' presence is ended, and he is going away, these future works will reach beyond the temporal scope of his presence in the world and so constitute an enlargement of that presence in some sense, an extension of his accomplishment into future time.

And now we meet the first fully Trinitarian formulation. The works that the disciples will do are founded on a relation with God, as Father, as Son and as Paraclete (John 14.13–16). As *petitioners*, they are placed directly vis-à-vis the Father, asking 'in Jesus' name'; that, at any rate is the unambiguous formulation of 16.23, and despite a degree of textual uncertainty, 14.13f. should be understood in the same way. Petitionary prayer is the foundational form that faith takes in action, the first way the agent lays claim on a world and a good that is not yet present but waits to be opened up in history. The Father has not disappeared *behind* the Son and the Spirit but is addressed in his own person as the ruler of history. But the believer's relation to the Son is described in rather different terms: 'if you love me, you will keep my commands' (John 14.15). And the relation to the Spirit of Truth is different again: it consists of 'receiving' him and being 'indwelt' by him (John 14.16).

Let us pause briefly over the striking language about the disciples' love for Jesus. In what follows, the Father himself is said to love (of course) both the believer and Jesus (John 14.21), and Jesus is said to love the Father (John 14.31). But the believer who *asks the Father*, loves Jesus rather than the Father. For it is in Jesus that the Father's presence *in the world* can be seen and known, and love implies a world of value, an objective order of good, to which it relates its object. What we have here, I suggest, in the sequence of faith in the Father and love for Jesus is a Johannine way of imagining the Pauline formula, 'faith working through love'. (At the centre of the discourse, in chapter 15, we shall find Jesus developing the point in terms of a 'friendship' between himself and the disciples; the importance of that concept is underlined when friendship returns in the famous exchange between Jesus and Peter by the Sea of Galilee in chapter 21: ἀγαπᾷς με; φιλῶ σε.) What may strike modern readers as unexpected is the strong insistence, here and again in chapter 15, on the connection between love and observing commands (John 14.21). Jesus' commands are, as he insists, the Father's commands too, and Jesus has kept them as well as given them (John 14.24). But they are *Jesus'* commands because they have disclosed the active will of God for life within the world, and Jesus it is who has done the 'works', who has lived in the world the human life that God created it for. This, then, is the connection, which in our voluntarist and emotivist age we so easily lose touch with, between 'loving' and 'obeying': meaningful and effective moral rules reflect and mediate loveliness and beauty in good order. *What* we love, when we love Jesus, is a perfect fittingness, a human life just such as the world was made to contain, and our love makes his active and effective human existence normative for us. He continues present to the disciples, dwelling within us, through his words (John 14.23). His commands are the normative formulations that express his own life, and in giving his disciples not only words (of disclosure) but commands (of normativity), Jesus opens for them a way to participate in the deep rationality of the world order God has made, the world order called forth through the Logos that became flesh.

Most of the second section of the chapter, which I take to run from verse 12 to 24, focuses on the continuing experience of Jesus in love and obedience even when 'the world' does not see him; that is, when his presence on earth is recalled as an object of faith, not sight. The third section (John 14.25–31) then moves into the more threatening terrain of the experienced absence of Jesus, with a recall of its threat to agency: 'let not your heart be disturbed, and do not shrink' (John 14.27). Here the presence of the Paraclete comes to the fore (John 14.26). But in the programmatic statement of verses 13–16 this third point of practical contact with God has already been announced: 'I will ask the Father, and he will give you another Paraclete, to be with you for all time' (John 14.16). 'For all time', εἰς αἰῶνα, introduces the future horizon when the one who has done the works is no longer present. If God is present to them on the past horizon of their accomplished experience in the works and word of Christ, he is present on the future horizon of their emerging experience in the guidance of the 'Spirit of truth', who continues with and in the Church. Emerging time and the absence of

Jesus, then, do not constitute a defeat for his and the Father's works, even though time defeats all the works of humankind. There is a progress with these works, the Spirit offering new knowledge as the time requires it but always bringing them back to the teaching and commands of Jesus (John 14.26). Though a fuller exposition of the Spirit's role is reserved for 16.7–15, the Spirit's place in the economy of divine grace and human action is clear from this point on.

What we see in this text, then, is the godhead really present in time, in the accomplished history of Jesus and in the emerging future of the disciples' lives, and yet no less in transcendent control of time. The living of the life of faith corresponds to this: rooted in love of the past world of Jesus' presence on earth, anticipating the disclosures of the Spirit within time as it emerges, always calling on the one who enables agency by allowing petitions. The correspondence between the shape of God's Trinitarian presence and the shape of Christian practical engagement is very evident. What may we conclude from this? Have we, to evoke a term heavy with resonances, stumbled upon an 'analogy' of the Trinity within Christian moral reasoning?

Let us construct our answer to that question in three steps.

1   Any account of human moral reason must speak of nothing less than what humans *as such* are made to be and do. No privileging of Trinitarian approaches should let us suppose that Adam and his progeny, innocent or fallen, could simply have been *without* agency. God did not create mankind like that. That practical reason should need to relate to the agent-self, to the world and to emerging time, is how things have been from the beginning. If we seek and achieve a better and fuller understanding of practical reason, then, that will, in the first place, be a better understanding of Adam, not an understanding of a better Adam. Yet because moral reasoning always involves reflection, both on the world and also on itself, its exercise is hindered by misunderstanding and empowered by truth, the truth of the world and the truth of itself. So we may say that in the second place a better and fuller understanding of moral reason enhances the possibility of exercising moral reason well, and helps us overcome our natural tendency to reason lazily, carelessly and impulsively. Moral reason must understand itself, if it is to fulfil itself; good moral theory, though not, as such, a proof of sanctification, does have a positive bearing on sanctification. There are a thousand ways of misconceiving human agency and action, and all of them tending to some typical loss of agency and miscarriage of action. It is possible to conceive our action as reactive need-satisfaction; it is possible to conceive it as creative self-expression. It is possible to conceive agency as merely resting in God; it is possible to conceive it as wholly godless, a function of our life 'without God in the world'. (Remember Plotinus, admired by Porphyry for his conscientiousness with domestic accounts, drawing him away from his aspirations as a φιλόθεος. Remember Luther in a bad moment: 'You do not have to ask Christ about your duty. Ask the imperial or the territorial law!'[3]) It is even possible to conceive ourselves as not agents at all but as centres of feeling to whom things simply happen. And there is a multitude of other misconceptions, none of them prima facie stupid and all claiming respectable philosophical advocates. It is possible, then, for men and women to be ignorant of their agency and therefore incompetent in its exercise, in sore need of a disclosure that will correct their understanding and so rescue them from their incompetence. All this without their having ceased at any point to be human agents, for whom practical reason, engaging with self, world and time, is their essential form of existence.

2   Of what kind will such a disclosure be? The contention of monotheism, decisive for any ethics, is that to understand ourselves as agents we must understand ourselves as existing before God, rather than in the midst of many gods. That said, it does not at once follow that we must understand ourselves as existing before the *Trinitarian* God of Christian belief as we have seen that existence sketched out in John 14. The time-structured conception of moral thought we find there is clearly anticipated, at least, among believers in the covenant of YHWH with Israel. To take just one example, the Long Psalm (119, LXX 118) is devoted to a patient exploration of a number of different foci of moral experience. As elsewhere in other psalms there is a difference made between the backward-looking and the forward-looking response to God's direction: statutes that have been founded for ever, on the one hand, which become the topic of reflection; paths that stretch out ahead into unknown futures, on the other; also the transcendent presence in which the expressed will of God stands guard over the poet in the face of hostility. Essential to this perception is the experience of covenant, with its historical reference back and its prophetic promise forward. And to understand how the doctrine of the Trinity might shape moral life, we have to see that it does so precisely as a fulfilment of the covenant, adumbrating the presence in time of the self-covenanted God. The correspondence between Trinity and human action that emerges from the discourse in St John is wholly

focused on the presence of the godhead to the community in covenant relation to God.

3   Which leads us to our third point. The theological tradition does not allow us to say that God present in covenant is the only reality of God there is; neither does it allow us to say that God acting as Trinity in history is the only Trinitarian reality there is. In each case it acknowledges a gratuity about the divine presence in history, and that presupposes God acting *from behind* his presence to us, not wholly accounted for by it. The covenant is as an act of grace that was not in itself covenanted. Our talk of God cannot make itself independent of the covenant but neither can it forget the 'always greater' that governs all we say about the acts of God in covenant. What we learn from life in covenant, then, is by no means everything that there is to be known about God, nor even about God as Trinity. Questions such as increasingly absorbed John Webster about the 'aseity' of God are not to be answered from a mirroring of the divine in human moral experience. Nor can human moral experience pronounce on divine decisions 'before the foundation of the world', or on divine omnipotence to make counterfactual worlds such as Lombard taught the scholastics to think about, and so on.

Those considerations should ensure that our claims for an analogy of moral reason remain modest. Yet within the scope of modesty there are real claims to be made. If we are not entitled to think ourselves in possession of an *imago Dei* through the structure of our moral reasoning, we may nevertheless find the promise of a *similitudo Dei* within them, an invitation to live out the conformity between God's gracious act and our responsive action. It is the glory of human action, we are told, to follow in the pattern of the divine. Because the acting God has in three persons entered covenant with us, we may claim our freedom to act more fully and comprehendingly. We may know our own freedom not as an empty idea to be asserted by self-positing bluster but as a way to live in community with God in Trinity, who meets us in our active relations to self, world and time. A clear grasp of the form of our own action, then, serves as a confirmation of the decisive self-presencing of God, a 'sign following'.

In conclusion, let us return to where we began, the mutual service of dogmatics and ethics in theology. 'In the order of knowledge', John Webster asserted, we may speak sometimes of a priority of ethics, sometimes of a priority of dogmatics. We should not think of them as having different 'material bases' – each listens to the word of Scripture interpreted through the Spirit within the Church, and its validity is dependent on the faithfulness of its hearing. But in my view, going a step further than John Webster was ready to allow, we may suppose different modes of reasoning, for moral reasoning is fundamentally inductive while dogmatic reasoning is fundamentally analytic. Yet there can be no challenging his judgement that 'in the material order' there is a disequilibrium between dogmatics and ethics that has to be respected. Dogmatics is responsible for accounting theologically for the *actual*, the work of God as it has been and is, the historical and the unchanging, the created and the miraculous, the fact of witness and the fact of promise. Ethics has to follow a train of reasoning from the actual to the *possible*, concluding in the purposing of a human action to be performed, and therefore in no way actual. But since possibility depends on what is actual, ethics must accept the position of *following* dogmatics, of seeking life on the basis of what it has learned of God's deed and promise. If it tries to break free it will become merely aspirational, an ethics of the abstract ideal, and so become a salt that has lost its practical savour.

Jesus spoke of two men going up to the temple to pray, one who gave thanks for the life he lived, the other who prayed for mercy. The second, as we know, left the temple with God's approval, the first was rejected (Luke 18.9–13). It can be tempting – to the ethicist, that is, and to those who suppose themselves to be guided primarily by ethics – to see the Pharisee and the publican as dogmatician and ethicist respectively, the one content to describe the way things are, the other aspiring to set what is wrong right. Augustine liked to say of the Pharisee that 'he went up to pray, but did not ask for anything.' He was not, that is, a practical reasoner, while the publican, for his part, 'reasoned and asked' (*cogitabat et petebat*).[4] Does that comment invalidate the attitude of praise and thanksgiving, which the Pharisee shares with the dogmatician? Not at all! The wise dogmatician – and I speak again, of course, of John Webster – knows what the Pharisee did not know, that though praise and thanksgiving are the ultimate form of reflection on God's works, they cannot – before the end of all things – be self-reflexive. Our praise on earth is about 'Thou', not about 'I'. The wise dogmatician also knows that knowledge inseparable from holiness and holiness inseparable from knowledge must take form before an eschatological horizon. Understanding the future *as promise*, he understands the renewed self *as promised*, a challenge to reach out from praise to practical trust. He understands the cognitive conditions of theology on pilgrimage, reining in the ambition for a comprehensive doctrine that might wrap up our selves and our actions into the created order without remainder, and pretend to find them as finished and entire as God found his work to be on the seventh day of creation.

Can the ethicist be as wise as that? It may be all too easy, as Basil Mitchell remarked 50 years ago, for the energetic moralist to imagine himself or herself in the role of the publican as entitled to thank God 'that I am not as this Pharisee'.[5] We are familiar enough with the temptation to assert peremptory moral conditions for belief in God: 'I could never worship a God who would do . . . this or that!' The wise ethicist will know that no one is ever in a position to dictate moral terms to reality. To do so is to pretend to take over the descriptive function that is the dogmatician's responsibility in theology, and to make description subservient to the needs of practical deliberation. Such an ethics would be worse than a salt that had lost its savour. It would be an ideology, dictating to experience rather than following experience, pretending to tell the truth about the universe on the basis of nothing more than a project of action. Balthasar once described such syntheses of ethics and dogmatics as a 'gnosis that claims to be as coextensive as the *agape* that works God's will'.[6] If, on the other hand, we avoid this primary mistake and find in theological ethics a more complete fruition of the gift of moral reasoning bestowed in common on Adam and his children, that can only be because ethics has first been able to listen to representations, both dogmatic and narrative, of an actual God, a God who 'besets us behind', and not only 'before' (cf. Ps. 139.5).

Notes

1 'Introduction: *Agere sequitur esse*', in *God without Measure: Working Papers in Christian Theology, vol. 11, Virtue and Intellect* (London and New York: Bloomsbury, T. & T. Clark, 2016), pp. 2–3.

2 'Theology and the Peace of the Church', in *The Domain of the Word: Scripture and Theological Reason* (London and New York: T. & T. Clark, 2012), pp. 152–3.

3 Luther, *The Sermon on the Mount*, WA 32.390; LW 21.110.

4 Augustine, *Sermo* 36.11, cf. 115.2.

5 'Ideas, Roles and Rules', in Paul Ramsey and Gene Outka (eds), *Norm and Context in Christian Ethics* (London: SCM Press, 1969), p. 365.

6 'Nine Propositions in Christian Ethics', in Heinz Schürmann, Joseph Cardinal Ratzinger, Hans Urs von Balthasar, trans. Graham Harrison, *Principles of Christian Morality* (San Francisco: Ignatius Press, 1986), p. 88.

Sermon

Foretaste of the New Creation

JONATHAN GOODALL

Evensong, Friday 1 July
Lectionary: Psalms 6; 7; 8; 1 Kings 13.11–end; Mark 9.33–end

> 'Whoever welcomes one such child in my name welcomes me, and *whoever welcomes me welcomes not me but the one who sent me.*'
> (Mark 9.37)

You have heard so much theology in the past three days that I really don't intend to speak for long, you'll no doubt be pleased to hear.

We meet Jesus in the Gospel passage we heard a few minutes ago with his disciples, entering Capernaum, half way through the long final journey from the far north to Jerusalem. It is a journey on which, with gradually rising intensity, Jesus is trying to confront the disciples with the *necessity* of his passion and death (Mark 8.31; 9.30; 10.33–34). In a world of injustice and violence, the righteous can only suffer and be condemned and delivered into unrighteous hands. They take some rest, and in that moment of tired intimacy Jesus asks, 'What was it you were arguing about on the road?' The answer is a shamed silence, because in the face of his incomprehensible suggestions of being given over to suffering and death, they had been arguing – of all things! – about the leadership of their group. They had *heard* him but not *comprehended* his words.

Then Jesus called them to him, especially the Twelve, to make a shocking gesture. He took a child, whose weakness everyone understood, embraced the child tenderly, and said: 'If you welcome one child like this you welcome me: and if you welcome me *it isn't me you welcome*, but the One who sent me.' A child was made to stand in the circle of the men intending to have the first place in Christ's community, to teach them that their estimates of greatness were upside down.

Whoever welcomes one such child in my name welcomes me, and *whoever welcomes me welcomes not me but the one who sent me*. The greatest, God himself, proves his greatness by stooping down to put himself in the lowest place. A child, the weakest form of human power, who calls out for care and acceptance, is the best image of such a God, and what is more, when such a one is loved, it is God who is recognized and accepted. Jesus is challenging the Twelve not only to accept the child as the image of the humbled Son of Man, on his way to suffering and death, but also to accept that in such a poor condition they will also meet the One who sent him, the Father, who accepted the humiliation of his Son for love of us. By this freely chosen condition, God demonstrates to all those who take refuge in power that he is supreme over all.

Now let's gloss over the obvious, the history that belongs to every Christian community: the tendency to look for our leaders among the most spectacular, brilliant, visible, spontaneous and strong – even bullies are not unknown in the history of the Church's leadership – and let us try to focus on what Jesus' words suggest in terms of our conference.

First, it is the particular role of the Son to carry out freely the will of the Father; that is, to be the One in whom uncreated and created life are brought together in a union that, while it is manifestly not a union of equals, is a real and indestructible communion of love. Because when we welcome the Son, it isn't him we welcome but the One who sent him.

And second, this union in the Son is made possible by the intervention of the Holy Spirit, who enables creation to overcome the limitations of its nature and the weakness of sin. So when we welcome Christ, it isn't him only we welcome but also the One whom the Father sent with him, the Spirit.

It is within this threefold movement – which the Father originates, the Son undertakes, and the Holy Spirit enables – that the Church is brought into being. Because of his Incarnation, the Son is at the centre of this movement, the Church is his body; a body, we could say, that truly exists nowhere other than in this threefold movement – of the Son's reconciling and gathering life, and the Spirit's unifying and directing energy, drawing everything back into the 'bosom' of the Father.

However, as Jesus tries to make plain to his disciples, in a world of sin, injustice and violence, the incarnate Son must suffer and be handed over to the wicked. In such a world the Son must pass through powerlessness, humiliation and death. To love the world, God must pass through the cross.

But it does not end there. In the Resurrection the Church becomes the foretaste of the new creation, the pledge of the kingdom it is the

Father's will to give us, a kingdom fully freed for life in God. Alarming as it must seem to us, the Father has destined the whole world to become the Church.

Jesus said: 'If you welcome me, it isn't me you welcome' but the transforming fullness of the life that embraces us, the kingdom of the Father and the Son and the Holy Spirit.

Conclusion
Knowing and Loving the Triune God

ROWAN WILLIAMS

I have been given the task of reflecting on the themes of the conference, and to do so within a finite space and ideally with a measure of coherence; the former may be possible, the latter a little more challenging. But one thing that has emerged very clearly in our discussions in the last couple of days is that speaking about God the Holy Trinity is both exhilarating and difficult – neither of which things should be news to us. From the very earliest days when people began to reflect on God in these terms, these two things – exhilaration and difficulty – have been very clearly in evidence. And as we well know, by the time the doctrine was beginning to achieve some sort of intellectual sophistication and rigour in the fourth and fifth centuries, those who were most responsible for pursuing such rigour were also the ones who were most eloquent on how little one could really say about it. By the time we get to the fifth and sixth centuries, this has become almost a commonplace in theology; and it is the Pseudo-Dionysius who reminds us that when we say 'One and Three' or 'Monad and Triad' of God it is not *pros hemon*, not what we usually mean by such words.

But let me begin by picking out two themes which have emerged in discussion this week that seem to me help us understand what the doctrine of the Trinity is *not*. Recall again those Dionysian phrases about how God is neither a Monad nor a Triad 'as we use such words'; and if we try to put that into slightly more contemporary terms, we could perhaps say that this means that God is not one *instance* of something, and neither is God *three* instances of something. The one thing we are not doing when speaking about the Trinity is enumerating anything: we are not adding separate elements to make up a composite God; we are not describing how many inhabitants there are in the Seventh Heaven. And whatever we learn to say about God as Trinity, we need to be perpetually on our guard against the temptation of speaking so as to imply that God is one or three 'cases' of an abstraction called divinity. To say there is one God doesn't mean that there is a category of 'divine beings' of which there happens to be only one instance; to say there are three Persons doesn't mean there is a category of beings called

'God' of which there are three instances. And the Cappadocian discussions of the fourth century, which Metropolitan Kallistos summarized so lucidly for us early on in this conference, are of course discussions that move in and out of the complexities of this particular conundrum.

And then there is another thing that talking about the Trinity emphatically is not, which has come up in connection with discussions such as we heard from Douglas Hedley about triads, the Neoplatonic tradition and so forth, presenting to us an intellectual world in which it was often quite tempting to treat the doctrine of the Trinity as an answer to the question of 'how God gets to the world' – how reality moves from the absolutely simple and undifferentiated to the complex, plural world we know: divine triads are a way of enumerating the stages of that process. A question came from the floor about what the influence was of 'divine-triad' language on early Christian Trinitarian theology; and the answer is not entirely straightforward. In terms of vocabulary, one can quite often trace an influence; yet in terms of substantive use and meaning, things are a great deal more complicated, because the early Christian theologians were wrestling with precisely the temptation to turn the Trinity into a sort of sequence, starting with the eternal, unified and simple, and ending up with the world. Those of you who know the controversies around the theology of Origen, for example, will recognize the degree to which Origen does and doesn't give way to that particular kind of temptation – the Father who is One and simple, the Son who is the ground of multiplicity and so on. As later theology illustrates, there are ways of dealing with that and ways even of incorporating some of that language into a theological mainstream. But it is not where the Trinitarian enterprise begins and it is important to be clear about the limited influence of triadic metaphysics on the theology we are considering.

Where the enterprise *does* begin, as Father Andrew Louth reminded us earlier this afternoon, is in the plain recognition that we are *standing somewhere*. Father Andrew spoke very movingly of that picture of Father Sergii Bulgakov standing in front of the altar, and his Trinitarian theology evolving from that point; and I want to suggest that a great deal of what we've been listening to – not least the fascinating accounts of the New Testament roots of Trinitarian language that we had from Jenn Strawbridge and Markus Bockmuehl yesterday – points to the fact that the beginnings of this language lie in an awareness of standing somewhere. And the doctrine of the Trinity is articulated as we begin to offer answers to three interlocking questions that arise as we stand. What do we see? God. Where do we stand? God. How are we joined to and lured into what we see? God. The language of the New Testament pivots around those questions.

What do we see? We've been reminded of the different kinds of answer to that question in various theologians. We see Christ, the works of Christ. We see the Father in seeing Christ. We see in some measure the infinite and unconditional, the uncaused welcoming love of the Source of all things, laid open before us. 'Behold, I have set before you an open door', as Scripture says. We see the One who without cause, without being persuaded, manipulated or shunted into position by us, simply opens arms of mercy. That's what we confront, and some of the difficulty of talking about God as 'Father' that was mentioned earlier on in discussion is surely the difficulty of talking about what you are looking directly into; talking about it can draw you away from gazing into it.

But we look into this mystery because we stand in a certain place; we stand in the place that is Jesus Christ. *Where* we are is defined by him; 'Where I am, there shall my servant be also.' And in the Fourth Gospel – about which we have rightly heard so much in the last couple of days – there is a clear connection between the way, in the first chapter, we're told that the only Son, or the 'only begotten God', is 'in the bosom of the Father', 'next to the Father's heart' as it's been translated, and that later promise that we will be where Christ is. So that is where we stand; but why and how do we stand there? Who is this Christ who has made space for us in this way? The one whose life, whose existence on earth is again pure grace, pure gift unconditioned. The coming of Christ is both the fulfilment of all human expectation and the overturning of any expectation; and so the 'place' we occupy is divine in that it is uncaused, unconditioned, not ultimately the product of finite processes. Christ comes, the gift of the Father into the world, and in turn gives the gift of the Spirit, whose work in us and for us – uncaused, unconditioned, uncreated – continues to draw us towards the mystery of the Father. Again: *uncaused, unconditioned*; a grace given – as the Fourth Gospel once again says – 'not by measure', the Spirit given to us not in carefully calculated and measured degree according to our merits and our achievement, but simply *given.*

So, as so many of the lectures we've heard have spelled out in their different ways and different idioms, thinking about God the Holy Trinity is thinking about where we are. It is a way of locating ourselves on a map of uncaused, unconditioned Love; a map in which there is a 'to' and a 'from' and a 'between' – and the lines thus sketched run in different directions at different moments, but it is a map with one fundamental direction in it. This is the world we now inhabit; and learning to talk about God as Trinity is learning to talk about where we are, the place we inhabit. We recognize in what we look into, in the place we stand, in the energy that moves us towards what we contemplate, the single fact of uncaused, uncreated, unconditioned Love, a love that acts not because of anything we do but because it is what it is. In all of that we hear the words we have heard alluded to in many of our discussions: *Ego eimi ho on*, I am the one who is. 'I am who I am.'

This is why we must also say, as Lucy Gardner reminded us on behalf of Hans Urs von Balthasar (and as we've heard from other speakers also), that the experience of *prayer* is where Trinitarian discourse begins – not the experience of prayer in the sense that we have all sorts of interesting and unusual spiritual experiences from which we draw interesting conclusions, but the strange fact of being where we are faced with the welcoming and terrifying mystery of God's uncaused embrace of us. And I say welcoming *and* terrifying because, as the New Testament makes perfectly plain, being confronted with the causeless love of God is something that drives human beings into murderous panic. It takes conversion to understand it as good news.

This language of God tells us who and what and where we are; and of course it tells us also why the Church is the Church. You could say that one reason for the development of Trinitarian language about God is the recognition that the Church would make no sense at all without the Trinitarian God. So it should not entirely surprise us that in some contexts where language about the Trinity tends to dry up, the reality of the Church makes even less sense than usual – but that is perhaps another story. Why is the Church unique among human communities? Why is the Church not just another useful human association where we club together, refine our ideas in conversation with one another and – more or less – improve our awareness about our own convictions? There are many human organizations in which we can refine and develop our convictions and even our spiritual skills if we want to talk in those terms – but the Church is different. Bishop Jonathan Goodall's homily at the opening mass flagged up this theme: the doctrine of the Trinity is in a very important sense a doctrine about the Church, indirectly, in that it is only if we understand how the doctrine of the Trinity makes sense of our being in this particular place and these particular relationships that we can truly grasp what it is that's different about the Church, and why we want to speak of the Church as a 'supernatural society', not just yet another human association.

The Church, the place where we stand in Christ, looking into the mystery of the Father, energized by the Spirit, is the place – and here

I am picking up some of Oliver O'Donovan's points this morning – where human action at its most fully active and free level is suffused by divine action, made to be active and purposeful as it is meant to be by that suffusion of divine act. So that indeed, if we want to make sense of the humanity we're living into, we will need the language of God as Holy Trinity – not as a speculation about a distant God but as our way of mapping the territory we inhabit. And, of course, if the Church is truly where human action is suffused by divine action, that has some implications about an issue that came up in the wake of Lydia Schumacher's beautiful lecture: are we talking about humanization, or divinization? Well, actually both. Because for human beings to become *human* – active, free, intelligent, loving – as they are designed to be, then in them there must be liberated the action of God. So as God's action becomes progressively freer, more evident, more shaping and creative in human life, what is happening is not that we are becoming more divine and less human – we are becoming more human by allowing the divine to come to life in us. So that the humanization–divinization polarity begins to melt away like snow in the sun.

Jeremy Begbie, in the unforgettable musical meditation that introduced us to dinner on our first evening, spoke eloquently about the non-competitive, non-rivalrous nature of the divine and the human; not battling for position, not more-of-one-less-of-the-other. And his allusion to what we might mean there by 'musical space' was profoundly illuminating in helping us see what we do and don't mean when we talk in these terms of divine action 'suffusing' human. But we need to take this just a little bit further, because when we speak about divine action suffusing human, about our becoming human as we become divine, we do not of course mean that we become divine in the abstract, simply bearers of divine qualities. We become divine in the way Christ is divine; that is to say we become divine as sons and daughters of the Eternal Source, the Father. Our destiny is 'filial' – again, a word that has come up in various discussions, especially of Augustine and Aquinas and, I believe, a crucial point of clarification in understanding the notion of *theosis* – divinization – in Christian theology, Eastern and Western. There are those who argue – some quite learned scholars among them – that *theosis* must be some kind of mistake; we cannot be partakers of the divine nature because God is God and we are not. But with due respect, this is in a sense the whole point of the doctrine of the Trinity: that God from all eternity is, has, enjoys a way of being that is dependent, responsive and loving, as well a way of being that is pure bestowal and outpouring. God is 'filial' as well as being eternally, unconditionally generative; God is 'filial' as well as 'proceeding' in communicative transparency. God looks at God with a filial devotion, a filial love. And so the holy life for us as loving and intelligent creatures is the full actualization by divine act of our lives as daughters and sons of the Father of Jesus Christ. This is not something that removes or destroys creaturely integrity; it realizes in us the capacity with which we are created, the capacity for contemplation of the eternal, unconditional Love that is the Father's.

And in so doing, it also realizes in us that capacity for self-emptying attention to the world itself. As Dietrich Bonhoeffer argues of Christ in his brilliant, incomplete lectures on ethics, Christ has no identity but who he is for others – which is not (as some have read it) a sentimental projection on to Christ of intense, deeply felt altruism; it is affirming that the very rationale of Christ, divine and human, is that he is who and what he is for the sake of the Creation and for the sake of the Father. To stand where Christ stands is not only to behold the Father in the sense we have been speaking of, but also to behold what the Father loves – which is the world – with the same single selfless, radical outpouring that is divinity.

This also bears on another question that came up in discussion – raised particularly in response to some of the remarks Paige Hochschild made after her lovely paper on Augustine: questions about the 'natural' knowledge of God. Do we know God in advance of revelation or not? It's a slightly silly question at the end of the day, in that it would be bizarre to suppose that God – whose making of us depends on nothing but his own nature and will – would make a creation utterly resistant and impenetrable to God's own nature and will. We suppose therefore that the capacity with which we are made – the *image* in which we are made – must somehow be orientated to the knowledge of God. This lays God under no 'obligation' – a familiar anxiety in some theological debates of the twentieth century and indeed earlier. It simply declares that when – freely, causelessly, unconditionally – the Eternal Word of God takes flesh this is, as I noted earlier, simultaneously a fulfilment of all that human being was ever about and a total renewal of all that human being is and ever shall be.

In the light of this, too, we can say some things about not only the Church in general but the sacramental life of the Church in particular. One of the advertised themes of this conference is *transformation* – how our knowledge and love of the triune God is a transforming reality for us. We have heard in several different contexts how the sacramental life of the Church sets out and embodies that growth into filial maturity in the New Creation that is fundamental to our thinking about God the Holy Trinity. We have heard – in connection with Balthasar, Bulgakov, Aquinas and others – how what is happening in the Holy Eucharist is the movement of the Son to the Father in the Spirit, and how our participation in the Eucharist is a very particular *embodied* manifestation of that entire realization of where we are and who we are as humans in Christ. The Eucharist above all is where our map of our position gets some clarity. But of course this applies more generally: we can speak about the implications of Baptism in these terms – and we have been challenged in some of the discussion to think about other sacraments in those terms too. So the question raised yesterday in connection with Balthasar's theology of how we might develop and refine a theology of human relationship, especially marital relationship, in the light of all this becomes a serious and an engaging question. I certainly don't propose to attempt to resolve it now but to note it as one of several possible implications of seeing the entire sacramental life of the Body of Christ in this light. What are the sacraments? They are all of them God-suffused ways of growing into filial maturity. All of them give the grace for which we are hungry, the grace we need, to grow more fully into that suffusion of all our lives by the shape, the form of the Son made flesh. *All the sacraments need to be thought through in Trinitarian terms.* And in thinking through this yet further, of course we come through to that other area of territory so effectively explored this morning by Oliver O'Donovan, which has to do with the social and the ethical – and (I would add) the ecological implications of all this. The map on which we locate ourselves, the territory we inhabit where the three questions I began with are raised – Where do we look? Where do we stand? How are we united with God? – is something that has to do with our reality within a world that is material and complex. It is not about living in our heads or living as detachable souls. If our doctrine is about our transformation as human agents – intelligent, free and loving agents – it is also about the world in which we are such agents, the world, the material, interlocking, interdependent world, which is to be transformed by our engagement with it; and transformed not by egotistical human will but by the Christlike agency we exercise in its midst.

And if what we are living out is human agency suffused by the divine life of the Son in the communion of the Trinity, then how we relate to and regard our neighbour, near and far, is transfigured by that fact. We cannot any longer define ourselves as living in a territory that has to be policed and fenced – we are living in communion. Going back to discussion right at the beginning in the light of Metropolitan Kallistos's lecture, this is not to mortgage ourselves to the very unsatisfactory language of human community imitating 'divine community'. We have heard enough warnings in the last couple of days about this kind of language (God is a very good example of community and we should like to be just as good if we can be). God, remember, isn't an instance of anything, nor yet three instances of anything: the Trinity is not an example of community. God is what God is. Nonetheless, we have to say among other things that what God is is 'communion'; and therefore, if we are immersed in the divine life, communion is what happens, and the life we find ourselves leading – the life of the Body of Christ – is a life in which, as in the life of the Trinity, we are engaged in life giving; in relations where the life of one is unintelligible and unreal without the life of the other. We're not thereby setting two *kinds* of communion side by side – perfect divine communion, imperfect human communion – but saying that the effect on human community of being embraced within the life of the Trinity is to change the quality of our relatedness with one another so that the giving, the sharing of life, the nurturing, the bringing alive of the other, becomes what is most natural, most profound and most lasting in us. We learn to live in a human relatedness where the most significant thing about our relatedness is how far it nurtures in the neighbour near and far the kind of filial liberty and dignity that we're made for. By grace we make the other alive; and we make the other alive so that the other will make another alive and so on. We're not simply in the position so wonderfully articulated by C. S. Lewis in that famous dictum: 'She lived for others. You could tell the others by their hunted look'; we live for others so that they may live and give in the same way.

Which is why we come back repeatedly to the theme of *kenosis*, of self-emptying. And perhaps it is important to put that word at the end rather than the beginning of the discussion. It's very appropriately a frightening word. We may throw around the language of kenotic love very freely, but whenever we stop to think about what it actually means we should be properly alarmed – judged, almost paralysed by the thought of it. But if we put it at the end of all this discussion, perhaps it becomes a little clearer that the self-emptying we speak about in the life of God the Holy Trinity is always life-giving gift. To put it in very simple terms: the Father doesn't 'empty himself' in generating the Son because that's what he wants to do in the abstract; he empties *life* into the *life* of the Son, declaring (as it were) to the Son: 'I am nothing and have nothing that is not for you.' The Son, in eternity and in time, says to the Father: 'I am nothing and I have nothing that is not for you.' The

Spirit declares to us, lives out in us: 'I am nothing but the witness that gives you, carries you, into the relationship between Father and Son.' This brings us back to the beginning of these scattered remarks and to the basic awareness of both exhilaration and difficulty, because thinking of *kenosis* in that light is, I dare to say, exhilarating; it is exhilarating to speak of that depth and radicality of joyful, loving gift. And yet it is as profoundly difficult as we could imagine, because while God is kenotic love and enacts it eternally, we are not, and we don't very much want to enact it. Which is why we need to ask God to do it in us and to pray for what I have been calling the suffusion of our action by God.

All I have sought to do in these reflections is to pick up some of the themes that have arisen in both the talks and the discussion in the past couple of days, themes that seem to weave together in a way that shows us how profoundly embedded Trinitarian language is in so many areas of our Christian thinking. When we speak about and pray in and into the life of the Threefold God, we're not simply addressing a theological topic – let alone a rather difficult and remote one. We are trying to make sense, as I said earlier, of where we are and who we are; to make sense in a way that recognizes that we have already been overtaken by a mystery we cannot control or manipulate into place; and to make sense of what is now unexpectedly, mysteriously possible for us in the light of our being placed here in this extraordinary new world where what we see is God, and where we are is God, and how we move Godward is God. In a sense, speaking about 'knowing and loving the triune God' just might, if we haven't been to this conference, lead us off in a wrong direction; because the triune God is not one of those things 'over there' that we know and love as an object. It is the world we're in and the air we breathe. And so if we want to speak – as we surely still do – of knowing and loving God the Holy Trinity, we must be clear that it is a matter of knowing and loving precisely this, this new world in which we are set – what Charles Williams in one of his poems called 'the land of the Trinity'. And it is to know that for all the uncompromising and alarming challenges this puts to our ambition and egotism, for all that we live most of our lives in what Augustine and the Augustinian tradition after him poignantly called 'the land of unlikeness', *this* is our native land because the God who made us and loves us made us in the divine image; made us in this way because there is absolutely nothing but God's own loving nature and purpose to condition what we are. If this is the case, what we are is as it is because of Divine Love from beginning to end; and this is what we have been celebrating for these last two days and will, I trust, continue to celebrate for the rest of our days on earth and beyond.

Biblical Reference Index

Name and Subject Index